THE STAR THROWER

THE STAR THROWER

*And Other Power Plays,
Solo Plays, and Monologues
for the Church*

Robert John Versteeg

Copyright © 2003 by Robert John Versteeg.

ISBN: Softcover   1-4010-6250-4

All rights reserved. No part of this book may be reproduced or transmitted in any form or by any means, electronic or mechanical, including photocopying, recording, or by any information storage and retrieval system, without permission in writing from the copyright owner.

This book was printed in the United States of America.

To order additional copies of this book, contact:
Xlibris Corporation
1-888-795-4274
www.Xlibris.com
Orders@Xlibris.com
15603

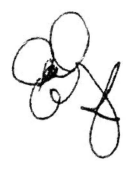

In honor of

Cassandra Lee

Unto my friends I give my thoughts,
Unto my God my soul,
Unto my foe I leave my love—
These are of life the whole.

Nay, there is something—a trifle—left;
Who shall receive this dower?
See, Earth Mother, a handful of dust—
Turn it into a flower.

—*Ethelwyn Wetherald*

CONTENTS

PREFACE 9

PART ONE: PLAYS

Introduction: 15
THE STAR THROWER 23
THE SURVIVORS 36
THE KING OF BABYLON 79
SAUL AT ENDOR 101
BALLOONS'N'TUNES 113
THE CHILDREN'S CHRISTMAS PLAY 125
BOXES 136

PART TWO: SOLO PLAYS AND MONOLOGUES

Introduction 151
Developing and Presenting Solo Plays and
   Dramatic Monologues: A Short Course in
   the Art of Dramatic Monologue 152
MEN OF FAITH 177
   WELCOME TO HEAVEN 181
   PAUL, A PRISONER 191
   DONNE TO DEATH 202

FATHERS AND SONS 217
   THE PRODIGALS 220
      SON 220
      BROTHER 223
      FATHER 225
   FOUR FATHERS 228
      ADAM REMEMBERS 228
      ABRAHAM FOLLOWS 232
      DAVID DECLINES... 238
      JOSEPH DISAPPEARS 242
WOMEN AND WONDERS 246
   LOT'S WIFE...251
   MARY OF MAGDALA 255
   THE GREATEST SHOW ON EARTH..............260
      TAMER 260
      CHARMER 262
      RING MASTER.. 264
      JUGGLER 266
      EMMETT KELLY 267
NOTES 269

PREFACE

My circus hero is the Roman rider, who rides astride two galloping horses. That's me. I live my life simultaneously riding two horses—theatre and church. My theatre has been a church, my church a theatre. To manage them both side by side is a challenge.

Part of that challenge is finding the right plays to do. I've never found it hard to find plays to do in the theatre that had exciting spiritual value. On the other hand, it has often been hard, indeed, to find plays to do in church that had *dramatic* value.

As a pastor, I look for powerful ways to share the faith. As a theatre director, I know that plays pack punch. So I look for plays that will be both faithful and effective.

One solution is to do in church plays that have spiritual value regardless of whether they were specifically designed for church production. All too many of the plays coming from and intended for a specifically Christian community are embarrassingly defective in either content or form—often in both.

Worse, I often encounter among laity, pastors, and play publishers an attitude of indifference—or maybe it's simple ignorance—about theatrical value in church drama.

If we are going to go to the huge labor of producing a play in church, the play ought to justify the expenditure of all that energy and resources.

By the same token, if we do a play in church, for God, it deserves our best theatrical effort.

But there is an industry in our midst marketing inferior plays for the church. That industry's hook is that their plays are "easy to produce." In one sense, namely, that they are unchallenging, that's true. But they are also easy to fail with—fail to produce dramatic impact or spiritual growth. They are pious parsley. Who said it was going to be easy? After all, it's "easy" to collapse.

Worse than the treacherous easiness of effortless drama, too often these plays also purvey easy theology. They allow our complacency. They let us hide from life's hard questions and harsh facts. They sacrifice significance for simplification. They permit us to remain, in the words of T. S. Eliot's Thomas à Becket, "safe by the fire." Again, they are spiritual Greyhound buses, designed to "leave the driving to someone else" over smooth paved roads. For life's deserts and jungles and craggy heights, we need sturdier vehicles.

The spiritual deserves our best of everything—including our best plays and our best efforts. And in this higher sense, it is "easier" to give our best efforts for something worthwhile. And also, consequently, it is "easier" to enjoy success—that is, to produce worthy fruits—with both good plays and good theatrical effort.

Because I couldn't always find the plays I wanted to do in church, I wrote some. I've collected them here to share with other Roman riders who seek both effective theatre and responsible spirituality.

My idea of "effective theatre" includes, first, that it "works" on stage. It grabs and holds people's attention (the derivation of the word *entertain*). But I want it to be *theatre*, not soap opera or sitcom, and not even a Sunday School lesson! Sunday School lessons are fine. Sermons are fine. Anthems are fine. But they're not drama. Further, I want spiritual drama to be contemporary, even daring. In the name of Christ, I want it to discover, claim, and explore the frontiers of the audience's imaginations. I want it to surprise them, if need be jar them, and always move them.

My idea of "responsible spirituality" is spirituality that knows its theology and also knows and respects people, their lives and struggles, as well as the real world in which human beings today have to live their theology. It also accepts responsibility to help persons grow in spiritual stature.

My experience gives me grounds to hope that you will find these blessings in these plays. But you will not find uncomfortably predictable dénouements. You will find "textual indeterminacy"— that is, you will find life's ambiguities that challenge the audience to become co-creators and to join in the *agon*, the struggle. You will find characters who are uncomfortable with cliché. Some voice disturbing feelings and thoughts. They struggle with doubt and, as Siam's king would have it, puzzlement. Like Job and other biblical persons, they complain. These plays are not tidy. Prophet Amos' direction remains valid for Roman riders, Christians, and play producers: "Woe to them that are at ease in Zion" (Amos 6:1).

Here are some uneasy plays. Read them, preferably aloud. Then start by producing the one that most excites you.

Giddyap and ta-da!

PART ONE:
PLAYS

"Whatever is not turned into art disappears forever."

—Arthur Miller

"And a lot of what is turned into art disappears forever."

—Donna Versteeg

INTRODUCTION:

Art Comes to Church

ACT 1

(*The lobby of a church immediately following Sunday worship.*)

PASTOR CHURCH: (*extending hand*) Welcome to Trinity Church! Good to have you worshiping with us today!

ART: Thanks! My name is Art. I'm new in town, and I'm looking for a church where I can be in ministry.

PASTOR CHURCH: Well, great! . . . What sort of "ministry" did you have in mind?

ART: I'm looking for a church that would like to have a drama ministry.

PASTOR CHURCH: Ah! A drama ministry!

ART: I have an undergraduate major in Drama, and a Master's in Radio, TV, and Motion Pictures. I've taught theatre in college, university, and professional theatre school. I've directed more than fifty full-scale productions. I've acted professionally. I'm an award-winning playwright. I'm also a seminary graduate and an ordained minister.

PASTOR CHURCH: Impressive. But I'm afraid we don't have the resources for another staff position.

ART: I'm self-employed. I expect to serve as an unpaid volunteer.

PASTOR CHURCH: (*warming*) Well, that does sound promising. Let's see. We could have skits to kind of set up the sermon—you know, introduce the topic, pique interest. Liven up the service. Maybe a puppet troupe. Or a spectacular Christmas or Easter production to pull in the community.

ART: Actually, I was thinking more in terms of what the church could do for drama.

PASTOR CHURCH: Pardon?

ART: Funny how we pastors think in terms of what drama can do for the church—part of our maintenance-over-mission mentality, I guess, our old self-fulfilling, self-defeating, scarcity mindset. Jesus was apt to start with what he could do for others. What if the church took that approach to drama?

PASTOR CHURCH: Not sure I'm following you here. What's the church got that drama needs?

ART: (*laughing*) The church can offer drama and theatre people the most important thing, a sense of significance, purpose, mission, meaning. Clement II gave Michelangelo the tomb of the Medici. Julius II gave him the ceiling of the Sistine Chapel. Paul III gave him the rear wall. St. Thomas' Church in Leipzig gave Johann Sebastian Bach an organ to play and choirs to direct. In modern times, the festival committee at Canterbury invited T. S. Eliot to use the cathedral as his stage and he wrote *Murder in the Cathedral*. By implication, all these gifts, being gifts of the church, included the gifts of the world's great themes. That water-cast bread returned inspirational art to enrich God's people inside and outside the church. And there's a creative synergy operating here. As

THE STAR THROWER   17

the president of Georgetown University said, "Art in the service of God is itself enhanced." You've been in plays, haven't you?

PASTOR CHURCH: (*modestly*) Well, I have; in school. I was Lysander in *A Midsummer Night's Dream*.

ART: Was it fun?

PASTOR CHURCH: Yes!

ART: And was it work?

PASTOR CHURCH: A lot of people worked hard to make it happen.

ART: Why? What did they get out of it?

PASTOR CHURCH: (*thoughtfully*) For one thing, the fun, the camaraderie. The sense of teamwork, of belonging, of being part of something big. And the sense of accomplishment.

ART: "Something big," you say. *Midsummer Night's Dream* is one of the world's great plays. It illumines the human experience, puts a spotlight on God's creation, even—or maybe especially—when Puck says, "Lord, what fools these mortals be!"

PASTOR CHURCH: I love that line!

ART: In that particular case, the ridiculous is the sublime. Theatre artists hunger and thirst for the sublime, for the spiritual. The church can give them a chance to pursue it pretty well unencumbered by the commercial constraints and trivial expectations that strangle secular theatre in its own vomit.

PASTOR CHURCH: Maybe we could talk about this some more. Could you come by my office this week?

ACT 2

(The Pastor's office later that week.)

PASTOR CHURCH: To tell you the truth, I got a bit edgy when I heard you talking about *Midsummer Night's Dream* as "sublime," and then "sublime" as if it were a synonym for "spiritual."

ART: As I see it, anything that has implications for the spiritual dimensions of life is "spiritual."

PASTOR CHURCH: You're not proposing that we perform Shakespeare in church?

ART: Why not? We could do worse.

PASTOR CHURCH: For one practical thing, it'd be too hard, wouldn't it?

ART: Is anything too hard for the Lord?

PASTOR CHURCH: Well, you know, I keep getting advertisements from people who will sell us church plays that are "easy to produce."

ART: Should we bring the Lord what's easy or what's best? "Easy plays" are bad plays. Good art is demanding. Paradoxically, the better the play, the "easier" it is to do because a strong play will carry you, whereas if you take on a weak play, you have to carry it. There are all kinds of great plays, plays with spiritual impact, that are in the public domain. Publishers don't push them because publishers can't make money selling them because they're out of copyright. Instead, publishers peddle plays with the "easy" bait. They'd like you to believe those easy plays require almost no work, no preparation, no rehearsal. What they neglect to add is that usually there's also no reason to do them. People rise to challenge. Tell people at the start, "We can't expect much of you," and you demoralize them and defeat yourself. But tell them, "We're going to do something great!" and watch them stretch to meet that expectation.

PASTOR CHURCH: We don't have professional theatre people in our congregation, you know.

ART: How many singers in your choir are professional musicians? Theatre is a field where "amateurs"—"lovers"—have made great contributions. I said "amateurs"; I did not say "dilettantes." That's precisely the problem with many of these "easy" plays—they're written by well intentioned authors who have neither practical experience nor expertise in theatre. I can think of only two significant playwrights in the history of world drama who have written under those circumstances. Ideally, in theatre the difference between an amateur and a professional is that the professional gets paid—or at least hopes to! We don't lack training resources and books. World drama is packed with treasures. And if the word should ever get out that the church is offering serious theatre people a chance to do really good theatre, they'll flock to us. Just put out the word and brace yourself for the response. The world's a stage full of playwrights withering on the vine for lack of playing groups who'll produce their work. Let them know you want good—not schlock—plays to do, and they'll beat a path to your door. But they won't come to do plays like "Susie Goes to Sunday School."

PASTOR CHURCH: Yes, but the question always is, are these plays, well, "appropriate" for church use?

ART: That's a decision every church is going to have to decide for itself case by case. The process of hammering out the criteria—for deciding what plays are "appropriate" for a particular church to use—might be a growth opportunity. Is your sole criterion that a play present some approved party line? If so, that might limit you. If a play is deemed "appropriate" only if it's homiletic theatre—plays that preach—then we're back to the premise that the church is only interested in what drama can do for the church, and not the other way around. There may be good propaganda that's also good art, and vice versa. But if it's not good art, is it good for the church, and is it good enough for the Lord? Would the church buy a defective bus? Why buy defective drama?

PASTOR CHURCH: It's probably naïve to imagine that any communication event, including any theatre event, doesn't embody some party line. Politics is built into language. Language is tinctured with positions. Jesus is the incarnate Word of God, but all words embody hierarchy.

ART: Understood. And remember that other communications axiom, demonstrated by experiment after experiment, that the more a given communication conforms to expectations, the less it communicates. It's the unexpected that leads to growth. We need to remember from the start that many people have their expectations shaped by television and simplistic skits. Real playing holds a real mirror up to real life. (Of course I don't mean that it has to be "realistic" in style—anyone who sees great plays or reads the Prophets and the rest of the Bible knows that nonrealistic styles are often superior tools for penetrating to the truth.) It may be that we see in drama's mirror darkly, but we walk not by sight, but by faith. Serious drama probes and perhaps inspires openness to faith. When people demand that we fulfill lesser expectations, they're demanding that we allow them not to grow.

PASTOR CHURCH: (*decisively*) OK; let's see if we can get something going!

ACT 3

(*The church lobby three months later.*)

FIRST AUDIENCE MEMBER: Can somebody tell me what that play was supposed to be about?

SECOND AUDIENCE MEMBER: I'd say it's about half an hour too long.

FIRST AUDIENCE MEMBER: I mean, this person's throwing starfish back into the ocean, right? So why is it called "The Star Thrower"? How come it's not "The Starfish Thrower"?

SECOND AUDIENCE MEMBER: What I want to know is who are these persons running around with the sticks and bags?

FIRST AUDIENCE MEMBER: And what's this Professor dude got to do with it? He wants to dance with his mother?

SECOND AUDIENCE MEMBER: I wish he'd dance instead of lecture. If I want a lecture, I'll go to college.

FIRST AUDIENCE MEMBER: If I want plays, I'll go to a theatre. This is a church!

SECOND AUDIENCE MEMBER: Maybe we're supposed to start saving all the starfish in the world! (EXEUNT *laughing*.)

PASTOR CHURCH: (*overhearing*) I don't think it's a hit.

ART: Groundlings.

PASTOR CHURCH: Pardon?

ART: Caviar to the general taste. Playwrights have to please a wide audience. At the same time, they have to educate. Just as a reader needs "literary competence" to read a book, an audience needs "theatrical competence" to view a play. Building that—growth—takes time, work. Nobody said it was going to be easy.

CURTAIN

THE STAR THROWER

Preface

My spouse introduced me to the writings of naturalist Loren Eiseley in the 1970s. I was enthralled. My favorite was his story, "The Star Thrower."[1] I even searched the atlas looking for Costabel—"the beautiful coast"—which I at last ruefully concluded must be part of the non-existent "Seacoast of Bohemia."

Some years later I used a cutting of "The Star Thrower" as a Sunday morning sermon. I published directions for making that cutting in a worship journal I was writing at the time.

I hope that my publishing of that cutting did not abet the story's suffering what is in my opinion a grievous fate—it became one of those "preacher stories." As of this writing I myself have heard it used in sermons four times. What's bad about this is that each time I've heard it, Eiseley's story was mangled, truncated, and butchered almost beyond recognition. Its heart had been cut out on the altar of sermon illustration.

Bad enough, to have pulpits purveying adulterated, even contaminated soul food. But this particular strain of evangelical e-coli invaded the halls of power. Ann McFeatters, chief of a Washington newspaper bureau, reported that the then President of the United States's "version of the optimistic anecdote is the boy and his grandfather walking along a beach full of starfish. 'And the young boy picked one of them up and threw it in the ocean. And the grandfather, looking down the beach, seeing all the starfish, said, "That's not going to make any difference." And the young boy looked at his grandfather and said, "It makes a difference to that one." And that's how you change America—one heart, one soul, one conscience at a time."' Compare that cartoon with Eiseley's highly textured original story!

Here is a cautionary example of how a work of art may degrade as it passes into everyday parlance. It is not too distant from those TV-schedule condensations of a classic film, for example, when *Hamlet* is advertised as "Young prince faces difficulties at home."

Like *Hamlet*, "The Star Thrower" deserves better. I felt—grandiosely, it may be—called to try to rescue and restore it for the church by preparing a chancel-drama version that would translate the essay into dramatic form faithfully. "Faithfully" involves not forcing this wonderfully nuanced modern myth into any simplistic mold, religious or otherwise. What Eiseley would think of my attempt I don't know. However, I believe he would have been outraged by those sermon-llustration reductions of his many-faceted and polished gem to a cubic zircon. For what it's worth, Eiseley's publishers have approved my adaptation.

In the central scene of *Man and Superman*, Bernard Shaw has Tanner/Don Juan excoriate those who are "not religious: they are only pewrenters." On the other hand are those who, like Shaw himself, are not atheists, only offended by shoddy representations of religion, and who may serve the Lord unknowingly (Matthew 25:37-40). Eiseley somewhere muses on the irony that he himself, who professed no religion, found himself to be a profoundly religious person.

Paul Brockelman defines religious experience as "mystically encountering in wonder the mystery of being."[2] Eiseley had seen, experienced, and responded to that mystery of being, just as surely as Moses was mesmerized by a bush in Midian, and just as surely as St. Paul was unhorsed on his way to Damascus.

Nevertheless, it would be unfair to press Eiseley into service as a soul mate aboard the Ship of the Church. But a lighthouse keeper on the shore of Costabel, he most certainly is. We can join him here on the tangled bank where walks his Star Thrower.

My play's chief departure from Eiseley's story is the addition of a high-energy Brechtian chorus of two. Projections or placards with the scene titles may be used. We performed the play in a chancel without scenery of any kind other than recorded sound effects. Our sanctuary presented a proscenium-like orientation. Therefore, we located the ocean where the audience sat. Our Mother and Child mimed rather than danced their pas de deux to the human voice. The Shellers' bags were plain canvas tote bags with handles that conveniently doubled as shoulder straps to transform the bags into Scholars' backpacks.

THE STAR THROWER

A Play in One Act
From the story by Loren Eiseley

RUNNING TIME: Twenty-five minutes

CAST OF CHARACTERS

THROWER
SHELLERS-SCHOLARS
SCIENTIST
MOTHER
CHILD

(Morning. The sound of a storm and pounding surf. Then calm. We see a beach in Costabel, littered with living debris after a storm. The sound of surf and gulls. A rainbow.)

PRELUDE

(The THROWER moves along the beach, bending, plucking, throwing. EXIT.)

A GATHERING OF GULLS

(Armed with pincers and bags, the SHELLERS ENTER.)

1 SHELLER: This is the best time—in the morning!
2 SHELLER: After a storm!

1 SHELLER: The beach—
2 SHELLER:—littered with life!
1 SHELLER: Hermit crabs—
2 SHELLER:—scurrying for new homes!
1 SHELLER: Octopi—
2 SHELLER:—tentacles a-tremble!
1 SHELLER: Starfish—
2 SHELLER:—spangling the beach—
1 SHELLER:—as if the night sky had showered down.
2 SHELLER: See that one there—
1 SHELLER:—that starfish in a pool of sand and mud!
2 SHELLER: See how it arches up on all five legs to keep its body out of the silt!
1 SHELLER: The sand will clog its breathing pores!
2 SHELLER: The rising sun will shrivel the mucilaginous body of the unprotected being!
1 SHELLER: How soundlessly it cries for life!
2 SHELLER: (*after a pause, jabbing viciously at the starfish with pincers*) Ha!
1 SHELLER: (*jabbing at the starfish with pincers*) Ha!
2 SHELLER: Gotcha!
1 SHELLER: (*grabbing at the catch*) Gotcha!
2 SHELLER: Hands off!
1 SHELLER: I saw it first!
2 SHELLER: It's mine!
1 SHELLER: I got him!
2 SHELLER: I got part of him!
1 SHELLER: Find your own starfish!
(*Between them they have torn the imagined starfish apart, each stuffing part in a bag.*)
2 SHELLER: (*running after another creature skittering across the sand*) Oh no you don't!
1 SHELLER: (*jabbing elsewhere*) Hi!
2 SHELLER: (*likewise jabbing*) Ho!
1 SHELLER: (*chasing another prey*) Hey, you beauty!

2 SHELLER: (*to a creature*) See? Mother Ocean don't want you, she throws you back to me!

1 SHELLER: (*straddling a creature in the sand while fending off what appears to be a poaching gull*) Stay away! This one's mine!

2 SHELLER (*a ruse to divert 1 Sheller's attention*): Watch out for that gull!

1 SHELLER: (*at the gull*) I'll wring your neck!

2 SHELLER: (*taking advantage of 1 SHELLER's duel with the gull to slip in and snag the object from between 1 SHELLER's feet*) Ah!

1 SHELLER (*protesting*): That's mine!

2 SHELLER: (*moving out of reach*) A treasure!

1 SHELLER: (*grabbing*) Mine!

2 SHELLER: (*evading*) Finders keepers!

1 SHELLER: (*holding bag high in triumph*) A kettle full!

2 SHELLER: A kettle full!

1 SHELLER: (*a war cry*) Light the fires!

2 SHELLER: Boil 'em alive!

(*EXEUNT running.*)

THE THROWER OBSERVED

(*The SCIENTIST, who has entered to observe the behavior of the SHELLERS, watches them go, surveys the scene, is about to move on when the THROWER reappears and the rainbow breaks through. The THROWER gazes down, stoops, picks something up, and with the graceful motion of a sower of seed flings it far out into the ocean and watches it sink in a spray of spume. The THROWER moves to a new position, again gazing down, stooping, picking something up, and is about to throw it too, when, becoming aware of the SCIENTIST, the THROWER stands still.*)

SCIENTIST: (*indicating creature in THROWER's hand*) It's still alive.

THROWER: Yes. (*Flinging it far out with a quick but gentle movement and watching it splash*) It may live on, if the offshore pull is strong enough. The stars throw well. One can help them.

SCIENTIST: Do you . . . collect?

THROWER: Only like this. (*Picks up another creature and casts it into the sea.*) And only for life. (*Looks inquiringly at the SCIENTIST.*) You?

SCIENTIST: (*uncomfortably*) Once upon a time. I used to collect. I gave it up. The only successful collector is death.

(*Silence. They regard each other. The THROWER stoops and flings, looks at the SCIENTIST. SCIENTIST EXIT. In a ballet of throwing, the THROWER moves on down the beach as the rainbow fades. EXIT.*)

THE SONG 0F THE SHELLERS

(*ENTER the SHELLERS, with bags stuffed full with shells.*)

SHELLERS: (*dancing and singing*) Twinkle, twinkle little shell!
I have cleaned you very well,
Scrubbed you in a great big sink
Till you lost that awful stink,
Polished you until you shine.
I'm so glad that you are mine!

1 SHELLER: We boiled 'em clean!

2 SHELLER: Dissolved the former tenants!

1 SHELLER: Evicted!

2 SHELLER: Evaporated!

BOTH: Eviscerated the former tenants!

1 SHELLER: Bleach and rub!

2 SHELLER: Scrub-a-dub!

SHELLERS: (*dancing and singing*) Crunch and crackle, little shell,
Now I've bleached away your smell,
You will generate small talk
When you line my garden walk,
All my visitors enthrall

When you're mounted on my wall!
1 SHELLER: (*displaying a trophy*) My shell!
2 SHELLER: My gem!
1 SHELLER: My ectoderm!
2 SHELLER: My treasure!
SHELLERS: (*dancing and singing*) Twinkle, twinkle, O so bright,
You'll look lovely in Lucite.
You will shine and radiate
When you are my paperweight.
Twinkle, twinkle, little star,
As a lamp above my bar.

(*They dance with their bags, from which they present field specimens to the SCIENTIST as the SCIENTIST ENTERS. The playing space becomes a university hall. The SHELLERS become the SCHOLARS to whom the SCIENTIST lectures.*)

THE LABORATORY
OF THE "TANGLED BANK"

SCIENTIST: Good morning, class. Those of you who have brought back field specimens, please make certain you have your name with them so you can receive proper credit. I see that some of you have brought back suntans. I'm glad you decided to come back at all and to take your exams. If I didn't have you to lecture and give exams to, what would I do for a living, eh? (*Holds up the ectoderm of a starfish in Lucite.*) What have we here? A starfish paperweight! No; this hardly captures the spirit of scientific inquiry. Someone's idea of a joke, no doubt. I trust you are all well rested from your spring vacation, and prepared for the big push to final exams three weeks from today. I, too, traveled to the seashore. Unfortunately, it rained. There was a rainbow. But it was a working vacation. No suntan for me. It was merely another laboratory, nature's laboratory, a real life example of Darwin's "tangled bank." (*Seque-ing into his lecture*) Darwin's "tangled bank," you may remember—take notes; you're going to have to remember! Darwin looked upon nature, and in nature Darwin saw the "tangled bank," a scene of silent, preconscious, but nonetheless serious warfare—violence, death, the survival of the fittest. The ocean is the savage mother of all living. In a storm she flings her offspring far from her bosom up on the shore. From the greatest to the least—from beached Behemoths to minuscule crustaceans so microscopic that they can dance their dance of death by the dozens on a single grain of sand. From all of them, the Mother Ocean withdraws herself, abandons her children on the tangled bank. Tough love, eh? There they struggle to survive. The fish flops frantically but futilely, and gasps tragic-comically, drowning dry. The single-legged shellfish hops heightlessly in its maddened but motionless yearning toward its mother. Moving, but unmoved, the tide withholds her maternal embrace. Meanwhile, the sun sautés these wave-flung waifs on its grisly griddle of corrugated beach. The sun's shafts pierce and pin the starfish to the sand in a piscatorial crucifixion. Predators pounce. They, too, struggle on that tangled bank. One against the other they strive for the privilege of picking the prey apart, dart down to peck out the delicious delicacy of an unblinking eye. Yummy! All the while, the redundant waves distantly dance a tantalizing tarantella in which they uselessly beckon those land-lost victims back to unreachable life. Surveying this sad and sandy battlefield, Darwin observed that here each species and each specimen must fight for its life. Only the most fit survive. Here where the ocean mother casts away the runts of her spawning, here nature sorts out those selected to survive. This pitiless process forms the future. However—however! Darwin also hypothesized, if one species or even one specimen ever could be born which would surrender its own struggle, lay down its own life, and instead devote its life to saving one other species or specimen—if ever that should happen, then the theory of the tangled bank, of nature bloody in tooth and claw, would, by virtue of that unlikely occurrence, have to be revised. A new factor would have injected itself into the inexorable equation. (*Gazes at the paperweight still in his hand.*) But there is nothing on the shores of science that remains unmeasured—nothing, that is, but the spirit of humanity. (*After a pause, beginning to follow a dawning thought*) In the midst of desolation emerges the awesome freedom to choose—to choose!— to contend for the destiny of a world. Thus, in spite of war and famine and death, a sparse mercy persists, like a mutation whose time has not yet come. (*Another pause.*) I have forgotten something. Actually, I have remembered something—someone. I have to go. That will be all for today. (EXIT.)

1 SCHOLAR: What happened?

2 SCHOLAR: Prof left.

1 SCHOLAR: Left?

2 SCHOLAR: We could've gone off and left you sleeping here all day.

1 SCHOLAR: Did you take notes?

2 SCHOLAR: Got every word.

1 SCHOLAR: Let me borrow 'em.

2 SCHOLAR: Take your own notes!

1 SCHOLAR: I fell asleep!

2 SCHOLAR: Tough!

1 SCHOLAR: Hey! Have a heart, will ya?

(EXEUNT.)

DIALOGUE WITH A DEAF MOTHER: A PAS DE DEUX TO THE HUMAN VOICE.

(*As the SCIENTIST speaks, the DANCERS—the mother and her child—move to the rhythm of reminiscence. In the absence*

THE STAR THROWER 33

of dancers, the DIALOGUE WITH A DEAF MOTHER ballet may be performed by actors moving in carefully choreographed mime correlated with the SCIENTIST's words. MOTHER and CHILD, being memories, do not interrelate with SCIENTIST.)

SCIENTIST: (*satchel in hand*) I have come dutifully home to the house from which the final occupant has departed. In a musty attic—among old trunks, a broken aquarium, and a dusty heap of fossil shells collected in childhood—I found this satchel, a shabby antique in whose depths I turned up a jackknife, a pile of old photographs, and a note written in a thin, ornate hand, a single message that the writer had believed important. The note says, "This satchel belongs to my child."

(*Without looking, SCIENTIST hands satchel to CHILD; CHILD gives satchel to MOTHER who takes from it dance slippers.*) And there were also two incredibly pointed slippers that looked as though they had been intended for a formal ball, to which I knew my mother would never have been invited. (*Speaking toward the MOTHER*) Mother! You have never heard my voice. How is it, to be a deaf mother, never to have heard the voice of your child? Perhaps when I was in your womb you felt the vibration of my voice. I have such clever things to say, now, and you can't hear. Ill-taught prairie artist, painting the dust devils and the twisters! The twisters that came from nowhere to make desolation!

(*CHILD mimes digging with a shovel, then mimes calling to MOTHER.*)

SCIENTIST: (*Calling in lip synch*) "Yes! I'm here! I'm digging a storm cellar!" But you wouldn't have a storm cellar. You had been battered by fate so many times, you felt that to prepare for disaster was to court disaster, to tempt fate. It was better to pretend that there were no twisters. And the dust devils that danced, tiny, twister-like phantoms. I wanted to dance like them—or like the Indians around the fire, the Indians shadowed by their trickster always moving behind them,

(*CHILD is now mimicking SCIENTIST's movements*) solemnly mocking every twist and turn, every step and stamp. I wish you had taught me to dance. The deaf don't dance? Not even to the rhythm of their own heartbeats? Not to the swaying of the leaves or the beatings of the waves or the risings of the sun? I never saw you dance, Mother. You plodded through your life in silent, unbearable difference and isolation, all your life balancing on the precipice of mental breakdown, your Via Dolorosa to the long crucifixion of life. (*The scene has begun to merge with the Costabel beach, the rainbow dimly beginning to return, and the figure of the THROWER in his dance of star-saving seen in the shadows.*) I, I wanted to move through life with some specialness, something more than mechanical movement from womb to grave.

(*CHILD moves in accordance with SCIENTIST's words, shadowed by the THROWER.*) I wanted to dance, I wanted to dance through life with some beauty, some grace, some overflowing, some unnecessary arabesque, some posture, some pose, some pace, a variation in rhythm, a lilt, a lift, a leap, a dizzying spin, a fall and recovery. The way we go is all the same, but the way we travel, that is the difference—some drudge and others dance.

THE SCIENTIST BECOMES A THROWER

(*Now the beach in Costabel comes fully back into focus and the rainbow returns full strength. The THROWER continues his ballet of throwing—stoops, casts, stoops, casts—slowly, deliberately, well.*)

SCIENTIST: You're still here.

THROWER: (*looking around*) And you.

SCIENTIST: (*acknowledging it with a shrug*) One person. Who are you?

THROWER: A star thrower.

THE STAR THROWER

SCIENTIST: Alone!

THROWER: No. Somewhere there is a Thrower of actual stars, an unknown hurler of suns. He smiles and casts forever into the bottomless pit of darkness. He chooses always to dance in desolation, but never in defeat. He hurls his stars for the sake of life.

SCIENTIST: Death outruns you on every seacoast.

THROWER: Still I throw.

SCIENTIST: Why?

THROWER: I choose to.

SCIENTIST: I understand. (*The SCIENTIST gazes down, searching, stoops, and casts out into the water.*) I'll be another thrower. After us there will be others.

(*Together they continue to throw, the SCIENTIST's motion and rhythm gradually merging with the THROWER's ballet. MOTHER and CHILD join in, and then the SHELLERS/ SCHOLARS.*)

CURTAIN

THE SURVIVORS

Preface

As a senior in seminary, I was honored to be named Seminarian Preacher of the Year by *The Pulpit* magazine, a subsidiary of *The Christian Century*. Editor Paul Hutchinson therefore had the odious task of introducing me when I preached the winning sermon to the Chicago Sunday Evening Club—odious to him because my sermon was about the confrontation between Jesus and the citizens of Gadara (Mark 5:1-17). Those citizens took exception when Jesus healed their demoniac by transferring the demoniac's demons to a nearby herd of swine—which swine thereupon took themselves for lemmings and dashed off to drown in the lake. Dr. Hutchinson, I was given to understand—although he clearly ought to have held someone besides me responsible for it—took a dim view of that entire transaction and the young theolog who called attention to it.

Then what, I wonder, did Dr. Hutchinson make of the drowning of every living creature other than Noah and his manifest? For that matter, what do I make of it? When I graduated from seminary, I knew everything. By now I have learned that I knew nothing, least of all what to make of such stories.

As an actor/playwright, I can put myself in Noah's place. But no need—life puts me in Noah's position willy-nilly. Every day my fellow humans disappear like bubbles from the stream. Some days the bubbles burst in disasters claiming dozens, scores, hundreds, thousands. Biblical scholars estimate that a literal Noah would have lived about 8,000 BCE. The estimated world population for 8,000 BCE is 5 million. In such absolute numbers as these we may speak of "a disaster of biblical proportions." Today almost 55 million persons die each year.

Still, as George Foreman said, "Here I is." Being here, or being there in Noah's place, is thus not an entirely comfortable place to be—not if I truly care for others, and not if I believe that God's gift of this life is good. Even the bereaved who believe their lost ones are in "a better place" mourn their loss. Spared in the flood, nonetheless one day Noah died (Genesis 9:29). So will we all.

Therefore, in spite of the fact that it is a cliché boast among us—"I'm a survivor!"—and in spite of a TV series that may or may not survive until this book is printed, survivalism and being earthly survivors prove to be potentially Pyrrhic and certainly not permanent values.

All the same, in addition to coping with the loss of loved ones—and for the Christian that must mean the loss of anyone and everyone—surviving does confront us with the Why and the Why-Not-Me? Why was I (for now) spared? And what am I supposed to do with the rest of my life?

For those of us who remember the Holocaust, this may be a life-shaping issue. It has been for me. In the concentration camp gas chambers we can see scratchings where the victims clawed at the ceilings with their fingernails trying to escape, trying to live. They would have given anything for one more day of life. And so I ask myself, What have I done with this day of my life? There is a part of humanity that knows that survivors have to begin a new life and go forward. Most of us can identify with the challenge Noah and his family would have had to face in starting over again.

The highest I can think is that survivors must live in such a way as to perpetuate with honor not only the memory but, in a sense, the lives of those who do not, at least not in earthly terms, survive. In this way, the survivors may not only perpetuate but incarnate them. Great is the survivor's loss, anger, and pain. Greater is God's power to heal, to renew, and to restore.

The Survivors needs almost no scene construction. Act One asks a bit of acting space; perhaps some sound effects—animal noises, storm, and maybe a musical chord; possibly a rainbow projection; and a practical (that is, weight-bearing) railing. A wooden box, a step stool, or the apron of a dais can substitute for the railing. Act Two wants no more than a "vat." It can be a choir loft, choir pews, an empty refrigerator box, or a low curtained area (a few stanchions or boxes with some material draped between them will do). It should be big enough for two actors to dance in and big enough to conceal Noah lying down.

The Survivors may be produced as a two-act play, or each of its two acts may be performed independently of the other. Act One runs fifty minutes, Act Two thirty minutes. With a ten-minute intermission, that makes a full-length modern play.

When we formed The Point Place Players (no longer surviving) in a disused sanctuary (likewise), we chose for our maiden voyage Andre Obey's wonderful play, *Noah*, and performed it as dinner theatre. Shortly thereafter I received a phone call from the local representative of a group which travels the country playing church drama. He wanted to hear about what we were doing so he could "do some pioneering in this field"! Like *The King of Babylon*, *The Survivors* is too long for a normal worship service (why do I assume that something like an hour is the "normal" time for a worship service?), especially when both acts are performed, but just the right length for a dinner theatre. A sponsoring group serves a church supper, and afterwards the audience repairs to the sanctuary or other playing area for the performance. Alternatively, the supper may be served between acts. The audience receives food for body and food for soul.

THE SURVIVORS

A Play in Two Acts

RUNNING TIME: Eighty minutes
ACT ONE . . . . The day the rain came
ACT TWO . . . . Twelve years later

CAST OF CHARACTERS
NOAH, a vinedresser.
MARA, his wife.

PRODUCTION NOTE

The play is in two acts, but is designed so that either act may be produced independently as a self-contained one-act play. When produced independently, the plays should be labeled: "*The Survivors: Act One*," or, "*The Survivors: Act Two*."

Act One may be performed on a bare stage with any weight-bearing object, the apron, or other feature, substituting for a "railing."

ACT ONE

(*The deck of a huge ship. NOAH plays with an imaginary bird. His play leads him to climb up on a railing. MARA enters.*)

MARA: Noah!

NOAH: (*catching his balance and coming down from the railing*) It's all right.

MARA: Please stay off that railing. Someday you're going to break your neck.

NOAH: Got carried away—chasing the bird. (*He mimes petting his imaginary bird.*)

MARA: Not with the birds again! Do you have to do that?

NOAH: I like it.

MARA: It scares me.

NOAH: I'll stay off the railing.

MARA: It's not just that. It's this thing with the imaginary birds.

NOAH: Don't watch.

MARA: How can I help it?

NOAH: She's a beauty, isn't she?

MARA: (*shuddering*) Don't. Why don't you get yourself *real* birds? I could stand that.

NOAH: I couldn't. They're messy.

MARA: Ham keeps real birds. He's got a raven he's teaching to talk.

NOAH: He keeps it in a cage.

MARA: What else?

NOAH: Birds should be free. Birds should be free. And look at the mess that raven makes all over the place.

MARA: Well, at least it's real.

NOAH: A real mess.

MARA: A real bird.

NOAH: So are my birds.

MARA: Noah!

NOAH: Mmm.

MARA: They are not!

NOAH: Not what?

MARA: Not real.

NOAH: Mmm.

MARA: You just do that thing with your hands.

NOAH: Mmm.

MARA: But there's no bird.

NOAH: Uh-huh.

MARA: No bird! You're just pretending.

NOAH: No bird?

MARA: You know it.

NOAH: If there's no bird, how can it bother you?

MARA: *It* doesn't.

NOAH: You said it does.

MARA: You! You bother me. Doing that. Acting like you have a bird.

NOAH: I *do*.

MARA: You don't!

NOAH: I think I do.

MARA: Then you're crazy.

NOAH: You married me.

MARA: So I'm crazy, too.

NOAH: (*offering the "bird"*) Want to play with my bird?

MARA: Don't do this.

NOAH: You want me to get rid of it?

MARA: Yes.

NOAH: Kill it?

MARA: What?

NOAH: Do you want me to kill the bird?

MARA: There isn't any bird.

NOAH: Then it doesn't matter, right? If there's no bird, then you don't care if I kill it, right? (*He mimes twisting a bird's neck.*)

MARA: Please don't.

NOAH: Why not?

MARA: Just don't.

NOAH: How can it matter?

MARA: Don't.

NOAH: I might as well.

MARA: (*giving up*) I don't care . . . . It's so quiet.

NOAH: The bird is dead.

MARA: (*after a pause*) I haven't heard you working.
NOAH: I stopped.
MARA: Are you tired?
NOAH: Yes.
MARA: How much more have you got to do?
NOAH: It's done.
MARA: Done!
NOAH: Yes.
MARA: Finished!
NOAH: Finished.
MARA: All of it!
NOAH: All of it. Have a look around.
MARA: No. I hate it.
NOAH: Better learn to love it.
MARA: It's drab, awful.
NOAH: It's roomy.
MARA: It's almost as big as the vineyard.
NOAH: You're jealous.
MARA: And it's better than the house we live in.
NOAH: Well, we're *going* to live *here*.
MARA: We're going to live here?
NOAH: We're supposed to. (*He begins to sweep with an imaginary broom.*)
MARA: Here!
NOAH: Yes.
MARA: Then you've changed your mind.
NOAH: What?
MARA: It's not going to be a boat.
NOAH: Ship. Yes, it is.
MARA: But now we're going to live here?
NOAH: That's what he said to do.
MARA: On a boat! On dry land!
NOAH: You just said it's better than the house.
MARA: Fine! And furniture? Where will we get the furniture? It's as big as a hotel. It's big enough for a whole resort.

NOAH: That, too.

MARA: That's what I tell people.

NOAH: What do you tell people?

MARA: I tell them you're building a resort. With a hotel. And a restaurant.

NOAH: You do.

MARA: I have to tell them something.

NOAH: No you don't.

MARA: I tell them you're going to call it "Noah's Ark."

NOAH: What?

MARA: I tell them it's a publicity thing to attract attention so people will stop.

NOAH: Good.

MARA: So they'll think you're shrewd, a good businessman.

NOAH: They believe that?

MARA: No. They think you're crazy. The boys believe it.

NOAH: They don't think I'm crazy?

MARA: Of course they do, but they think you're crazy enough to build a resort. Ham wants to be the bartender. Shem wants to be the chef—"Shem the Chef."

NOAH: But it's not true.

MARA: You're just teasing again, aren't you? I've been telling myself all along it couldn't be a boat—

NOAH: (*correcting her again*) Ship.

MARA:—a hundred miles away from water. And we're going to live here . . . Noah, it *is* a resort, isn't it?

NOAH: Noah's what?

MARA: Resort.

NOAH: No, I mean the other thing—what you tell them I'm going to call it.

MARA: Oh. Ark. Noah's Ark.

NOAH: Ark.

MARA: It sounds nice, much nicer than boat—Noah's boat!

NOAH: Ship. It's a ship. Noah's ship. When it's this big, it's a ship.

MARA: But ships are for water.

NOAH: And birds are for air.

MARA: And we're on dry land.

NOAH: True—so far.

MARA: It'll be a marvelous hotel!

NOAH: I thought you hated it.

MARA: What I hate is a boat—ship. But if we're going to *live* here . . . . A resort hotel! Oh, you are clever! (*She throws her arms around him in a dance of joy.*) It will be our living!

NOAH: (*stopping her*) No.

MARA: No?

NOAH: No. I didn't build it for a hotel.

MARA: (*deflated*) Then why? Why have you made this thing? It's consumed you. It's consumed us. And never once have you told me why!

NOAH: I told you, I didn't know why.

MARA: Who builds such a thing without knowing why?

NOAH: But I know now.

MARA: Will you talk sense!

NOAH: When I was building it, I didn't know why I was building it, except to be building it. Because he told me to.

MARA: He told you to!

NOAH: But he never said why. He just said do it. And I did it. You're crying again.

MARA: You play with birds that aren't there. You talk to gods that aren't there. You build boats for water that isn't there.

NOAH: Ship. It's a ship. And it was one God. And he is there—here. He was. And he said build a ship. So I built the ship. He didn't say why.

MARA: This God wants a ship built, so he comes to a farmer like you?

NOAH: I'm not a farmer—not merely a farmer. I am a dresser of vines.

MARA: But no ship builder.

NOAH: The principle's the same. One vine, many branches.

THE STAR THROWER

Only by that design principle could you build a ship this big.

MARA: God comes to a vinedresser instead of a ship builder because he wants a ship built like a vine?

NOAH: Because no ship builder could imagine it—a ship like no other ship before. He chose me to do it because I didn't know it couldn't be done.

MARA: If he's God, how come he didn't make it himself?

NOAH: He makes in my making. He gave me the vision. Together we cleared the field. Beam by beam we hewed the wood. Plank by plank we laid it in. Peg by peg we put it together. We made this together. And I loved it. This ship existed in the mind of God who put the plans into my brain. Then it became a thing you can see and touch and live in. This thing was not. Now it is. I loved making it.

MARA: (after a pause) Noah.

NOAH: Yes.

MARA: I don't mean to criticize—

NOAH: Then don't.

MARA: Now that you're done making it, don't you think a bit of . . . decoration . . . would be a nice touch?

NOAH: You mean curtains?

MARA: Just like you! No, I don't mean curtains. I mean something grand. Something great, like the boat itself—the ship. Maybe . . . a figurehead!

NOAH: What?

MARA: A figurehead! Silly! You really don't know anything about boats at all!

NOAH: Only how to build the biggest and best one ever! . . . What's a figurehead?

MARA: A figurehead is a carving, a statue, a sculpture. You carve it out of wood, you paint it, and you put it on the front of the boat.

NOAH: The prow. Ship.

MARA: Pardon?

NOAH: The front is the prow, and this ship doesn't have one.

MARA: Doesn't have what?

NOAH: Front—prow.

MARA: There, you see? Wherever you put the figurehead, you can call that the front.

NOAH: Prow. Why should I call it one if it isn't one? What's it for?

MARA: The figurehead?

NOAH: Yes, of course, the figurehead!

MARA: Appearance. Aesthetic value.

NOAH: Ha! The vision itself, the thing itself—look!—that's aesthetic value! Don't need a statue stuck on the front!

MARA: Prow.

NOAH: Whatever!

MARA: (*pouting*) I still think it might make it look a little more pleasing, less austere.

NOAH: Pleasing to whom?

MARA: To everyone.

NOAH: I didn't build this ship to please everyone. I built it for God. Built it to his own order and his own specifications. Not to show off some petty effigy, some idol. This ship is God's grace. This ship is the means of our salvation!

MARA: I don't know what you're talking about. You don't care what people think?

NOAH: Think! My fig tree, woman! What makes you think people think? They don't think. They . . . they wuffoe.

MARA: I don't think I heard you.

NOAH: They wuffoe. That's the sound they kept making all the time I was building this ship. They stood around and they watched me build it. And they kept crying out in loud voices saying, "Wuffoe! Wuffoe, Noah! Wuffoe you doing that, Noah, wuffoe?" And they laughed at me. They danced rings around me. They performed pantomimes against me. They said, "You building a wooden bird, Noah? Wuffoe, Noah? How you fixin' to make it fly, Noah?" And when I

THE STAR THROWER

said, "I'm building a ship," they said it was a good thing I built it on dry land because it sure would never float.

MARA: They hurt you.

NOAH: Yes.

MARA: Maybe God hurt you by making you a laughingstock.

NOAH: I'd rather be a laughingstock with my ship than to be like them, the wuffoes, the ninnies and the nannies who huddle by their fires and gnaw their meat and cackle over their droppings.

MARA: You're mad at them.

NOAH: No I'm not; I hate them.

MARA: Noah!

NOAH: Is that what it's all for—this wonderful world—to spawn those misconceived mutations, those cesspools of self? If I had my way, I'd wipe them out. Human beings should dream dreams and see visions. All they do is chatter and cheat, whimper and whine, cackle and curse.

MARA: (*looking about*) It would make a wonderful hotel.

NOAH: It would.

MARA: Do it!

NOAH: (*turning, pacing to the other side of the deck*) He was here again.

MARA: (*in mounting alarm*) No! No, No, No, No, No! . . . When?

NOAH: This morning.

MARA: Where?

NOAH: Here.

MARA: Exactly where. Where did he stand?

NOAH: He doesn't stand.

MARA: Sit? (*NOAH shakes his head.*) Hover!

NOAH: What?

MARA: He hovers, is that it?

NOAH: He doesn't have a body.

MARA: You mean he's like your birds?

NOAH: No.

MARA: What does he look like?

NOAH: I told you, he doesn't have a body.

MARA: Well, what do you see?

NOAH: I don't see anything.

MARA: Because there's nothing to see.

NOAH: Right.

MARA: Because he's not really there.

NOAH: He is there.

MARA: How do you know he's there?

NOAH: He talks to me.

MARA: What does he sound like?

NOAH: There isn't any sound.

MARA: How can he talk to you if there isn't any sound? He's got no body, there's nothing to see, there's nothing to hear!

NOAH: All the same, he talks to me.

MARA: How do you know?

NOAH: I hear him.

MARA: How can anyone else know he talks to you? How can I know?

NOAH: Look!

MARA: Again?

NOAH: Look at this ship! You're standing on it. It's proof. I built this ship because he told me to.

MARA: Noah, there are such things as hallucinations.

NOAH: This ship is no hallucination.

MARA: The voice may be.

NOAH: Can something come from nothing?

MARA: Yes!

NOAH: I know he was here.

MARA: I know you think he was here.

NOAH: (*after a pause*) Look, would you feel better if I got rid of it?

MARA: What?

NOAH: Say, if I burned it. Would that make you feel better?

MARA: What do you mean? I don't know.

THE STAR THROWER   49

NOAH: Because I think, I think that's what I'm going to do.
MARA: Is that what he told you to do—to destroy it now that
    it's finished?
NOAH: No. He told me to move into it.
MARA: Move into it.
NOAH: All of us.
MARA: All of us.
NOAH: With . . . food.
MARA: (*suspicious*) No wine?
NOAH: Food. Enough for a year.
MARA: What do you mean, all of us?
NOAH: (*hesitating*) You, me, the boys, and their wives . . . .
MARA: Just us?
NOAH: And . . . and the animals.
MARA: What animals?
NOAH: Every kind of animals. Two of each. Seven of the clean
    ones.
MARA: (*laughing nervously*) You mean like your birds?
NOAH: No. Like Ham's.
MARA: Real ones?
NOAH: Ones you keep in cages. Ones you can see and hear and
    touch—and smell.
MARA: (*laughing again*) I won't do it.
NOAH: I don't blame you.
MARA: I mean, it's all right for *us*, if you say so, but forget the
    animals.
NOAH: He wants the animals.
MARA: Fine! Let the animals move in with him, not with me.
NOAH: He wants them in the ship with us.
MARA: Sure! . . . All kinds?
NOAH: Every kind.
MARA: You're mad.
NOAH: Loony.
MARA: In the ship with us.
NOAH: That's what he says.

MARA: No!

NOAH: But I don't think I'm going to do it.

MARA: (*perplexed*) Not do it.

NOAH: No.

MARA: Thank God! Why?

NOAH: You may not believe this, but—

MARA: Not believe this! Why should I not believe this? Have you ever said anything the least bit unbelievable?

NOAH: Today he told me why—why he had me build this ship.

MARA: To move into.

NOAH: Yes.

MARA: With animals.

NOAH: He's going to wipe everybody out.

MARA: (*frustrated to tears*) Noah! You've got to stop this! You can't go on talking like this! I can't keep listening to this! It isn't healthy!

NOAH: Right. It's not . . . . He says he's going to make it rain. Hard. For forty days. Flood, flood the earth, everything. Cover the mountains. Drown everything. Drown everyone. Drown everyone.

MARA: Noah, you're imagining all this!

NOAH: Oh, God, I hope so!

MARA: Noah, God wouldn't do that.

NOAH: God says he's going to do that.

MARA: That's what I mean. Don't you see? You're not well. You're not thinking clearly. You're hearing things. You're thinking you're hearing things that simply can't be so. I mean, even if you were hearing them, they couldn't be so. Who is this, this person?

NOAH: The Lord God.

MARA: Yes. You think you hear the voice of God.

NOAH: I hear it.

MARA: And this is the God who made everything?

NOAH: He made everything.

MARA: Everyone.

NOAH: Everyone.

MARA: Well, if he did, why would he destroy everything, everyone?

NOAH: (*shrugging*) Why do we all die?

MARA: But what you're talking about, it's catastrophe, it's, it's genocide, it's the end of the world.

NOAH: Whatever you want to call it.

MARA: Noah, I have children. They came out of me. I'm going to have another. I would never harm them, never! You see? Would God kill his own children?

NOAH: He says he will.

MARA: Why? Why would he do such a thing?

NOAH: I didn't say I knew why. I said he said that's what he's going to do.

MARA: He must have said why. He must have given you some idea.

NOAH: Punishment.

MARA: Punishment! For what?

NOAH: For being corrupt and full of violence.

MARA: Whose fault is that? He made us!

NOAH: Yes, well, he's recalling us. The manufacturer has determined that the product is defective.

MARA: Then let him repair us, not destroy us! When my baby soils his diaper, I change him and bathe him. I don't drown him!

NOAH: Right. I agree completely.

MARA: Oh, thank heavens!

NOAH: He's wrong. He shouldn't destroy them.

MARA: (*apprehensively*) Noah, listen to me. Did he say—I mean, did you hear him say, why he wanted us to go on this boat?

NOAH: So we'll survive.

MARA: Survive! Why?

NOAH: Yes, why?

MARA: I mean, why us? He's going to destroy everyone but us?

NOAH: That's it.

MARA: Why is he going to spare us?

NOAH: I don't know.

MARA: He didn't give a reason?

NOAH: When you're God, you don't have to give reasons.

MARA: Did he say it's because we're not corrupt and violent?

NOAH: No. He just said to get ready. (*Making up his mind, decisively*) I'm going to burn it.

MARA: You built it. God told you to get on it, and now you're going to burn it?

NOAH: Yes.

MARA: Why?

NOAH: Suppose it happens. Suppose I'm not crazy. Suppose he really wipes everybody out. Think about being the only ones left in the world. Just us, our family—the boys, their wives— and the animals, and I guess whatever swims. No one else. We'll be alone. All our friends, all the others we never knew— the ninnies and the nannies, the wuffoes—they'll all be . . . (*He shudders.*) And we alone . . .

MARA: You said *you'd* do it. You said you'd wipe them out.

NOAH: That's what I said.

MARA: If you had the choice—dying with the others or being saved all alone—you would, wouldn't you be saved?

NOAH: I don't even want to think about it.

MARA: What about us, your family?

NOAH: I should wish that on you?

MARA: What about your own life?

NOAH: Miserable!

MARA: See? You're a really good person. In spite of what you say, in spite of your hurt and your disappointment, you care about others. Noah, wouldn't God care about them, too, just the way you do?

NOAH: I don't know. He's God.

MARA: I can't believe it.

NOAH: Then that settles it. If you're right, I am crazy, and it's not going to happen. So we don't need this ship. So I'm going to burn it.

MARA: I don't understand why, now that you've built it, you're all of a sudden obsessed with the idea of burning it. You loved building it, you said so. It's well made. It'd make a wonderful hotel, a resort. You could fix things up, take care of it, greet the guests. Shem could be the chef. I could help him. I could do the laundry. It'd be our living. It'd be our own family business—something to start the boys off in.

NOAH: What I really want to do is vineyards.

MARA: You could do that, too. I mean, the investment's already here—the lumber, the pitch, all the labor.

NOAH: But if I burned it, it'd be like renouncing my visions.

MARA: You'd also be admitting to all the world that they were nothing but hallucinations. But if you go ahead and open it up as a hotel, everybody'll think that's what you really meant to do right from the start, and they'll think how clever you were all along.

NOAH: Yes, but every time *I* look at it, I'll think how all those people might have died if it'd been true. No. I'll tear it apart. If that's what you want, I'll use the lumber to build a proper hotel—you know, something box shaped, flamingos, a pool. Scratch the pool. Tennis courts. And a playground for the kids.

MARA: Noah, you don't have to change it. Why go to all that work? Just change your mind a little. The ark is really a—

NOAH: Ship.

MARA: —the ship is really a wonderful advertisement, so visual and all, especially out here so far away from the water. Talk about a novelty! Please, Noah. For me. For the boys. For us.

NOAH: Well, we'll see. (*He looks about.*) It would make a marvelous hotel, marvelous! (EXIT)

MARA: (*looking about and then up at the sky*) And if it ever did rain—for forty days—and if there ever was a flood, we'd be safe! (EXIT.)

(We hear animal sounds. Or dancers or stagehands representing animals begin to sneak and then stampede on board. The sound and-or activity builds in a crescendo climaxing in storm.)

(NOAH enters and slumps over the rail. He speaks to the heavens.)

NOAH: Still at it? Lightning! Thunder! Rain, rain, rain, rain, rain, rain! Day and night, week after week—rain. You call that power? I call it boring, petty, contemptible. You've done it; you've really done it, haven't you? You pulled the plug. The waters above the earth and the waters under the earth, they rushed together. The houses, the shacks went ripping away, people perched on top of them like trapped chickens. When it began, the neighbors shrugged it off. When it kept coming, they grumbled. When it started to wash everything away, they scurried like screeching rats. Inside the ship we could hear them. The family from the other side of the hill, I wanted to let them in, take them with us, and we were afraid to do it, because there were hundreds of others with them, thousands of others, sloshing in the mud, squealing in the rain. So we sealed the hatch—stout gopher wood! I did that—me, a decent sort of man. I sealed the hatch against them. It didn't just happen to them; I did it to them. They pounded on the sides. They clawed. Look there—you can see the scratchings where they tore at the seams with their fingernails. And the waters kept coming. And they splashed about. They clutched at the sides until they couldn't hold on any longer and they swirled away. They clung to the treetops until the treetops went under. They held out their babies and they begged us to take them. They tore their clothes and lashed their children to limbs and they pushed them across the water at us, and the current crashed them away. And every fool who climbed onto something to float was swamped.

THE STAR THROWER

And every floating family was attacked by flailing arms and thrashing legs like sharks going after the bloody gunwales. They were bloody because the people on top bit off the fingers of the ones trying to get on. But then they ripped the rafts to splinters and dragged them under the waves with them. Oh God, let me forget their eyes! Let me not hear their screams! And their silences, their terrible silences when they slid under the water. And I was glad—glad to see them go—because I was in the ship. That's what really sickens me, you know that? That is what makes me sick. I make me sick! I am sick because I'm glad it wasn't me. And now you're going to make me live, aren't you? You're going to make me live knowing that about myself. My miserable self! And where were you, God, you no-body God? You can't drown, can you? Oh, no; but you can watch babies drown. Aren't you ashamed of yourself? You shut your heart just the way I shut my hatches, when your children were out there dying. How could you be safe and dry? Why didn't you leap into the water and save them? How could you not do that? How could you be as small and as evil as me? And call yourself God! Is that the best idea of yourself you've got? Murderer! You murderer! You mass murderer! Answer me! I dare you! I accuse you of murder! Order, order in the court! I hereby summon before this bar of justice—this bar of injustice—I summon here the Lord God almighty, maker of heaven and earth, creator and ruler of all that is—the earth, the sky, the sea, the beasts of the field, the birds of the air, the creatures that drown in the depths of the sea. At such-and-such a time, this Lord God almighty did willfully and with malice aforethought cause to fall, for forty days, rain—thereby engendering upon the face of the earth a great flood, which great flood did most horribly and cruelly drown every living creature outside of Noah's ship—drowned them, killed them—each and every one of them murdered by his Divine Majesty—horrible! Let the accused appear to answer this indictment! Stand forth, murderer! . . . No? You do well never to show your face . . . . Never ask for justice! Never pray for mercy! Never beg for pity! Heaven drops no gentle dew. Heaven rains down death. And I further accuse you of making me your accomplice! You made me watch you do it. You made me consenting unto their deaths. You made me glad to be alive to watch them die . . . . You think I can't do anything about it. That's where you're wrong. You know what I can do? I can stop you! I can end it. You pulled the plug; well, I can pull the plug, too! I can scuttle this ship with all hands! Then where will you be? . . . Maybe you think I can't do it . . . . Maybe I can't. I'm not like you. But if I can't kill the others, then, just as a little gesture, God, just as a tiny protest, one man's protest, I think I will jump overboard. Yes, I'll jump ship. This is where I get off. Better a clean death in the water than alive and strangling on the vomit of self-hate. Yes, that's what I'll do. I'll jump in with all your other victims. And I'll leave you, almighty God, I'll leave you with your great, almighty, godly triumph! (*He climbs up on the railing.*)

MARA: (*entering*) Noah!

NOAH: What?

MARA: The animals!

NOAH: What?

MARA: The lion is roaring at the lamb and tearing at the bars of its cage!

NOAH: Again!

MARA: You'll have to separate them further.

NOAH: (*to Heaven*) For the sake of your lamb! You won't let me go, will you? (*He climbs down and goes inside.*)

MARA: (*singing to the baby bundled in her arms*)
    On the waves
    To and fro
    Gently rock

Sleeping.

Gone the sun,
Shine the stars.
Gently rock
Sleeping.

See? Hasn't the rain begun to ease up? Can it ever stop? Of course it can. It will! It's better out here in the rain than inside. You can't get your breath in there. It's a zoo in there. Or a tomb. No, it's a nursery. How beautiful you are, Japhet, my little chick! How beautiful your face, your eyelids, your mouth, your tiny hands. I love it when your incredible fingers close on my breast. How beautiful your skin! How beautiful, how very beautiful you are! Alive! Life of my life! Alive! How precious it is to be alive! Once many others were alive, too, and now they are dead. It was—I can never tell you how it was—the night you were born and the waters came. Even here in the ark I could hear them. Over the cries of our own birthing . . . I could hear the screams of those outside who were drowning. I wept for them while I rejoiced for you— my beautiful one. They're gone, and you are here . . . Your father carries such pain, but out of my pain God has delivered me you—my beauty, my joy, my life! What a miracle you are! Your father thought God was going to destroy everything, but for me God had a different word. To Noah's ears God spoke destruction, but to me God spoke through my womb and God said, "This is a beginning." You are the new beginning. I know his secret, God's secret. As you grow, I'm going to teach it to you, my chick, my own. This is God's secret—are you listening? Are you? In all creation there is no solid ground where you can stand safe; our only salvation is to rest in the ark and be carried by God's power. We have to trust. That's what you must learn, not only from me, but especially from your father. You must honor your father for that—he obeyed the word of God, even though he heard it only in the imaginings of his heart. Those who did not obey God have perished. They were corrupt and violent. God is the judge of all of us, and God did not judge them fit to survive. Their dying was hideous. But we, we have to be . . . buoyant. We have to trust and go on. One day—some day—the waters will go back. Then we'll see the mountains again, and the trees, and the land, dry land! And you, my chick, you'll enter a world that's clean. Everything evil washed away. You'll have no enemies. The corrupt and violent ones, the strife, the wars and hatred—they'll all be gone. You'll be the new beginning—you and your brothers and their babes—you'll be the firstborn of the new humanity, to start all over again. No violence, you hear me? No hate, no coveting, no envy, and above all no killing—your mother tells you. Each one must live in the land in peace, everyone beneath his vine and fig tree. Oh, what a paradise! Yes! You'll take your first steps on this bright new world. Your beautiful little foot will press its print into the shining sands of the new-made shore. You'll run beside the sea, you'll lie in the sun, you'll build castles and dream dreams. You'll grow and increase. Oh, what a race of beings must spring from beauties like you—soft and beautiful and serene! You'll be something wonderful! You'll become that beautiful boy David and play your harp! You'll become that wrinkled wisdom Socrates and set mankind's mind free! You'll become that magical Michelangelo and bring stone to life! You'll chant for Beatrice and you'll sing sonnets to the Dark Lady! You'll compose a tragic symphony, my little genius! You'll paint pictures of the starry night! You'll stand among the lilies of the valley and preach parables to the multitudes! You are the promise that God's dreams will come true! At a great and terrible price your new future has been purchased, the price that had to be paid, to wash the world clean, and you shall be worth it! Oh, my goodness! Now you've gone and done it, haven't

THE STAR THROWER

59

you? You've gone and soiled yourself! Well, come inside. We'll just wash you and change you and make you all dew-drop fresh again, my little Rose of Sharon! (EXIT.)

(*Enter NOAH hiding a saw in one hand and with the other hand lugging a huge bucket from which he averts his nose. He sets his burdens down, wipes his hands, and complains to Heaven.*)

NOAH: You create. Then you wash it out. And who is down in the hold cleaning up the filth? Your humble servant, that's who! Your sea slug—that's what you created me! I get to clean up your mess. Thanks a heap—some heap! Whatever happened to that "dominion" idea, I'd like to know? I'm the lowest of the low. (*He picks up the huge bucket.*) I suppose elephants are your idea of a joke, right? Just listen to me laugh! And seasick elephants at that! (*He makes as if to empty the bucket over the rail, remembers to stop and wet his finger to test the wind direction, then dumps the contents over—or, better, performs the old circus clown act of throwing the contents directly at the audience; but the contents had better be nothing, or if something, then confetti which has to be swept up later!— and looks after, meditating.*) Scavengers—the sharks—the sharks and me. I remember how it was—for weeks the corpses of your killing clogged the waterways, their stench unendurable until your stupid sharks gulped down their offal. (*He looks toward the hatch where MARA has gone.*) The woman nurses her baby with never a thought to those who died. (*Laughing*) How does she know but her slaughter-spawned small fry might grow up to be a shark? Why not? We're the ones, we're the scavengers who're supposed to live on all your droppings—the miseries, the failures, the corpses—the corpses. You don't know what it's like. You can't die. If you could put yourself in our place! Well, you'll know soon enough—the woman and the baby and his brothers and their wives and the animals and Noah—alone together in what's left of your rotting world. Your regurgitation—I'm supposed to drain it all off and plant it all over again, am I? Like that play toy Shem made—he calls it a yo-yo! There's a yo-yo, all right! You, too! You would spin the world out time after time to amuse yourself to all eternity, huh? Well, I've got news for you. I have cut the string! Yes! I'm sick unto death of your planetary yo-yo and your galactic carnage—sick and tired! And I'm too old to start all over again. I'm too old to be a Daddy. I won't do it. I won't! Listen to me, God. I have pulled the plug. I have scuttled this ship. (*Defiantly, he displays a saw.*) I've cut a hole in the hull. You hear me? It's sinking, this ark, it's sinking—right now, right this moment, even as I speak, it's sinking! Going down, all hands aboard! Down, down we go like the last leaf sucked into the stinking primordial slime! Down! Down! (*He staggers as the ship apparently strikes something solid. He regains his balance and realizes what has happened.*) Oh God! You've put a mountain under me!

MARA: (*entering*) Noah! We've struck land!

NOAH: Something like that.

MARA: The water's going down!

NOAH: Yes.

MARA: Soon we'll be starting over!

NOAH: Maybe. It's late.

MARA: When the water's gone, the horrible ones, there're all gone, aren't they? It's going to be so beautiful!

NOAH: It's going to be so muddy.

MARA: The sun will shine!

NOAH: The sun will burn.

MARA: We can set the animals free.

NOAH: Well, loose, set them loose.

MARA: And our family, they'll increase, they'll be fruitful and multiply.

NOAH: And divide.

MARA: There will be crops!

THE STAR THROWER 61

NOAH: God knows I've sent down enough manure—to mingle with his own fertilizer.

MARA: (*holding her cupped hands out toward Noah*) Here.

NOAH: What?

MARA: Take him.

NOAH: What's that?

MARA: Ham's raven.

NOAH: There's nothing.

MARA: Yes. See?

NOAH: What are you doing?

MARA: Set him free. If he doesn't come back, he's found a place to land, and the water's down!

NOAH: More likely he'll lose his way and drown.

MARA: Why won't you do it?

NOAH: There's nothing there!

MARA: You used to think there was before!

NOAH: I'm older now. Now I'm a man.

MARA: You're afraid!

NOAH: Afraid! God, yes, I'm afraid!

MARA: But you have to trust!

NOAH: I did. I trusted!

MARA: And here we are!

NOAH: Yes, here we are.

MARA: Set the bird free to see if it's time—time to land and start again.

NOAH: Start again, and end again, and start again, and end again? What for? No; if I'm going to start again, I've got to have some kind of guarantee. I've got to know it's not all going down the drain again.

MARA: Noah, we've survived!

NOAH: Why?

MARA: I don't understand.

NOAH: Neither do I. Why were we spared?

MARA: You found favor with the Lord.

NOAH: Favor! Great! Great! I've been favored to watch all the others drown. I've been favored to hear their screams, their gurgling screams. Now I'm favored with the memory, the ineradicable memory, of all of it. I've been favored to see their bodies bob back to the surface, favored to smell their stench while they were ripped apart by the things that swim in the midst of the sea. To see them, to hear them howl forever, I am favored! God slaughters, and I am favored to swallow all the guilt of the man who was favored to be spared! I'll be favored to slog through the sludge and the slime. I'll be favored to roast in the sun! I'll be favored to raise up another generation of victims. I thank God for all God's favors!

MARA: God has favored us with a new child. Japhet is God's promise. Our new child is God saying, "Yes! Go forward! Here's your future! Spread your wings! Go forth once more, unconquerable spirit of humankind!"

NOAH: What would you do if I tore your baby from your breast and threw him to the sharks?

MARA: (*recoiling*) You're unspeakable!

NOAH: That's what God does! That's what God does! It's his sole occupation. And he is not unspeakable; he's ineffable! And he makes us accomplices in his atrocity!

MARA: Noah, you can't live in the past!

NOAH: You call this living?

MARA: Oh, I know, I know! The pain! (*She holds NOAH.*) But you have to let it go. It's over.

NOAH: It will happen again. It will be the same, eternally the same.

MARA: How do you know that?

NOAH: How do I know anything different?

(*They are silent while she holds him.*)

MARA: (*looking up*) Noah, look!

NOAH: What?

MARA: There!

NOAH: What is it?

MARA: I don't know. A bird, maybe. I'm not sure.

NOAH: I don't see it.

MARA: There! Sweeping out of the sun.

NOAH: Where?

MARA: Blazing a trail of color in the sky, gliding down toward us—

NOAH: I see the color—like a bow.

MARA:—straight toward us! Like the Spirit of God, coming nearer, nearer!

NOAH: Where?

MARA: Here!

(*MARA mimes catching a bird. They look at it.*)

NOAH: But what kind is it?

MARA: You're the expert.

NOAH: I don't know.

MARA: You've seen every creature on earth.

NOAH: But not this one.

MARA: How did you miss getting it for the ark?

NOAH: I can't imagine.

MARA: Where could it have nested through all this flood?

NOAH: Where could it have come from?

MARA: From God!

NOAH: It's like no bird I ever saw—pure white, plump, and pounding with life.

MARA: A winged newness, a never-known creature that wasn't here before, and now it is here. Something newly made from God, a new creation, altogether new, and he sent it to us! (*She puts the "dove" into his hands.*)

NOAH: (*looking to the horizon*) New. Then I guess we'll have to go see what else is out there.

MARA: Isn't it beautiful!

(*They begin to leave. NOAH stops to speak to Heaven.*)

NOAH: You're not going to take it back, are you?

(*An answering chord of music sounds and a rainbow appears.*)

(EXEUNT.)

(CURTAIN.)

ACT TWO

A wine press on a hilltop. NOAH sleeps in the sun.

MARA: (*off*) Noah! Noah!

(*NOAH begins to waken. ENTER MARA carrying a basketful of grapes.*)

Oh, thank God! I was afraid you'd fallen into the vat again!

NOAH: (*shaking out the cobwebs*) What's the matter?

MARA: Have you been drinking?

NOAH: Dreaming. I have been dreaming. Alabaster towers! A city coming down out of heaven from God, and a throne with a rainbow 'round it!

MARA: Noah, wake up!

NOAH: What time is it?

MARA: The middle of the day—too early for drinking.

NOAH: Tasting the wine is not drinking.

MARA: (*setting down the basket*) It is, the way you do it.

NOAH: The wine must be tasted! Merely an occupational hazard, my love, nothing more.

MARA: You're not drunk?

NOAH: Of course I'm not drunk. I'm hung over—a little.

MARA: Noah!

NOAH: Well, a little wine tasting, a little nap—someone has to do it. (*NOAH holds up an empty wineskin.*) When I perfect the process, when I get it right, the right ingredients, the right treatment, then the wine will grant inspiration without intoxication. We will shake off the nightmares of death. We shall dream dreams of life! (*He struggles to rise.*) One will be lifted up (*sinking back*) without being let down.

MARA: I need you with a clear mind.

NOAH: A clear mind! Why?

MARA: (*helping him to his feet*) The boys are at it again!

NOAH: (*unconcerned*) Of course they are. Did you bring the grapes?

MARA: A basketful.

NOAH: (*examining the grapes*) Ah!

MARA: Noah, you've got to do something!

(*NOAH eats a grape.*)

Ham has been threatening Shem!

NOAH: Mmm.

MARA: He says he'll do something terrible!

NOAH: Ham has been threatening something terrible ever since the day he became lord and master of his own valley.

MARA: And Shem is threatening back!

NOAH: Shem always threatens back.

MARA: It's different now. Ham spends morning to night making spears!

NOAH: Mmm.

MARA: Spears, spears, and more spears!

NOAH: And swords.

MARA: And swords.

NOAH: (*he knows all about it*) And Shem does the same.

MARA: And Shem does the same.

NOAH: I know. I know. I watch them. Industrious lads! (*He hauls the basket of grapes to a spot where he can sit down to sort them.*)

MARA: And you're going to do nothing about it but sort grapes?

NOAH: Sorting grapes is doing something about it.

MARA: (*pacing*) I've tried to think it out, to understand it. When did our sons become enemies instead of brothers?

NOAH: (*thinking it over*) They always were rivals, even as boys— trying to see who could jump the highest, run the fastest, throw a stone . . . but enemies . . . I don't know. Maybe it was when each one became lord and master of his own valley.

MARA: And you should see the valleys!

NOAH: (*bored*) Should I? (*He bites into a sour grape.*) Why do you think I gave Ham (*he tosses the remainder of the sour grape Right*) that valley, and Shem (*he examines another grape and scowls*) that valley (*tosses the grape Left*), and took for myself (*he pops a grape in his mouth*) this hill between them? Up here I can keep an eye on both of them.

MARA: (*gazing into the valley Left*) Beautiful valleys! Fields and water enough to feed everyone with almost no work at all! They neglect it. They're too busy making swords and spears. They don't take care of the fields and flocks. All their people are making them, too—swords and spears, spears and swords! And they have almost nothing to eat. When I see little Elam with his ribs all sticking out, it makes me furious!

NOAH: Tell them.

MARA: I do tell them.

TOGETHER: But they don't pay attention.

NOAH: Taste these grapes.

(*MARA tries one.*)

Well?

MARA: It tastes all right to me.

NOAH: All right? All right? Magnificent! The secret is in the pruning. No harvesting for the first three years, but each year prune the branches that are barren. Let the fruitful branches rest high in the sunlight. It's the sunlight that does it! (*Popping a grape into his mouth*) Magnificent!

MARA: Sometimes I think it's all just a game.

NOAH: (*examining the grapes*) Ah, but what a magnificent game!

MARA: I mean Shem and Ham.

NOAH: Oh, them.

MARA: Especially Ham.

NOAH: Ham likes to play soldier. Always has.

MARA: But they're grown men now.

NOAH: Playing grown-up soldiers.

MARA: But it's not just playing.

NOAH: You just said it was.

MARA: Only in a way. It's dangerous.

NOAH: *Life* is dangerous.

MARA: (*looking down into the valley Right*) I don't think Ham loves his wife anymore.

THE STAR THROWER 67

NOAH: (*defensive*) What's that supposed to mean?

MARA: I just don't think he—well, knows how to give her what she needs.

NOAH: What does she need?

MARA: Caring—listening to—taking notice of.

NOAH: Recognition.

MARA: That's she's a person, valuable. Same for their children. Ham doesn't know what to do with them.

NOAH: Who does?

MARA: So he goes off and makes spears. He's just like you and your winemaking.

NOAH: I'd say that winemaking and spear making are two rather distinct activities.

MARA: It's his excuse to ignore them, escape them.

NOAH: He's creative, like his father.

MARA: He is not; he's destructive.

NOAH: He *makes* things.

MARA: To destroy . . .

NOAH: (*softening*) His brother.

MARA: (*nodding*) That wasn't the idea at the start. At first it was just his excuse to get out of the house. Then he thought he had to find a reason for making all those spears. So now he blames Shem for being his enemy.

NOAH: Mmm.

MARA: He tells everyone that Shem and his household are planning to conquer them all—all of Ham's household— take away their valley and make them slaves.

NOAH: He says that.

MARA: And Shem says the same thing about Ham. And they both spend all their days making swords and spears. And they both neglect the very households they pretend to protect.

NOAH: We all pretend.

MARA: I think they've frightened themselves into believing it . . . . Ham's making something new.

NOAH: I told you, he's creative. What is it?

MARA: Something new and terrible.

NOAH: Ah! A new spear?

MARA: No.

NOAH: New sword?

MARA: No. Some kind of machine. He calls it—I forget. He says it's going to be powered by horses, and it'll be made out of something new, with wheels of something called "iron," whatever that is. It'll be—he calls it "The Ultimate Weapon."

NOAH: That ought to be something!

MARA: (*stifling a sob*) He says it'll destroy Shem.

NOAH: Mmm.

MARA: And Shem's sending spies to try to find out Ham's secret so he can steal the idea and make the new weapon first and destroy Ham!

NOAH: Well, then, there'll just be a stalemate, won't there?

MARA: No; just more neglect and more destruction.

NOAH: (*going back to sorting through the grapes*) You think winemaking is my excuse to ignore you?

MARA: Me, everything. Isn't it?

NOAH: Of course not.

MARA: Oh?

NOAH: It's my work, it's my task, my calling.

MARA: And what am I?

NOAH: Certainly not my work!

MARA: Maybe I should be.

NOAH: (*going to her*) I'm not a good husband.

MARA: You built our home.

NOAH: Our ship. I love building. Building this winepress— the basin here, the wall, the drain, the vat—pure joy, pure joy! I'm a prideful man. I take great pride in my craftsmanship. And I'm afraid there's no limit to my ambition. I would build houses and halls, villages and roads, bridges and dams! I'd like to build a whole city—a shining city—a nation! I have this.

MARA: And you live here . . . . Why do you make the wine?

NOAH: Ah! My dream! My dream is to perfect the wine, to make it so that it won't cloud the mind, but clear it, not lull us into a stupor, but wake us to a vision!

MARA: Noah, you know how I hate the wine.

NOAH; And I love it!

MARA: Wine leads to drunkenness!

NOAH: The wine brings dreams of divinity!

MARA: It makes men beasts!

NOAH: It could transform us into angels! Why not? In the wine is the gift of God himself. Rooted in holy ground, it grows by God's grace. God's tears water it, God's kiss warms it. If only we could distill away the impurities! If we could drink the fruit of the vine and have the life of God flowing in our veins!

MARA: It frightens me when you talk like that.

NOAH: It heartens me! What a gift to give to our sons! (*Sits.*) You see them often.

MARA: The boys? Every day.

NOAH: How can you . . . well, tolerate it?

MARA: Is that why you don't go to see them—you can't stand them?

NOAH: I can watch them from up here. I'm busy with my own creating.

MARA: Drinking wine.

NOAH: Making wine. What about Japhet?

MARA: Japhet lives with us.

NOAH: I know Japhet lives with us. Does he see his brothers often?

MARA: They try to bully him, but it doesn't seem to bother him.

NOAH: What does Japhet think of his brothers—and their games?

MARA: Why don't you ask him?

NOAH: All right; I'll try to remember to do that.

MARA: Strange—I think Japhet feels . . . sorry for them. But he wants his own valley the day he becomes a man.

NOAH: And he will have it! Have a valley of his own he shall! There's plenty for everyone!

MARA: Ham and Shem tease him.

NOAH: Bully him and tease him.

MARA: They say they'll make Japhet work for them, make his valley their farm.

NOAH: And what does Japhet say?

MARA: He says he won't. But he's warmhearted. He loves his brothers. I don't think they love anything but power. Japhet doesn't know whether to battle them or befriend them. He looks to you to know what he should do. Japhet depends on you. We all do.

NOAH: (*examining another bunch of grapes*) It takes a supple branch to support so much weight. (*He carries the grapes to a bucket and begins washing them.*) Do you suppose they remember?

MARA: Remember what?

NOAH: (*shaking water off the grapes*) The flood.

MARA: I think for them it's a long time ago, almost like a dream.

NOAH: A dream! Ah, yes. We only dreamed them, the corpses. That's how it begins again . . . . (a *news flash*) God has commanded, from this time forward, no more killing.

MARA: Oh, God! My boys!

NOAH: (*squeezing grapes over the wine vat*) How could God blame them? Ham used to play at being God.

MARA: He made a bow and shot arrows. He called them lightning.

NOAH: He thought God displayed his power in the lightning— shaking heaven and earth, riving the rock, shattering the oak, drowning the world. (*He wipes his hands.*) But that was a shameful abuse of power. Now God has grown wiser.

MARA: Does God do that?

NOAH: Do what?

MARA: Grow?

THE STAR THROWER 71

NOAH: I think so—grows wiser. So may we. Maybe we're like God in that. God is in the vine.

MARA: (*looking about*) Where?

NOAH: I mean when it grows—slowly, silently. God's power is there, too, there most. Not in the shattered oak, but in the growing vine. And if in the vine, why not in the wine? And if in the wine, why not in us?

MARA: In us!

NOAH: Who knows?

MARA: (*after a pause*) Does he . . . visit you anymore?

NOAH: God? No; not the way he did in the old days. No more shipbuilding, no more floods, no more heroics.

MARA: He's not involved anymore?

NOAH: Well, yes, he's still involved, but in a different way, now. (*He scoops wine from the vat.*) With this, he tells me to break ground, tells me to plant, to spread compost, to water, to prune, to pick, to press, to taste, to dream—he tells me. I like him better now, now that he speaks not in raging rivers, but in the fruit of the vine. (*Drinks, reacts.*) Mind you, there's a strength there! I believe if he wanted to he could be almost as horrific as he was back then—almost, not quite. You know, it was too much for him, too. He has grown. I'm sure of it. (*Belches.*)

MARA: (*coming to him, relieving him of the wine and setting it aside*) I remember as well as you do how dreadful it was. But it's past. Now we have to concern ourselves about now. What are you going to do about them, about Ham and Shem?

NOAH: What do you think I should do?

MARA: You could talk to them.

NOAH: I have talked to them.

TOGETHER: But they don't pay attention.

NOAH: They have to live their own lives.

MARA: If only they will! You live up here on top of your hill with your vineyards. You remove yourself from their struggles in the valleys. You leave your own children to fend for themselves.

NOAH: I leave them to live their own lives.

MARA: You're neglecting your responsibility.

NOAH: That is my responsibility.

MARA: How can you just stay up here drinking wine and ignore what's happening down there in the real world with your own flesh and blood? You're a part of that, too! Trying to forget the past, you'll lose the future. Winemaking isn't your calling. Peacemaking is your calling. You said it yourself— God commands no more killing.

NOAH: You're right. I have an obligation to them—to all life in the valleys—and I have not forsaken them. When I perfect the wine, it will bring them peace!

MARA: I'm telling you, Noah, the boys are growing more dangerous by the day—catastrophically dangerous!

NOAH: I can see that. (*He stirs the vat.*) But there's an age when the child no longer needs the parent, doesn't want the parent. The fruit matures. It falls away. It leaves the parenthood branch bare. Now: what is the unemployed parent to do with his time? Prune! Cut away the empty branch so something new can grow in its place. I am no longer in the parenthood business!

MARA: So what business are you in?

NOAH: (*posing*) You see before you the first of a new breed of men. Behold the vintager!

MARA: The what?

NOAH: The vintager. The maker of wine, drafter of dreams, alchemist of amity, visionary of the vineyards!

MARA: My madman?

NOAH: Yours.

MARA: (*going to him*) Have you lost your stomach for the struggle?

NOAH: What makes you think this isn't a struggle, a different struggle, my struggle? Have I not been ever the struggler?

MARA: Of course you have. You did . . . you were heroic! You carried us through the deluge!

THE STAR THROWER 73

NOAH: (*more chagrined than pious*) Actually, God did that.

MARA: You believed in him when no one else did. Believe now! You endured when no one else endured. You were strong!

NOAH: Well, almost.

MARA: Assert yourself again, now, in this crisis, before the valleys drown in blood! You brought us through it before! You are our captain!

NOAH: So memory, that flatterer, insinuates. Memory suggests that I was managing things; that I cut quite a figure; that I was heroic, doing some great thing. But then in my dreams reality returns and I can see again the way it really was. I was nothing more than a floating zookeeper.

MARA: You were master of the ark!

NOAH: I shoveled manure.

MARA: You obeyed God!

NOAH: It's the same thing . . . . And when it was over and the water went down and we could plant the land, I scratched the soil. And I shoveled more manure. And I pruned the vines, and I pressed the grapes, and I fermented the wine. But it was the wrong wine, and I got drunk. And then the boys—Shem and Ham and Japhet—then they saw me as I really was, instead of the way I wanted to be. Maybe that's when they became enemies.

MARA: Anyone can have a letdown. They can't blame you for their hatred.

NOAH: Surviving the flood. You know, I'm least proud of that, worse even than getting drunk. There was a reason for getting drunk. But finding a reason for surviving, finding a reason for living, now that really was heroic. That was when I began to grope after greatness. That was when I really, for the first time, really began to pay attention to God. Then he sent, and you gave me, the dove. In the dove God showed me what I should do. (*He loads more grapes into the vat.*) Like God, I was to grow. Like God, I was to create something new. You see, it's not enough to beget the generations to come. We have to create a reason for them to live. We have to transform the heart!

MARA: So Ham and Shem won't study war anymore!

NOAH: This, this will be for them. The wine will save them. As soon as I perfect it—discover the secret—sublimate the substance—etherealize the essence—distill not the wine of drunkenness, but the—the elixir of inspiration. That's it, the elixir of inspiration. When we taste God, and that drink goes to our heads and makes us dream God dreams—dreams of things that never were, visions of life as God sees it possible.

MARA: (*after a hopeful pause*) I don't understand.

NOAH: It's too much for the mind. This concept must be comprehended with the feet! Come, my love—we shall dance, you and I!

(*NOAH leads MARA to the wall of the vat where they sit and with tub and towel wash each other's feet.*)

This little piggy went wheeeee!

(*MARA and NOAH rise and gird up their loins.*)

NOAH: Up we go!

(*Holding on to the overhead ropes and to each other, NOAH and MARA climb into the winepress.*)

MARA: Careful!

NOAH: It's slippery! Whoops!

MARA: Hold on!

(*Laughing, NOAH and MARA begin to trample the grapes.*)

NOAH: We dance, and grapes give their lifeblood to make us live! We live! We dance! We live again!

MARA: We live by the grace of God!

NOAH: We live by the grapes of God!

TOGETHER: (*singing*) Sparkle and sing!
> Every good thing
> Lives in the wine!
> Hop! Hop! Hop!
> What love can bring
> 'Round in a ring

Lives in the wine!
Hop! Hop! Hop!

(*Carried away by his enthusiasm, NOAH leaps mightily in the air, slips, and splashes out of sight. Alarmed at first, then laughing, MARA pulls NOAH back to his feet. They climb out, slipping, sliding, and whooping. They sit on the wall laughing as MARA dries NOAH with a towel.*)

MARA: That's what I like about you—you do throw yourself into your work.

NOAH: (*pointing to his anatomy*) Head, heart, and sole! (*They laugh.*)

MARA: (*noticing*) Oh! You've cut yourself!

NOAH: It's nothing.

MARA: It's bleeding!

NOAH: (*wrapping the wound*) It's nothing, really! (*Quietly*) Why have you stayed by me?

MARA: Where should I go?

NOAH: There are other hilltops, valleys, meadows . . .

MARA: There were always the children.

NOAH: And now?

MARA: Now there's you. Someone has to take care of you. Someone has to save you from drowning yourself in your own wine.

NOAH: (*drawing wine from the vat*) Ah, yes. Women have the care and nurture of children—and husbands. Men—men have to invent other reasons for living.

MARA: (*after a pause*) Why do our sons look for reasons to kill?

NOAH: They are young. They have no memories. They don't understand the reasons for living.

MARA: It's not enough just to live, to dance?

NOAH: Not for me.

MARA: Then what do you think life is for?

NOAH: I've told you.

MARA: Tell me again.

NOAH: Life is for finding the purpose for life. (*NOAH takes a great swig of wine.*)

MARA: Noah, don't drink.

NOAH: I'm tasting.

MARA: I wish you wouldn't.

(*NOAH sits bolt upright, then comes to his feet transfixed.*) (*alarmed*) Noah! What is it?

NOAH: Something's happened to the wine!

MARA: What? What's the matter?

NOAH: (*pulling another deep draft*) Nothing. I mean, I'm not . . . I don't feel anything, no kick. But I see—I see visions! Visions! Visions of such beauty!

MARA: You're drunk!

NOAH: No! See? (*NOAH tiptoes an imaginary line and touches his fingertips to the tip of his nose. He stares up, entranced.*) Oh! I see a city! A city set on a hill—gleaming! I hear singing, such music! And there are people, so beautiful! And there is such fulsome, fruitful peace!

MARA: (*screaming*) Noah! Look! Down in the valley!

NOAH: (*coming to her side and peering after her pointing finger into the valley Right*) What is it?

MARA: Horses! Raising such a dust cloud! Pulling something . . . terrible!

NOAH: (*breathless*) It's Ham's new machine—his ultimate weapon!

MARA: (*crossing to look in the valley Left*) There, too!

NOAH: (*beside her*) Shem's spies have done their work!

MARA: (*distraught*) Shem has one, too!

NOAH: (*thunderstruck*) It is indeed terrible!

MARA: Oh, God, what destruction!

NOAH: Oh, God, what creativity!

MARA: They'll kill each other! They'll kill everyone!

NOAH: They can't get from valley to valley without coming over this hill!

THE STAR THROWER 77

MARA: You've got to do something!

NOAH: (*gripping a wineskin*) I am going to do something! Oh, it'll be something indeed! (*NOAH rushes to the vat and refills the wineskin.*) It's time! Now you'll see!

MARA: What are you going to do?

NOAH: I'm going to give them my great gift! (*holding aloft the wineskin*) I am going to unleash the awesome power of the new wine! Hurry! Go fetch Japhet!

MARA: Japhet! Why?

NOAH: He shall carry my gift!

MARA: Noah, I'm afraid.

NOAH: I know. (*Brandishing the wineskin*) But it's time! It is time!

MARA: They'll bully Japhet. They'll hurt him!

NOAH: They won't dare! Japhet, my son, their brother, bearing my gift, Japhet will represent my own person!

MARA: Take it yourself!

NOAH: My son shall have that honor! It is his mission, his reason to live!

MARA: They'll kill him!

NOAH: He will live! He'll bring them my great gift!

MARA: What gift?

NOAH: The wine! The gift of the wine! Now I know how to perfect it! It is the blood in the wine! When they taste this wine, they will see visions of a new life. They'll leave off making new weapons and they'll begin to make new worlds! (*NOAH throws more grapes into the press.*) Hurry! Fetch Japhet! Wait! Before you go—

(*MARA comes back to NOAH at the winepress and hurriedly helps him wash his feet.*)

I'll make the wine new! (*NOAH kisses her.*) Now off you go! Fetch Japhet!

MARA: Be careful!

NOAH: (*He dips his finger in the wine and tastes it. Then he unwraps his wound, touches his finger to his blood, and tastes*

it.) So that's the secret! That's how the wine is transformed! It's a great price to pay—but not too great a price for love to pay. (*NOAH climbs into the vat and begins prancing on the grapes.*) Run, wine! Ooze and flow! Come on, Japhet! Gather it up! Take it to your brothers! Give them life! Sparkle, liquid sunshine! Sing out, grapes! This is the dance divine! Whoever drinks of this wine will cease from killing! Drink of this wine and live eternally! Ham! Shem! You down there! You have invented engines of death! (*laughing*) But I have discovered the wine of life!
(*singing*)
What love can bring
'Round in a ring
Lives in the wine!
(*NOAH releases his hold on the overhead ropes, spreads his arms wide, and sinks into the vat.*)

MARA: (*returning*) Noah! Noah! Japhet's on his way! He'll carry the wine to his brothers! Noah, your dream is going to come true! Noah? Noah?

CURTAIN

THE KING OF BABYLON

Preface

Aeschylus (525-456 BC) was the first playwright to use two actors on stage at the same time. Sophocles (c. 497-405 BC) was the first to use three. Throughout history, many playwrights have continued to write even large-cast plays made up mostly of scenes for two actors.

The two-scene can be wonderfully clear—as direct as a tug of war or an embrace. Two-scenes can be efficient, intense, and focused. They are also convenient to rehearse.

However, two-actor plays may inhibit variety and complication. Further, by definition, the two-handed play often makes it difficult to present those situations or stories that call for on-stage multiple live characters. In Brutus' garden or tent, two actors get along very well, but they are stretched to present scenes of a plebian mob or a murderous conspiracy—not that it can't be done!

Although *The King of Babylon* (a two-character play originally intended for Good Friday) throws most of its verbal burden on The King, this in no way diminishes the importance of the Water Carrier's more laconic role which makes different and possibly even greater demands. For example, the second character in Strindberg's *The Stronger* is important, is the stronger, despite the fact that she never speaks at all.

Don't even think about directing or performing *The King of Babylon* until you have performed the exercises in Keith Johnstone's chapter on "Status" in *Impro: Improvisation and the Theatre*.[3]

THE KING OF BABYLON

A Play in One Act

RUNNING TIME: Ninety minutes
CAST OF CHARACTERS
THE KING OF BABYLON
A SLAVE

(*The throne room in Babylon. Through an opening in one stone wall a finger of light points to a fantastic dial flanked by figures carved on another wall.*)

KING: At midnight, the king of Babylon will die. I am the king of Babylon. If you were the king of Babylon, and if you knew that at midnight the king of Babylon would die, what would you do? Eh? Precisely! I abdicate. I quit. I descend from the throne. In my place, I install my successor. His reign will be regrettably brief. As prophesied, he will die. After his midnight departure, I shall reinstate my royal self. I shall become king once again. The king is dead; long live the king! I have sent for a slave—a stupid slave. Stupid—that is a prerequisite. I said to the Royal Overseer, "Go to the quarries. Sit by the well and watch the water carriers. The most chowderheaded water carrier who passes from the well, bring him to me. Then see that no one interrupts us until the hour of midnight has come and passed." At this moment, the slave is on his way. The slave is at hand. And now the slave has arrived.

THE STAR THROWER

(*ENTER SLAVE carrying water container.*)
>Kneel!

(*SLAVE kneels. KING looks SLAVE over.*)
>Rise!

(*SLAVE rises.*)
>I am king; you are slave. But these things are relative. It's a world of change. Can you speak?

(*SLAVE nods.*)
>Well, say something! (*silence*) You have my royal permission. (*silence*) I command you; speak!

SLAVE: God bless the king.

KING: Amen. Quite right. God bless the king. And give him a long life. Do you know why I am king? (*silence*) Look here, this won't do. I want to have a conversation with you. That means that when I ask you a question, you are to answer. I command you to answer. Have you got that? (*silence*) Speak!

SLAVE: God bless the king.

KING: Yes; well, good. But you'll have to answer to the point. Do you understand?

SLAVE: I understand.

KING: I know you have been taught not to speak in the presence of your betters, and there is no one better than I, but in this case I require conversation from you—and in fact quite a bit more. Now, we'll try again. Do you know why I am your king?

(*SLAVE shakes his head.*)
>Because I was born king. My father and my mother had me—and my father was king before me—a jackal! Therefore, the jackal having some years ago pushed off in the midst of a binge, I, the jackal's son, am now king. The question, then, is, why did my father and my mother have me and why did they not have you, eh? And the answer is, that is the accident of birth. You have probably never thought of it, but we both of us appear to be men, you and I—both of us male human beings born of women. As the proverb says, when the game is over the king and the pawn go back into the same box. I

dare say that you and I have all the same, well, similar parts, of human animals, and all the same functions. Yes. And yet I am a king and you are a slave. Curious, isn't it? And good thing for me, too, although I would have you know that being king does have its minor inconveniences, one of which is . . . You are well made. Who was your mother? (*silence*) Who was your mother?

SLAVE: I don't remember.

KING: Hmm. And of course you don't remember your father. To whom do you belong?

SLAVE: I belong to my king.

KING: To me. Have you ever seen me before?

(*SLAVE shakes his head.*)

Of course not. How do you suppose the accidents of birth are arranged, hmm? The gods, perhaps? Marduk, certainly, being himself king of the gods. You see, it is pre-ordained, this business of being king. Have you ever thought about it? No, I don't suppose you have. Yet it should be a matter of some interest to you. You belong to the king. Yet has it never entered your mind—why should I be the king and you the— ah—thing? Why should you belong to me, instead of the other way around? Why should not you be king and I belong to you? Just the two of us here alone together. What is it here and now that makes me your king and you my slave? I have my dagger, but if you were brave enough . . . foolhardy enough . . . strong enough, you might take the dagger from me and kill me. But that would not make you king. That would make you a corpse—as well as me. The guards would kill you. Then another—my imbecile child, in point of fact— would become king. Why? Why would my imbecile child become king? Because he is mine, devil take him, and for no other reason. So you see it is something quite beyond the two of us that makes me your king. Can you run fast? We are all of us fleas on the backside of the camel of existence, and yet one flea differs from another in glory. You are a water

THE STAR THROWER

carrier, hmm? Your legs are strong. In a footrace you might outrun me—if you dared. However, kings do not race with slaves. But if we did, and if you won, that still would not make you king, any more than if you killed me. It is not a matter of endowment. It is not a matter of ability, nor of action, nor of achievement. It is simply and exclusively a matter of the chance of birth. The only way you could have been king would have been to enter into my mother's womb. So then you would have been I—and perhaps I would have been you—and maybe we are! Maybe I was born you and you were born me. What do you think of that? That is called philosophy. Perhaps in reality you are the king and I am the slave! And if I were to die, they would come and bury you. That is philosophy. Well! But as this world judges, here we are: I ostensibly the king, and you obviously the slave. So it seems. Just the two of us, and yet because I am king and you are slave, we behave in totally different but equally predictable ways. We play our roles. I command; you obey. Kneel!

(*SLAVE kneels.*)

Then there is the matter of social training. You were taught to carry water in the quarries, and I was taught to rule from the throne. That is specialization. I rule rather well. Don't suppose you agree? What would you know? It is built into your brain. You have no choice, have you? Choice! Do you know what it is, slave, to choose? Answer me!

SLAVE: Yes.

KING: Ah! You do, do you? You know what it is to choose! What choice does a slave have? Tell me!

(*SLAVE touches his temple.*)

Oh, you can think, can you—choose to think . . . what you choose? I doubt that—at least, not if the question were to come to a point. No matter. After all, the true slavery is in the mind. But you harbor secret thoughts, do you? . . . You belong to me. Your life is mine. What would you do to serve me? What!

SLAVE: What do you wish?

KING: An answer! That is what I wish! Is there anything you would not do to serve me?

SLAVE: I carry water.

KING: Water! Say, for example, that I were to command you to take a life—to kill. You would obey my command.

SLAVE: You ask me . . .

KING: Yes.

SLAVE: You ask me whether I can choose.

KING: But you see you can't. It's kill or be killed—or worse.

SLAVE: Then that would be my choice.

KING: What! To be killed!

SLAVE: Yes.

KING: Marduk almighty! How morbid! You set your own life that low, do you? On the other hand, I don't suppose your life is worth much. Fairly miserable, are you?

SLAVE: No.

KING: Probably don't know any better, don't know enough to be miserable. Work all day—bread and water—sleep—work all next day. Hmm! Have you been tortured?
(*SLAVE nods.*)
What was it like, being tortured? . . . Tell me!

SLAVE: I was beaten.

KING: Whipped?

SLAVE: Yes.

KING: Scourged?

SLAVE: Yes.

KING: Why?

SLAVE: It was a mistake.

KING: Yes, it always is. All the same, I have ordered the torture of many. I never think about it. Rise!
(*SLAVE rises.*)
You see, authority—a great thing! I command; you obey. Holds society together. Do you place no value at all on your life?

THE STAR THROWER

SLAVE: Yes.

KING: Yes what? You do or you don't?

SLAVE: I do value life, all life.

KING: I have no idea how much you cost in the market—I don't buy or sell slaves myself—but I suppose there is a price. Now you—what would you give me for your own life, if you had it to give, that is? What exactly is it worth to you, your life? Tell me, do you have a life? You carry water. You sleep and feed.

SLAVE: Yes.

KING: And that's all.

SLAVE: I think.

KING: You think. What else?

SLAVE: I talk.

KING: Really? Better and better. What else?

SLAVE: I see. I hear. I touch.

KING: So does my donkey! You do run on, don't you? You have women, do you?

SLAVE: No.

KING: Oh? Just as well. They can be a nuisance, always— well, never mind. But you do have sex? I mean, with men, or . . . ?

SLAVE: No.

KING: Are you a eunuch?

SLAVE: No.

KING: Hmm. But you say you do touch—things?

SLAVE: And people.

KING: I thought so! You have feelings?

SLAVE: I care for people. I bring them water.

KING: So they can maintain their wretched lives in the quarries! See here! I myself have women . . . and men . . . and—never mind. I am a husband and a father, worse luck. Yet I care for no one—no one. It is a weakness . . . . Would you exchange it, your life—your entire life—would you exchange it for, say, one hour of my life?

SLAVE: No.

KING: So quickly! It loves its life after all! Suppose I were to put you in the army. Well?

SLAVE: I would not make a soldier.

KING: You're afraid to die?

SLAVE: No.

KING: Hmm. Neither am I, but I don't want to, all the same. The fact is, now that the subject has come up, the fact is there's a . . . problem. Yes. You see, there's this custom—this asinine custom—lethal, actually, fatal. (*He indicates the dial carved in the wall.*) You see this calendar? Awful, isn't it? No sense of line. Well! And you see this patch of moonlight falling on the wall? It comes through that slot in the stone over there—some astronomical mumbo-jumbo cooked up by the priests centuries ago, really. And whenever it should happen—as it does happen precisely at midnight every once in an epoch or so—whenever it should happen that that patch of light there should fall upon this skull here (*pointing to part of the dial design*) the king of Babylon must die. Must, mind you, must. Must die. It is prescribed by inviolable custom: a celestial but slaughterous game of chance . . . . As you were brought into the palace tonight you came past six tall fellows down at the end of the hall. You remember them? The ones with the lances, the long spears.

SLAVE: Standing near the great water fountain.

KING: I'm afraid that's not exactly a water fountain; rather, an altar, a somewhat rococo altar—although I can see the similarity, yes. Now, when the moonlight strikes this skull at midnight, as it will tonight, full upon it—so says the Royal Astronomer, a royal nincompoop, but annoyingly accurate when it comes to predictions—, at that moment, the king of Babylon is to don his robe of state and his crown and he is to march to the end of the hall—the end of the hall at the . . . ah, fountain . . . , and there those six tall fellows with the six long spears will . . . ventilate . . . the King of Babylon. Now

THE STAR THROWER 87

is that not a bizarre custom? Barbaric! I have protested, you understand, but it seems that when ancient usage—no matter how absurd—dictates, even kings must obey. That is irony. We are really in very much the same position, you and I— both of us slaves: you to me, and I to custom, to obscure, immemorial, irrevocable custom!

SLAVE: I am sorry.

KING: Are you? Are you? Good. Good! Because that is why you are here. You don't think I sent for you because I was thirsty? I don't need water. What I need is a substitute king, a king for tonight. I am going to make you king. How do you like that idea? I think it's brilliant. Because there is also another custom—my private custom—of self-preservation. I honor it devoutly. Not for myself, you understand. For the good of my people. I suppose you have never seen my son—the royal prince? The royal prince is a royal boil on the Babylonian behind. The thought of that becoming king! And there is so much I haven't accomplished yet! Now here, then, is our dilemma, yours and mine. How are we to avoid this bloodthirsty old custom with which the priests of the past have cursed us? I suppose I could abdicate in favor of the royal boil, and let that royal boil be lanced, but its mother raises such a fuss where it's concerned. So I'll have to think of some other way to puncture the princely pile. Meanwhile, you, my slave—you shall become the king. A happy but truncated regime. (*At the dial*) From here to here—I'd say, an hour? Oh, there is precedent. I had the Royal Historian look it up. The last time this cursed coincidence occurred, my great, great grandfather (*indicates figure carved in wall*)— well actually, he tried to send a pig in his place, but the royal court wouldn't go for it—said you couldn't make a pig king— whereas the fact is all kinds of pigs have been kings. But they went right ahead and spitted the old boy six ways from Sunday and then they barbecued the pig for good measure. But you are not a pig. You are a man—well, a human being . . . . a slave, that is. I am pleased to tell you that this need not be for you an unmitigated misfortune. Inside the bitter cup of calamity the ancient priests did put a dab of honey. They promised that the hereditary victims of this senseless custom—the noble sacrifices—immediately they have poured out their blood at the end of the hall in the . . . fountain . . . you saw—at once—so runs the primeval proclamation—the king—the former king—under our arrangement, that would be you—you become a god. Yes; it's true—officially a god!—with effigies and shrines and rites and holidays and all that sort of thing—prayed to, groveled before, blessed for babies, blamed for blemishes, importuned for fortune, poured libations for luck and lamentations for losses—a household name, (*indicating the sculptures*) your likeness carved on the walls of the palace and installed in your very own temples, the object of dread and desperate devotion! Think of it: a god! You shall be a god! From slave to god! By Marduk, I call that getting on. Not that you don't richly deserve it; you do. After all, the sacrifice you are making enables me, the rightful king, to reclaim the vacant throne and continue to rule—a task to which I am divinely ordained by birth and for which I am superbly equipped by talent and training. Besides, I like it. For your selfless contribution to the welfare of the state, you have earned your apotheosis. You shall be a god hereafter. Are you pleased? (*silence*) Awed?

SLAVE: No.

KING: Wonderful! Perfect! A man who disdains death and deification alike! Why are you unmoved? Because your life is so miserable? Speak!

SLAVE: My life is elsewhere.

KING: Elsewhere? (*suddenly suspicious*) What do you mean?

SLAVE: Not in my body. Not only in my body.

KING: Oh, well, that's good; splendid! Because you see that's all I require, your body. Look, I really am going to let you be king, you know—the real king. I wouldn't treat you shabbily.

For example, I thought we'd have a little coronation ceremony, just the two of us, you know. And then you will be the king, with all the rights and privileges appertaining thereunto—until the moonlight strikes the skull. And that means that until then you can have anything you like: you can send out for food . . . wine . . . a woman . . . women . . . anything . . . gold, tons of it . . . whatever you want. You could make gifts . . . you don't have a family?

(*SLAVE shrugs.*)

Well, what do you think you would like?—I mean anything besides your own abdication. Tell me.

SLAVE: I have everything I need.

KING: Everything you need! You! Then you are the richest man in all my kingdom—or in all the world! There's nothing I can give you? You are rich enough to give to everyone else! . . . Look; how would you like to make a few laws—you know, pronounce some edicts, enjoy a sense of power? We'll change places. You'll be king, and I'll be your servant, your amanuensis—your scribe—and you can promulgate a law or two. And I tell you what: just to show my appreciation for your splendid spirit—or body—I'll see to it as a point of honor that your law becomes, well, law—the law of the land. And all the others will have to obey that law—your law— we could name it after you. And everyone for all time would obey you slavishly, albeit posthumously. How do you like that? It's the least I can do. You'll go down in history. Your name will—. Have you got a name?

SLAVE: I am called carrier.

KING: Well, that won't do. We'll have to call you something, something impressive, something like, uh, Son of Marduk . . . or Mardukson. How does that sound? In the chronicles of history you could be Mardukson the First—I think it's a first, or how would you like to be Mardukson the Great? Now there's a name with some oomph!

SLAVE: Carrier—a carrier of water.

KING: Oh, well, it's your kingship. King Carrier. It does have a common touch to it. And alliteration. Well, then, it's agreed, isn't it? You'll do it . . . quietly . . . without objection . . . no struggle . . .

SLAVE: You command.

KING: My dear boy! Wouldn't hear of it! One doesn't command a king. Come on, then! Oughtn't waste precious time. Ready for your coronation? I have the robe and the crown . . . . Look here, you won't try, you're not going to trick me, are you? You will honor the bargain? (*silence.*) I do wish the Royal Overseer had found someone a bit more addled. I did specify stupid—and I meant tongue-lolling, slobbering stupid. Not that you're not cooperative and all that, but—ah—not as addlepated as I'd . . . (*on guard*) You know I haven't been trained to obey, so as soon as you are King you can't command me to go get killed in your place; that won't work. (*silence*) And you can't make me take it back at the last minute. What else might you try? . . . I suppose I've got to rely on your good faith. And on this (*touches his dagger*) . . . . Then let us proceed with the coronation, the coronation of King Carrier. (*He takes the king's robe and approaches the SLAVE.*) I do wish I'd thought to command a shower. Do you ever think about bathing in some of that water you carry? I suppose you'd be whipped for that, too. I'm afraid you're going to get my beautiful robe terribly—well, what of that? We can always get new robes—for a new king. Going to have to anyway, aren't we? This one's going to be full of holes and . . . Here; wrap this around you . . . No; not like that; like this . . . Ah! The royal signet ring! (*Places ring on SLAVE's finger.*) Now let's see. In this coronation ritual I say, or the priests . . . Wait! I'm forgetting the ceremony. It was a long time ago. Terribly long speech . . . a lot of incantations . . . something like (*chanting*)

Upon your shoulders the mantle of those who

THE STAR THROWER

have gone before,
As you will lead us onward forever more.
Ceremonies like this . . . are a bit of a bore . . .

I'm afraid I don't remember much of it—but that's the general effect. . . . And then you put your arms out—like so. Very good! Ah! Now the crown. You kneel here. (*chanting*)

Your head now shielded from evil
And your mind fitted for heaven . . .

and so on. Now you rise. Yes, go ahead, rise. Good. And you ascend your throne . . . . There; up there . . . . Ah! And all others kneel—blast it! Where's the scepter? Knocking about here someplace. The devil! Where's it got to? Well, here, this will have to do (*He fetches and presents a dried flower stalk*). (*chanting*)

The royal wand of power,
Father of your people,
Prince of . . . uh . . .

and so on. Now all kneel—hmm!—all kneel! (*He kneels.*) I haven't done this since I was a child . . . . Uh! . . . Your Majesty might say, "All rise" . . . You could let me up.

SLAVE: It is you who keeps yourself down.

KING: The weight of centuries of ceremony and custom keeps me down.

SLAVE: (*after a pause*) I lift from your shoulders the weight of centuries of ceremony and custom.

KING: As easy as that! What power lies in the word of a king! Then I will stand upon my feet. (*He stands.*) Ever ready to serve you, Your Majesty—ever, that is, until midnight . . . There! It's done! How do you feel?

SLAVE: I am well.

KING: No different?

SLAVE: No.

KING: Well. (*He walks about. There is an awkward pause.*) Hungry?

(*SLAVE shakes his head.*)

KING: Wonderful! Well now, let's see how you get on at the business of ruling.

SLAVE: I do not wish to rule.

KING: (*mimicking and mocking him*) "I do not wish to rule"! No! Not like that! You're a king. You must speak in a tone of command, with authority—like this: "I do not wish to rule!"

SLAVE: (*placidly*) All authority is given to me, but I do not wish to exercise authority.

KING: (*again starting to coach*) I do not wish! . . . Not exercise authority! Well, that does let the blood out of the bladder, doesn't it! How do you expect to rule if you don't exercise authority? They're the same thing; it's the sine qua non.

SLAVE: It is a sin.

KING: With one word you have just toppled the towering edifice of human governance! You have undermined all of human society. You have annihilated law and order. You are an anarchist, an anarchist king! It's like saying you'll carry water but you'll never go to the well. You see, you *have* to command, and others *have* to obey.

SLAVE: I will not command.

KING: "I will not command!" Better. You think then no one will have to obey, hmm? That's where you're wrong. The others are *made* to obey. They are created to obey, destined to obey, born to obey—they love to obey. It's all they know. They obey their leaders. They obey their spouses. They obey laws. They obey customs. They obey fads. They obey their whims! They beg to obey. They need to obey. And if not you, then someone else. In fact, that's the chief thing—to make certain they obey you and not someone else.

SLAVE: Then I shall command them not to obey.

THE STAR THROWER 93

KING: Aha! There I have you! That is a logical paradox, isn't it? They obey you by not obeying, and if they don't obey you, then in that disobedience they do obey you. You see? It's inescapable. That's logic. All the same, that would destroy authority, and they can't abide that. They'll look about till they find someone else who will command them to obey. Or to put it the other way, since you have suddenly become the philosopher king: if they don't obey, then you can't be said to rule, can you? At least, not effectively. You see? The jig is up. It is the business of a king to command, and it is the business of subjects to obey.

SLAVE: I do not wish it.

KING: I hope you won't mind my telling you this, but really you're not getting into the part. It goes with the territory, like wetness with water. It's what kings do: kings command.

SLAVE: I do not wish to command.

KING: (*sighing*) Well, there, you see? You've just done another of those logical paradox things. That's an internal contradiction. When you are king, your *wish* is a kind of command. So when you say you don't wish to command, you're really saying, "I *command* that I shall not command," and the whole thing just falls apart again. You see, all you have to do is express your wish—if you don't want to command, you just wish; that's quite all right. It's the same thing. And then your slave—your obedient servant—will write down your every wish—sometimes even when you don't express it, even when you don't wish it, he will write it down—and when it is written, when it is inscribed in the royal records, when you impress your royal seal upon it, lo and behold! it has become your royal edict—a law! Your universal command! A respectable, an unimpeachable authority—the command of law! All must obey. All of them: your slaves! Isn't it marvelous!

SLAVE: (*slowly, after a pause*) I wish to free all slaves.

KING: (*aghast*) You can't mean it.

SLAVE: Yes, I wish to free all slaves.

KING: (*dismayed*) Is this your trick? Are you trying to get out of it?

SLAVE: I free you.

KING: Confound you! I don't want to be free; I want to be alive! I'm not sure you understand exactly what the implications . . . the ramifications . . . Look here: Babylon is a slave society. Babylon is built on slaves. Babylon runs on slaves. Without slaves, Babylon would disintegrate, collapse. I don't know—it's the most absurd! . . . What a thing! I don't know who would be worse off—the owners or the slaves: the owners who can't take care of themselves and the slaves who can't take care of themselves. We need each other. If I were to publish an edict that all the slaves are free—well, it's just impossible. That's all: impossible! Unthinkable!

SLAVE: It is what I would do, if I were king.

KING: Well, maybe you would, but I—. Oh, but you are king— yes, you really are! There must be no doubt about that! (*He checks the position of the light relative to the dial.*) You are the king. Midnight requires a king in Babylon, and you are it! Robe, ring, and ritual—you are the king of Babylon! And being king requires obedient subjects; otherwise, it's a bit thin.

SLAVE: You are wrong.

KING: (*bristling*) You dare say that—! Ah! It takes hold! It works, does it? The sense of power rises to the head. If the King says his servant is . . . wrong, then the King is right, and I, his servant, am wrong. Will Your Majesty be pleased to instruct me in the error of my thought? I beseech you.

SLAVE: If there is no king in Babylon, no king can die in Babylon.

KING: (*anxiously*) On the contrary! With all respect, Your Majesty, the custom expressly decrees that when the moonlight falls on the skull the King must die. So you see the custom demands that there *be* a king to do the dying. Considering Your Highness's background, along with the

THE STAR THROWER

bleak—but glorious!—prospects for your future, I can understand why you would take little interest in perpetuating the institutions of our venerable society—in perpetuating society itself, for that matter. But if you will summon up just a bit of compassion and approach the subject from the standpoint of your humble servant . . . . Maybe you don't care about society, but I do. As I was your predecessor, so I hope to be your successor, and it would be just peachy if you would deign to leave me my kingdom to rule. As king, I really do need a kingdom, complete with loyal, obedient, abject subjects. And they do need me—and we, all of us—all of us!—need you in your rapidly approaching manifestation, apotheosis, and epiphany as a newborn god. That, after all, is what gods are all about, isn't it: to uphold society?

SLAVE: If there were no king, what would be lost?

KING: Everything!—from my point of view, everything. From yours, naturally, nothing. But I dare say every objective observer will tell you that there must be authority, rule, a king—whatever name you call him—or society will collapse.

SLAVE: Your society. Your kingdom.

KING: Well, I didn't make it, you know. Marduk ordained it; I was born into it. Take it up with Marduk when you are a god yourself. (*suspicious*) . . . Or is that your game—that the *gods* shall rule? Could you have been planted by the priests? What could they promise that I can not? I must say I don't think you've seized onto the possibilities in your present position. Think! Imagine the good you might do this very moment with your brief—with your regrettably brief—authority, if only you grasp it! Instead, you take a notion to free the slaves (*giggling hysterically*)—a disaster, for the slaves most of all! How would they live? Food—bread: who would give them bread? Now look: here's an idea! What do people really need? You, a water carrier—a former water carrier—you of all men ought to know that. You want to do something for the people so they'll remember you with gratitude, with warmth? Then pass an edict—let's see—an edict that you will pledge the royal granaries to guarantee that every man, woman, and child in the kingdom each day will receive, let us say, one-half an omer of barley. Now there is a revolutionary idea for you! Rid the kingdom of hunger! Isn't that a thing worth doing? Isn't that worth being a king for? That is philanthropy. You have only to command, and their bellies are full. And as your successor I would be bound to let your generous edict stand for, well, at least for a month or so, and the devil of a time I'll have rescinding it, too—people are so easily spoilt, don't you think? Of course, there are problems: will the dogs continue to work with the same enthusiasm? There is something about living on the edge, the edge of starvation, that renders them marvelously sharp and eager to please. And then there is the question of where all this barley is going to come from, no matter how hard the slaves work. Of course, when you become a god, perhaps you'll favor us with more bountiful harvests, hmm? Thank you very much! Or it could be we'll have to support the new food distribution by marching the troops off to some neighboring country—expanding the agricultural base. But if you're any kind of a king, you know how to call out the troops when it's necessary.

SLAVE: Disband the army.

KING: (*after a stunned pause, ironically*) Oh, certainly! Immediately! Of course! That's just what we'll do! We'll disband the army. You are still—. Your Majesty must forgive me—the habits of slave thought . . . you must divest . . . Now, Your Majesty must no longer think like a slave; Your Majesty must think like a king. I thought we'd already gone over this business of authority, and here you are bringing it up again! The army, you see, *is* your authority. The army is your guarantee of the obedience of the subjects. What do you think enforces the master-slave relationship if not the army? When you were a slave, no doubt it seemed a good

THE STAR THROWER

idea to weaken authority. But now that you are a king, you must think like a king—the enforcement of law, the preservation of order, the consolidation of power, the expansion of influence, the preservation of your royal rear! Disband the army and you not only dissolve the state, you erase the borders; the property and persons of every inhabitant you expose to plunder and foreign enslavement. Devil take it, man, we do have neighbors, after all! And our neighbors are bloodthirsty, voracious, insatiable devils! Disband the army! What do you think prevents our neighbors coming in here and carrying you off into . . . Well! Take my advice—I know about these things. If you want to be great, if you wish to leave behind you a name to live in history, so that at the mention of your name even the slaves, even the prisoners in their dungeons will remember you with patriotic pride, then so far from disbanding the army, you attack! Overcome! Win victories! A word of caution: attack only those who are weaker than yourself. Now, if *I* know that, then every king of every other state knows that as well. Each one lurks like a hyena drooling over the sheep, hungering for a taste of victory, waiting to gobble up a juicy victim. Therefore, the king and Babylon must never present an enticing display of weakness. You must appear to be too tough—no tender lamb, but a great, iron-horned ram—too great a risk for the hyenas to dare to attack.

SLAVE: You will not disband the army.

KING: This is your trick, isn't it? You hope to get those six tall fellows with the spears discharged, cashiered, sent home. Well, it won't work. They're not in the army. They are the private guard of the temple. They belong to the priests. And even if you are in league with them, they'll betray you. They'll stay until the deed is done. Nothing short of blood will satisfy them . . . . You've asked for nothing for yourself.

SLAVE: You tell me that everything, all of it is impossible.

KING: Freeing the slaves, disbanding the army—yes, those things are impossible, can't be done. It would destroy the kingdom, and without a kingdom, there is no king, and without a king, no kingdom. Besides, there must be a king to die at midnight. You see? There are limits to what even a king can do.

SLAVE: The king is not free.

KING: Free? The king free! Least of all, the king. The king is immured in his kingdom. Noblesse obliges! The king must command, must wield authority, must preserve himself as king for the sake of preserving the kingdom. The king is nailed to his kingdom the way a criminal is nailed to a cross.

SLAVE: Then if it is possible, for myself I ask the end of this kingdom.

KING: Oh, how I underestimated you! The height—the depth of your destructiveness! You would save your own miserable hide at the expense of this entire kingdom! Now that's the difference between us: I must live to preserve the kingdom from the princely pustule. I live for the sake of this kingdom, and you shall die for the sake of it. Those are the responsibilities of kings. So it has always been; and so it ever shall be.

SLAVE: Was there ever a time when there were no kings?

KING: Never!

SLAVE: Or slaves?

KING: Never!

SLAVE: Or armies?

KING: Never! Nor there never shall be! Always there will be kings and slaves and armies. That is why I am necessary. And you.

SLAVE: But I am not made after your likeness.

KING: (*patronizing*) Well, I can see that these things don't come easily—without the proper training and all. You're just a little slow getting started, that's all. Understandable, given the circumstances. I dare say if you had time to grow into it . . . .

THE STAR THROWER   99

Well. We all have to die, even kings. But not gods. They don't die, isn't that so?

SLAVE: And if I were not to die?

KING: (*affably*) Ah, but you will die. I make that my major program. If you were not to die, then I would die, and immediately upon my demise . . . the princely pustule, he's expecting it, you know. Licking his chops! His mother has already told him that when he wakes up tomorrow she will be a widow and he will be the king—that little titular tumefaction would drain its pus all over my beautiful throne. It must not be! . . . You are not such a bad fellow at all. Too bad. I wish . . . I find myself wishing . . . that the Royal Overseer had found someone else, a different man—instead of you. I would have preferred someone who was disposed to at least take advantage of the opportunity . . . a few women . . . a little wine . . . a lot of wine . . . some food . . . going off to glory with a buzz and a bang! You've scarcely had your fun; seems a shame. But the hour is late, and there is no time to search for another candidate . . . (*sizing him up*) Do you have a trick? If you have a trick, I advise you to trot it out pretty quickly.

SLAVE: No.

KING: Some stratagem to thwart the tall fellows with the spears . . . some substitutionary swine of your own . . . some way out . . . some . . . (*He comes to one of the carvings in the wall.*) Wait a moment! An effigy! An effigy! We could substitute an effigy! Make a dummy out of straw— a scarecrow—a ritual substitute, you see? Of course! How much more humane that would be! Then the whole thing would be done symbolically, you get the idea? We could hide you away, and afterwards the supposed executioners could themselves be killed to keep them quiet—or banished . . . . No; killed! And I could . . . . And you . . . . (*He trails off.*)

SLAVE: You have already chosen me to be your scarecrow, your ritual substitution. The law requires a king.

KING: And you really are a king, a kind of king.

SLAVE: You have said so.

KING: This has become decidedly difficult. Devil take it, I hope you don't think this is easy for me! The unfriendly eye might see in our . . . arrangement . . . a tinge of, well, cowardice—some might even call it cowardice—, but when you consider that through your generous . . . cooperation—either it is me on that throne, or else at my death the crown passes to that primogenital pustule—well, then my continuance as king is, is as expedient for the health of the kingdom as are sunshine and rain. You do understand that?

SLAVE: I must die so that you may live.

KING: Yes, and all the others. That's it, precisely. Do you hate me? (*silence.*) What does that matter? . . . The moonlight is on the skull. (*Touches his dagger.*) Will you go quietly?

(*SLAVE descends from the throne, stoops to pick up his water container, and brings water to the KING. KING declines the offer, takes the container from SLAVE, and offers water to SLAVE. SLAVE sips, then again offers water to KING who also sips. They are silent a moment.*)

KING: Goodbye—King Carrier.

(*EXIT SLAVE. KING brings a basin, pours water from the Water Carrier's container into the basin, and washes his hands.*)

CURTAIN

SAUL AT ENDOR

Preface

Saul's history was written by his victorious enemies. If not to redress this prejudice altogether, at least to restore a bit of balance, Jungian analyst John A. Sanford seeks to reconstruct the supposedly suppressed side of the Biblical account, Saul's side. Sanford sees Saul as a tragic hero.[4]

No less a giant of drama than Racine himself wrote a tragedy with Saul as its hero. Someone else once claimed, in fact, that Saul is the one and only truly tragic hero in the Bible. I'm not convinced that Saul is the only tragic hero of the Bible, but I think he is one. Julian Jaynes tends this way, too. He calls the book of I Samuel "perhaps the first written tragedy in literature," whose hero "subjective Saul" at the dawn of consciousness in a still bicameral era, "seeks wildly about him for what to do," only to commit at last "that most terrible subjective act, the first in history—suicide . . . ."[5]

It is not my purpose in *Saul at Endor* to engage in this interesting discussion. Rather, I want to explore the desperate spiritual condition of a person who, although anointed at God's command and an ecstatic, nevertheless lacks a personal experience of, or relationship with, God, and therefore must deal with God at secondhand, through intermediaries such as priests and mediums.

We're told that the words *theatre* and *theos* share a common root meaning "to see." A theatre is a place for seeing. Theos,

God, is sometimes symbolized as an all-seeing eye. One result of an encounter with Theos may be "I see!" Enthusiasts, those filled with Theos, see visions. Thus Christ as Theos is the light to enlighten everyone and make sight possible.

But the nearer to the light, the darker the shadows. Consequently, saints suffer dark nights of the soul. King Saul's namesake, Saul of Tarsus, will meet God as a light that, before enabling him to see, first blinds him. (If we note that Jesus is named for Joshua, why should the fact that Paul the Apostle was named for King Saul be any less auspicious—for King Saul as well as for Paul?) To begin his new life, Paul had first to experience total eclipse—though perhaps only, as the Unidentified Guest says in T. S. Eliot's *The Cocktail Party*, long enough to rid himself of "the illusion of ever having been in the light."

God may be without shadow, but, Peter Pan notwithstanding, humans do have shadows. Shakespeare calls actors shadows. *Saul at Endor* is a play of shadows shown by two shadows.

(Directors should not take this as a lighting plot. There may be shadows in the playing space, but the playing space should not be in shadow. Instead, directors should follow the lead of Konstantin Stanislavski. When an admirer of that great director asked why he had invented the coup de theatre of bringing up the lights at a climactic moment, Stanislavski replied, "So the audience could see the actors' faces.")

In this play, our shadows show two dark sides of the failure to see God. One shadow is the controller. The controller seeks above all to control God and, through God, others. This figure is Lucifer, ironically named "the light-bearer." Seeking to supplant the light, Lucifer trespasses so near the light that he casts nothing but a huge shadow.

As a prophet, Samuel occupies a privileged position. He is God's mouthpiece. Consciously, he may be sincere. We all like to think well of ourselves. Samuel may conceive himself to be what the victor-penned scriptures portray him—God's devoted servant. He may see himself as God's agent to exercise God's

THE STAR THROWER   103

control. He is and he intends to remain the power behind the throne. Power is a witch's brew.

King Saul is a shadow figure, too. He knows God only through Samuel. Saul is the existential person, but not the authentic person. Once upon a time God chose Saul—at least Samuel told him so. Now God casts Saul off—at least Samuel tells him so.

Saul comes to Endor to learn how his story will end. He hopes that the Witch of Endor has foreknowledge of fate. Of course all our attempts to peer into the future betray our lack of trust in God's providence.

But maybe Saul's more compelling need is not so much to know how his story will end—after all, we all know that all our earthly stories end in a death—but to know what his sleep-rounded story *means*. What has it all been about? Can Saul know or discover what Christians know, namely, that God is lovingly present and active even in—or especially in—our defeats?

I assume that Saul doesn't know this until that day when Christ came to release him from Sheol. Until then, excepting only that Saul tries to take a kind of desperate control of his life by taking his own life, Saul remains in the dark. The Christian proclamation assures us that, even as Christ had the power to take *his* life yet take it up again (John 10:18), so God has the power to give the existential person new, eternal life.

But here in Saul's struggle is no happy ending, no sunshine. Saul is on the dark side of the earth amid shadows in a cave—in great darkness and in need of a great light.

There are many valid ways to distinguish those segments of the dramatic spectrum that we generally label with the words *tragedy* and *comedy*. One way is to say that comedy tells us "The Sun Also Rises." Tragedy tells us it also sets—or, in Antonin Artaud's stark words, tragedy tells us that the sky can fall on our heads. Both, of course, are true. The gospel tells us that Christ is the light who defeats darkness.

If I may presume to borrow from Samuel Beckett's superior

stagecraft, appropriate music for *Saul at Endor* may be found in the largo of Beethoven's Piano Trio No. 5 in D, Opus 70, No. 1, commonly known as "The Ghost." I include here Andrew Buskey's original music for the melodies sung by David on pages 110, and 112.

I wrote *Saul at Endor* as a two-person play. It might be convenient to have different actors play The Witch, Samuel, and David. But if one actor—or, preferably, actress—plays all these roles opposite the actor playing Saul, that actress may represent a force of nature transforming itself. That actress may seem to be an incarnation of the principalities and powers that encompass and bedevil human beings.

Yet Samuel and David, although they are Saul's enemies and imperfect human beings, are anchorage points between whom Saul forms the bridge. Thus Saul plays a necessary, if unknowing, role in God's historical drama. It is his human unknowing, unenlightened by faith, that constitutes the pathos of Saul's position. And it may be his unknowing which diminishes his stature as a tragic hero.

It is important for every human being who has to make up in her or his own body the sufferings of Christ to understand the real and tragic—even if triumphantly tragic—cost of playing that role.

Melodies to "Saul at Endor"

Music by Andrew J. Buskey

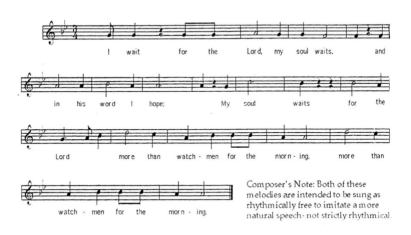

Composer's Note: Both of these melodies are intended to be sung as rhythmically free to imitate a more natural speech- not strictly rhythmical.

SAUL AT ENDOR

A Play in One Act

Original Music by
Andrew Buskey

CAST OF CHARACTERS
KING SAUL
WITCH OF ENDOR
SAMUEL
DAVID
(*NOTE: The characters of WITCH, SAMUEL, and DAVID
may be played by one actor.*)

(*A cave with a fire. Enter SAUL in armor.*)

SAUL: Who's there?
WITCH: (*appearing from the shadows*) Who's there?
   (*SAUL and WITCH eye each other.*)
SAUL: Can you raise the dead?
WITCH: Can you slay the living?
SAUL: Can I—yes, by God! There was a day when I could slay . . .
   by the thousands! Forgotten now. Can you raise the dead?
WITCH: (*cautiously*) There was a day . . . a soul or two. I could
   bring them back.
SAUL: Back? From where? Where do the dead live? In Sheol?
WITCH: It is forbidden now. King Saul has forbidden
   witchcraft.

THE STAR THROWER

SAUL: Have no fear of Saul.

WITCH: Who would not fear Saul?

SAUL: Saul will thank you. I know.

WITCH: What do you want?

SAUL: Bring back Samuel.

WITCH: Samuel the prophet.

SAUL: Samuel the prophet. Bring him here. Let me talk to him.

WITCH: Saul forbids it.

SAUL: Saul commands it . . . . There shall come no punishment. None. I swear. Bring me Samuel.

(*WITCH considers, then gestures. SAUL lays aside his armor and sword.*)

WITCH: (*handing SAUL a pouch of powder*) Offer the sacrifice.

SAUL: To whom?

WITCH: To the God of all.

(*WITCH begins to beat a drum. SAUL sways, moves, falls into a trance, and begins to dance a clumsy, shuffling dance which grows wilder until it reaches a climax at which Saul throws the incense into the fire where it explodes. SAMUEL emerges from the smoke.*)

SAMUEL: What have you done?

SAUL: Samuel?

SAMUEL: What have you done? I told you not to go into battle until I came to offer the sacrifice.

SAUL: But you didn't come! Seven days I waited. The enemy gathered at Micmash—30,000 chariots, 6,000 horsemen. My people hid in caves, among the rocks, hid in pits and high places. You didn't come. I said, "The Philistine will come down on me, and I have not made supplication to the Lord before battle." I forced myself. With my own hands I offered the sacrifice to your God. Then—only then!—you came.

SAMUEL: Fool! You broke the commandment of the Lord God which he commanded, saying, "You shall wait until I, Samuel, God's own prophet, until I have offered the sacrifice." Did you imagine the Lord God would accept the sacrifice from your hand? Did I not strictly charge you, "You shall not commit your warriors to battle before I, Samuel, have offered the sacrifice"?

SAUL: You did not come! Your God had his offering! What matter whose hand offered it, yours or mine, so it were offered?

SAMUEL: (*offering to leave*) You have no need of me.

SAUL: (*clutching and tearing SAMUEL's robe*) Stay!

SAMUEL: As you have torn my garment, so will the Lord God tear the kingdom from your hand. You have cast him off, and he will cast you off.

SAUL: It may be your God will repent. Choose me again. Restore me. Why did your God choose me in the first place? You—you came like a raven to snatch a mouse from the field. Why?

SAMUEL: (*The scene has changed.*) You! Hiding there! Come here! (*To the audience as if they were the people of Israel*) Hear, O Israel! Thus says the Lord God. I brought you up, O Israel, out of the land of Egypt. I delivered you out of bondage, out of the hand of them that oppressed you. And this day you have rejected me, your God. You have gone awhoring after a king. You have cried out and you have said, "Set over us a king so that we may be like the nations of the world. Give us a king!" This is the head of all your sinning. Now therefore array yourselves before the Lord God by tribes and by thousands. (*He casts lots.*) Let the tribe of Benjamin come near! (*He casts the lots again.*) Let the family of Matri come near! (*He casts the lots again.*) Let Saul the son of Kish come near!

(*SAUL slowly comes out of hiding and approaches.*)

Behold the man whom the Lord your God has chosen to be your king! (*To SAUL*) This people lust to become like the nations of the world. They would have a prince. They reject God as their king. Now God gives them you to rule over them. You shall be their king, but you shall not be a king like the kings of this world. You shall not put your foot on the neck of the people, but you shall fight the Lord God's battles.

THE STAR THROWER   109

At his command shall you fight. And he, the Lord god, will give the victory into your hand. (*To the people*) Behold, the Lord God has set over you a king. Yet turn not aside from following the Lord God, but serve the Lord your God with all your heart. And for the sake of his great name, the Lord God will never abandon his people. As for me, God forbid that I should sin against the Lord God by ceasing to pray for you. But I will teach you the path of good and the path of righteousness, lest you do wickedly and be consumed, both you and your king. (*To Saul*) The Lord God sent me to anoint you king over his people. (*SAMUEL causes SAUL to kneel, then anoints him.*) Now hear the word of the Lord. Thus says the Lord God of Sabaoth: I remember that which Amalek did to Israel. I remember how when Israel came like a lamb out of Egypt, Amalek lay like a wolf in wait. Now, therefore, Saul, son of Kish—King Saul—go you and smite Amalek. (*He begins to drum.*) Destroy utterly all that is Amalek's. Spare not one life. Kill them. Kill their men. Kill their women. Kill their infants, suckling. Kill sheep and ox, kill camel and ass. Every living thing that is Amalek's, you shall kill! (*Drum crescendo and stop.*)

SAUL: (*The scene has changed.*) Blessed be the name of the Lord! I have performed the commandment of the Lord!

SAMUEL: Is Amalek destroyed?

SAUL: Annihilated! Total victory!

SAMUEL: Every living thing?

SAUL: Every living thing!

SAMUEL: (*listening*) What means this bleating of sheep? What means this lowing of oxen?

SAUL: They have brought them from the Amalekites—the best of the sheep, the best of the oxen—the people have brought to sacrifice to the Lord your God. All the rest we have slain.

SAMUEL: The Lord God commanded you, saying, destroy the Amalekites. The Lord God commanded you to fight against them until they were utterly consumed—they and every living thing that is theirs. Why did you not obey the word of the Lord?

SAUL: I have obeyed the word of the Lord! But the people, they took of the spoils, these oxen and sheep, to sacrifice to the Lord your God.

SAMUEL: Does the Lord God delight in sacrifices or burnt offerings? Does the Lord God not rather delight in obedience? Obey! Obey! Because you have rejected the word of the Lord, the Lord has rejected you! You have spared Agag, King of Amalek.

SAUL: I have brought him here to your God.

SAMUEL: Why did you not kill him?

SAUL: Then or now, what difference does it make?

SAMUEL: Obey! Bring Agag here to me! (*SAMUEL begins to beat the drum as though he were hacking Agag to pieces. With each stroke, SAUL convulses until he collapses and the drumbeat ceases. SAUL sleeps fitfully. SAMUEL as DAVID begins to sing.*)

DAVID: (*singing*) Trust in the Lord and do good;
    so you will dwell in the land, and enjoy security.
Take delight in the Lord,
    And he will give you the desires of your heart.
(SAUL *cries out, wakens.*)

SAUL: Jonathan! Jonathan, my son, is it you?

DAVID: No, sir. It's me—David, my Lord's servant.

SAUL: You wear my son's clothes.

DAVID: Your son gave them to me.

SAUL: Who are you?

DAVID: David, a son of Jesse.

SAUL: That was you singing?

DAVID: I was sent to sing for you.

SAUL: Good. You sing well. I don't sleep well. Nightmares. The drum. War. Killing kings. The butcher sword. Above the field, a raven with a mouse impaled on its bloody beak . . . A

THE STAR THROWER
111

son of Jesse? Your brothers, they're with me here, fighting the Philistine?

DAVID: They are.

SAUL: They fight. You sing.

DAVID: I can fight, too!

SAUL: (*with a bitter laugh*) You! Fight! Sing, boy! Better be the singer who celebrates both the slayer and the slain.

DAVID: I have courage!

SAUL: You do. Wait until you hear the sword sing—a biting song, a piercing melody, a drunken song that sucks blood until it strangles and vomits. When the sword sings, strong men scream. They bray obligatos to gurgles. They howl curses. They yawl lovers' names. Then they squeal, and they gag, and they choke, and they puke, and then they die.

DAVID: I am skillful. I have defended my father's flock.

SAUL: Oh! You want to be tested! Come. Stand here. We'll make you a soldier. (SAUL *arms the boy with his own equipment.*) Armor. Helmet. Sword. (SAUL *laughs.*)

DAVID: (*staggering*) It's too heavy.

SAUL: Now, soldier, I am a Philistine—your enemy, a powerful man, a giant. The armor that weighs you down is to me as light as a shadow. We face off, man to man. I rush you! (*Spear in hand, SAUL makes a mock-menacing pass at DAVID, who nimbly slips under the charge and then backs away. SAUL turns toward him again.*) Now, boy, would you rather fight or sing?

DAVID: I can't play the song of the sword. I sing the song of the sling. (DAVID *slips out of Saul's gear and produces instead a sling.*)

SAUL: A toy! Would you toy with a giant?

(SAUL *hefts his spear and makes as if to charge again.* DAVID *whirls his sling.* SAUL, *as if stricken, halts, clasps his forehead, and sinks to his knees.*)

DAVID: (*rushing to him*) My Lord!

SAUL: It's all right, boy—a pain that comes to me sometimes.
I'll rest. You sing. (*Sleeps.*)

DAVID: (*singing*) I wait for the Lord, my soul waits,
      And in his word I hope;
      my soul waits for the Lord
      more than watchmen for the morning,
      more than watchmen for the morning.

(DAVID *takes* SAUL's *spear, stands over him, raises the spear as if to strike, and changes his mind.*)

SAMUEL: Shall I kill a king? You disobeyed my command. In tomorrow's battle, you and your sons will come to me in the place of the dead. The Lord God will give Israel's army over to the Philistine. Thing of my making, you defied me. I gave you a throne. Now I'll give you a grave. No. No; I'll nail your carcass crucified on the city walls.

(SAUL *rises, dons his armor.* SAMUEL, *standing behind Saul, reaches in front of Saul with his sword, his intention ambiguous.* SAUL *seizes Samuel's wrist.*)

SAUL: Ancient enemy! Your hand! Your hand chose me, anointed me. Your talon seized me, controlled me, shook the life out of me, cast me aside. Raven of God, behind my throne, beak in my back!

(SAUL *wrests the sword from Samuel and holds it high.* SAMUEL *takes Saul's spear and jabs at Saul four times, wounding him.* SAUL *staggers away, then deliberately falls on his own sword.*)

I take back my life. (*Dies.*)

SAMUEL: Sleep. I'll sing. (*singing*) Trust in the Lord and do good;
      so you will dwell in the land, and enjoy security.
      Take delight in the Lord,
      And he will give you the desires of your heart.

CURTAIN

BALLOONS'N'TUNES

Preface

Mystery Plays—plays of that medieval dramatic genre in which "Mystery" refers to the trade or vocation of the group that sponsored the particular play—hold a world of wonder.

None is more wonderful than *The Second Shepherd's Play*, written by a playwright who evidently cared so little for self-promotion that s/he wrote anonymously. A grateful posterity has dubbed him or her "The Wakefield Master," thus immortalizing both the author and the town where the play was performed.

In *The Second Shepherd's Play* we see a shepherd/scamp named Mak and his wife, Gill, attempt to conceal their theft of a lamb (of course call it "kidnapping") by disguising the purloined loin as a baby in a cradle. This same scoundrel Mak—finally let off with a mere tossing in a blanket instead of the customary medieval death sentence for sheep stealing, and without being sanctified—is then invited to go worship the Christmas babe.

Balloons 'n' Tunes aspires to partake of this same spirit of naïve but deep faith as well as the impulse to reenact a Biblical story for a contemporary audience.

Theatre historian Oscar Brockett tells us that, of the four songs used in *The Second Shepherd's Play*, "The Shepherds' first song and Mak's lullaby would have been contemporary [medieval] popular songs. The Gloria sung by the Angel, and the Shepherds' final song would have been taken from contemporary church music."[6] In this, medieval stagecraft foreshadows the development of eighteenth-century England's ballad operas, the most famous example of which is *The Beggar's Opera*—reworked in the twentieth century by Kurt Weill and Berthold Brecht as *The Threepenny Opera*. In ballad opera, "lyrics were interspersed with dialogue much as they are in modern musical comedy, but, . . . unlike musical comedy, they were sung to old tunes."[7]

For its form, then, *Balloons 'n' Tunes* is indebted to both of these traditional theatre types, the Mystery and the ballad opera. Its title it owes to the name of a shop adjacent to the University of Cincinnati.

I like to keep the entire cast in view of the audience. In a chancel setting exits and entrances aren't always feasible. In *Balloons'n'Tunes* they aren't necessary. For example, an "exit" by Gabe may be simply a move from one area of the playing space to another.

Pictorially, the Boss on the upstage ladder dominates the play.

Balloons'n'Tunes preserves the convenience and efficiency of rehearsing in two-handed scenes.

The centuries have indeed risen up to call Mary blessed, and with reason! After all, how easy is it to find a person willing to be totally vulnerable and available to the Spirit of God? Finding that person is the task we set Gabe here. "[W]hen the Son of Man comes, will he find faith on earth?" (Luke 18:8b). Like those invited to the King's feast (Matthew 22:1-14), we and other potential Marys are quick to excuse ourselves, slow to yield. Dostoyevsky notwithstanding, Mary is no fool. She is a servant saint.

When I've directed *Balloons 'n' Tunes* in a worship setting, I've had the entire cast come forward at the end—when the Tree of Life blazes and Gabe explodes in a glittering shekinah—to lead the congregation in singing the Gloria and then the entirety of "Angels We Have Heard on High."

BALLOONS 'N' TUNES

A Modern Mystery Play of the Annunciation

CAST OF CHARACTERS
THE BOSS
GABE, A Balloons'n'Tunes Man
MARY I, A career woman
MARY II, A party girl
MARY III, A maid.

A Note on Properties

I phoned a number of party-supply stores and asked for the technical name of that wonderful party toy—the little whistle with an attached rolled-up cylinder of paper (sometimes sporting a feather at its end) that extends when the whistle is blown. The city's acknowledged party-toy expert assured me it's called a "party blow-out." Other dealers referred to it as a "musical blower," a "party whistle," or (my favorite) a "squeaker." Whatever you call it, it's what GABE toots. The instrument can be bought in most stores that sell party supplies.

GABE also packs a pen with a plume (he uses his cuff for a note pad), trails colorful helium balloons, wears a timepiece, and has, on his person or secreted on the set, easily opened vials full of glitter confetti. THE BOSS has Christmas tree ornaments to handle. MARY I carries an attaché case, MARY II has a makeup compact, and MARY III lugs a bucket and mop.

(Standing on a stepladder upstage, THE BOSS hangs Christmas ornaments on a tree.)

THE BOSS: *(singing to the tune of "O Christmas Tree")*

The Boss' Song
O Tree of Life, my Tree of Life,
You stand in great black danger.
Your branches there are bleak and bare,
You need my dearest loving care.
You need a lift, a special gift,
You'll find it in a manger.

(ENTER GABE, dressed in gala attire and wafting behind him a multicolored cloud of balloons emblazoned with such greetings as "Congratulations!" "It's a Boy!" and "Happy Birthday!" He trumpets his arrival with a mighty blat of a party blow-out. Startled by the tootling, THE BOSS nearly fumbles an ornament and barely maintains his perch on the ladder.)

THE BOSS *(Continuing)* : Must you do that?

GABE: *(brightly)* Sorry, Boss! Just getting into the spirit. You sent for me?

THE BOSS: *(closely examining a spherical ornament)* I think something's wrong with this one.

GABE: *(shrugging)* So toss it out.

THE BOSS: No, it's special.

GABE: Oh, that one. *(moving to peer at the ornament)* I wonder what it's like to be one of them.

THE BOSS: *(after a pause)* I want to send a birth announcement.

GABE: Where?

THE BOSS: *(holding up ornament)* Here.

GABE: There?

(BOSS nods.)

GABE: Now?

THE BOSS: Now.

GABE: This is the time?

THE BOSS: Yes.

GABE: (*keen anticipation*) *The* announcement? The *special* birth announcement?

THE BOSS: They're all special. But yes, *the* announcement.

GABE: Yes, sir! (*He whips out plume and shoots a cuff to write on.*) The lady's name?

THE BOSS: Mary.

GABE: (*writing*) Mary. Last name?

THE BOSS: Saint Mary.

GABE: Mary is the last name?

THE BOSS: From this moment on I've decided to know people only by their first names.

GABE: Address?

THE BOSS: (*pointing to a spot on the ornament*) She lives in Nazareth.

GABE: (*wrinkling his nose*) Nazareth! (*mollified by the reprimanding eye THE BOSS turns on him*) Well, can you narrow it down?

THE BOSS: Nazareth is already narrow.

GABE: (*making a note of it*) Nazareth is narrow. Husband's name?

THE BOSS: She doesn't have a husband.

GABE: (*suppressing his reaction and writing*) No husband.

THE BOSS: She's betrothed.

GABE: Oh. (*consulting his notes*) Mary—that's a pretty common name. How will I know which Mary?

THE BOSS: My servant Mary. You'll know.

GABE: O.K. (*starting to leave, but coming back*) I get paid on a per-call basis; this could cost.

THE BOSS: I'll pay.

GABE: Have it your way! I'm off! (*EXIT GABE with a parting toot causing THE BOSS again to bobble the ornament before he makes a juggling catch. GABE calls back:*) Nice save!

THE BOSS: (*singing as he returns to his decorating with a star*)

O Universe, my Universe,
In Satan's curse you grow much worse
Creation groans with sighs and moans.
Her fondest hopes are just dry bones.
Though darkness now may frighten you,
A shining star will brighten you. (*The star shines.*)

(*ENTER MARY I, stylishly dressed for success, attaché case swinging energetically. She crosses busily until she is halted by GABE's tootling. She glares at him.*)

GABE: (*pointing*) Mary!

MARY I: Do I know you?

GABE: Hey, have I got good news for you! (*He sings to the tune of "Joy to the World" and then "Happy Birthday."*)

Gabe's Song

Joy to you, girl, great happiness!
The one the Lord will bless!
The one through whom he brings
The King of all the kings!
You'll bear the holy babe,
You'll bear the holy babe,
You'll bear, you'll bear the holy babe.

Happy birthday to you!
Happy birthday to you!
Happy birthday, dear Mary,
Happy birthday to you!

(*He holds out a Congratulations balloon which MARY I declines to accept.*)

MARY I: Sorry, you've got the wrong person. It's not my birthday.

GABE: (*laughing*) No, but it's going to be! Get it? (*starting to sing again with special emphasis*) Happy *birth*day . . . .

MARY I: Not until May twenty-first.

GABE: Not that soon. (*counting on fingers*) Not until December (*checking his timepiece*) twenty-fifth. See?

MARY I (*suspicious*) What exactly is on your mind? Who sent you?

GABE: The Boss.

MARY I: No way.

GABE: No, *my* Boss. Everybody's Boss. The bosses' Boss.

MARY I: (*shaking her head*) Not my boss. I'm my own boss.

GABE: (*laughing*) Oh, yes! Look, what I'm trying to tell you is, my Boss—our Boss—(*spacing his words for emphasis*) wants you to have his baby!

MARY I: I'll have your boss up on harassment charges so fast he'll never know what hit him.

GABE: No, no harassment. It's strictly up to you. It's only an offer.

MARY I: Well, I don't like it, I don't like your boss' come-on, and I don't like you. I've got other things to do with my life besides having babies. I find the mere thought of baby bearing . . . unbearable. (*She sings, to the tune of "Tempus Adest Floridium" ["Good King Wenceslaus"] at a presto tempo, metronome setting = 184*):

The Career Woman's Song

Got no time to have a child,

I am on the fast track!

Diapers would drive me wild,

A baby would hold me back.

I have built this great career

And you know it can't wait.

If you want a baby dear,

Find another surrogate!

120   ROBERT JOHN VERSTEEG

I can't take the mommy track
Up the corp'rate ladder.
Pregnancy, my aching back!
Nothing could be sadder.
Motherhood is one big Owe—
Why should I pursue it?
You can tell your C E O
I'm not going to do it! (*EXIT.*)

(*GABE, his squeaker clipped in his teeth, gazes forlornly after her and gives a dispirited toot. ENTER MARY II. Her makeup is too thick, her hair is flamboyantly styled, and her clothes are calculated to catch male attention. MARY II sees GABE, and under the pretense of examining her makeup in her compact's mirror, sizes him up.*)

MARY II: Looking for somebody?

GABE: Oh! Yeah. Hi!

MARY II: Hi. Like me?

GABE: What? Oh! Yeah. Sure. Nice.

MARY II: You bet I am!

GABE: Right! (*He inflates the tootler.*)

MARY II: You got a name?

GABE: Oh, yeah. Gabe. Short for Gabriel.

MARY II: Gabriel! (*chuckling*) I'll bet you're no angel!

GABE: Well, actually—

MARY II: I'm Mary.

GABE: Right! Mary. Saint Mary!

MARY II: (*laughing*) More like Madonna.

GABE: Yeah! That's it! Madonna! You're it! You're the one I'm looking for!

MARY II: (*teasing*) Looking for me, are you? Well, maybe I'm taken.

GABE: No; I've got a message for you.

MARY II: Sure you have.

GABE: (*singing*) Happy birthday to you! Happy . . . (*He thrusts a birthday balloon in her direction.*)

MARY II: (*declining the gift*) It's not my birthday.

GABE: No, but it's going to be. Get it? (*He extends the balloon again.*)

MARY II: Don't you be too sure of yourself.

GABE: This is from the top.

MARY II: Oh, I get it—they sent you over from the lab, right?

GABE: Oh, no; I came straight from The Boss' office.

MARY II: Uh-huh. So your lousy rabbit turned belly up, did it?

GABE: Pardon? Look, I'm telling you, this is straight from The Boss. The Boss wants to kind of, you know, make the scene. He wants to give the world his Son, his only Son. And he's picked you—you! It'll be a great honor! This baby is good news which shall be to all people!

MARY II: Well, I've got some news for your boss. No fuddy-duddy and no big daddy is gonna intimidate me. His baby, huh? I'll tell you, the daddy could've been any one of a number. But I'll get along. I'll survive. I know what to do. (*Singing to the tune of "Greensleeves."*)

The Party Girl's Song
My life style's filled with the nicest things,
Gold chains and diamond rings.
I date this fellow who really swings
And I love what every night he brings.
Thanks, thank you for dropping by—
I love the look in your bedroom eye.
Parting now gives us such sweet sorrow,
But what are you doing tomorrow?

I'd like to help you, but can't you see
The one that I love is only me.
I've got a boyfriend, got two, got three.
They swear I'm sexy as I can be.
Why should I bear someone's baby?
Don't even know who the dad may be.
I'm heeding this early warning,
I'm taking the pill in the morning! (*EXIT.*)

(*ENTER MARY III with bucket and mop. GABE, discouraged, starts to leave, then comes back.*)

GABE: 'Scuse me.
MARY III: Yes?
GABE: Know anybody else around here name of Mary?
MARY III: No . . . (*Begins to mop floor as GABE turns to leave.*) Just me.
GABE: (*starting off*) Well, thanks anyway. (*take*) Are you Mary?
MARY III: No, but I'm betrothed.
GABE: I said, Are you *Mary*?
MARY III: Yes.
GABE: And betrothed?
MARY III: That's right—to Joseph Carpenter.
GABE: Would you happen to be Saint Mary?
MARY III: (*laughing*) What?
GABE: Saint Mary.
MARY III: (*smiling*) I don't think so.
GABE: (*offering one*) Would you like a balloon?
MARY III: (*wiping her brow with the back of her hand*) I don't know. I guess not, thanks anyway.
GABE: Don't like 'em?
MARY III: Oh, yes!
GABE: Here. Take it.
MARY III: I don't think I should.
GABE: It's all right. It's not from me. It's from The Boss.
MARY III: The Boss?
GABE: The Boss of all of us. The giver of every good and perfect gift.
MARY III: You mean . . . from Him?
GABE: He told me to give it to you.
MARY III: (*delighted and relieved*) You're a believer!
GABE: You better believe I'm a believer!
MARY III: So am I.
GABE: I'm glad to hear that, very glad. Look; would you believe that you're going to have a baby?

THE STAR THROWER

MARY III: Someday, I hope, but not yet. I'm only betrothed.

GABE: Understood. But you know The Boss can do whatever he chooses to do, and he wants you to have his baby—spiritually and, ah, bodily. He can do that. Do you believe?

MARY III: (*after a pause*) Yes.

GABE: I know this could get you into a lot of trouble . . . with Joe—it's Joe, isn't it?—and your family, the townspeople. But believe me—or believe The Boss—some day people all over the world will rise up and call you blessed!

MARY III: (*solemnly*) If this is what He truly wants, then I am His servant. Let it be so.

GABE: (*slowly*) It shall be so! (*He hands her a balloon with a picture of a dove on it.*)

MARY III: (*singing to the tune of "Silent Night"*)

The Song of the Maid

Now sings my soul,
"Great is the Lord!"
He is my joy.
He is my joy.
He has looked down on his handmaiden here.
Those who come after will call me blest.
He that is great has done great things!
Holy is his name!

He has shown power,
Scattered the proud,
Put down the mighty,
Lifted the low,
Filled up the hungry,
The rich sent away,
Helped his servant Israel.
He that is great has done great things!
Holy is his name!

THE BOSS: Let light shine!

(*The Christmas tree, star on top, blazes.*)
GABE: (*flinging up his arms to release bursts of glittering confetti*)
Glory!

CURTAIN

In a worship setting, the Cast may now come front singing a rousing chorus of "Gloria in Excelsis Deo" to introduce the spontaneous congregational singing of "Angels We Have Heard on High."

THE CHILDREN'S CHRISTMAS PLAY

Preface

I wrote *The Children's Christmas Play* because I needed children's Christmas material that would:

- honor both Christ and children
- involve the children without engaging them in extensive preparation (nothing wrong with extensive preparation, but in this particular case circumstances precluded it)
- free the children from "performance anxiety"

Our Creator God who accepts the sacrifices of broken and contrite hearts nevertheless deserves to be honored with our best efforts, and our children deserve to learn this.

But I don't believe the church should exploit the cuteness of children and/or the indulgence of their parents and church family in order to foist off trite or embarrassing material on a church audience inclined to be charitable (nothing wrong with being charitable, but something wrong with exploiting charity).

In this world we work under limitations. With sufficient commitment, almost any limitation can be overcome. But sometimes, because of constraints of time, space, travel, resources, or leadership, we don't always have the kind of conditions necessary to present a polished pageant.

As a child actor, I was distinctly unhappy being laughed at when I gave what I imagined was a thoroughly Stanislavskian performance as a bluebird in a Sunday School play. And as a *Children's Crusade* chorus member I regarded the honor of singing with diva Lily Pons so little that I went hysterical before curtain time. I am therefore reluctant to subject children to the pressures of stage performance. But in this day when children see so much television, maybe my reluctance is obsolete.

Please read the word *Play* in this piece's title in its original meaning. Children play naturally and effectively (it's what they do) without special practice or stress. Hence our format here combines modes that are natural for children—storytelling and the kind of playing to be found on any playground but which, in order to admit it to academia's rarefied precincts, we dub "creative dramatics." (Nothing wrong with Creative Dramatics; I once spent a happy summer teaching teachers how to teach it.)

In *The Children's Christmas Play*, the only rehearsed person is the Storyteller. When my son directed this play in his church, he divided the Storyteller's role among several Readers. This gave him several adult leaders in the midst of the children. The Storyteller(s) may work with script in hand. If the children have any sort of rehearsal at all—perhaps taken aside for a brief period before the program—it should be used only in some theatre games.[8]

One director suggested printing the words to the songs in the bulletin for members of the congregation to help with the singing.

Preferred properties are:

- a globe, large balloon, or beach ball to represent the world (it is possible to buy either an inflatable globe or a collapsible geodesic globe)
- an "It's A Boy" balloon
- a pail with a *small* amount of water in it
- flashlight(s)

THE STAR THROWER 127

- a claxon, bell, or whistle—the harsher sounding, the better. A vocal noise, perhaps amplified, can be used
- a star of fantastical design: perhaps a flashing tree ornament mounted on a pole.

Resist the impulse to multiply properties. Arming tiny players with shepherds' staves, for example, is asking for trouble. Likewise, costume pieces clutter things up and slow things down. One director reported that since his church owned a stock of costumes, he decided to go ahead and use them, but ran into a snag. "One child cried and refused to participate when I told him that somebody else had already spoken for the donkey's costume."

Although it's unlikely, it's possible that a child who has already represented one character, that of the innkeeper, for example, may (unlike Bottom) hesitate to "double" as another character, say, a shepherd, on the grounds that he or she is still the first character. Simply giving permission—"You can be both, if you'd like"—ought to free the actor. Or a child may wish to exchange roles. Or maybe more than one child will want to play the same character simultaneously. No problem—this is *avant garde* theatre!

In many churches children routinely come forward to participate in a Children's Time, and the size of the group is open. For *The Children's Christmas Play*, a group as small as five or six is large enough, while a group larger than three dozen probably proves that enough is enough and calls for multiple Readers. In some churches the children are also accustomed to repeating a prayer phrase by phrase. Throughout, the children should feel encouraged but not compelled to hum and sing along and to join in the playing.

It goes without saying that the Storyteller must be a person of rapport—that is to say, respect—who can lead others in play and so guide (without pressuring) the children to create appropriate action, especially the trek to Bethlehem, the angels' appearance to the shepherds, and the visit of the Wise Men. Approached in a spirit that allows and accepts their creativity, the children will respond with contributions more original and truly inspired than any adult writer or director could calculate—gifts worthy of the Christ child.

THE CHILDREN'S CHRISTMAS PLAY

For My Grandchildren—and Theirs!

CAST OF CHARACTERS
STORYTELLER(S)
CHILDREN

(*STORYTELLER invites the children to come forward and sit on the floor. As the action of the play requires, STORYTELLER and CHILDREN move about, otherwise sit—but they won't all sit when they're supposed to!*)

STORYTELLER: Where do you think I could find some children to help me tell the Christmas story? Will you help me tell the Christmas story? OK; to begin with, we need a sound track. Where do you think I could find some children to help make the sound track? Will you be a singer? Do you know "Away In A Manger"? The words come later, so let's start off with a hum. Sometimes in church we sing a hymn. Now let's sing a hum. Do you know what a hum is? Right! A hum is singing without words, like this: hummm. Ready? "Away in a Manger."

(*They hum "Away in a Manger."*)

Once upon a time the world fell sick. (*Displays a globe or partially deflated large balloon or beach ball representing the world.*) Look at that! Just lies there, too weak to move, scarcely breathing! Same thing for all the people living there. (*to the world*) Feeling bad? (*hand on globe*) I think it's got a temperature! And look!

Poor thing's breaking out all over. Here's a war wound, and here's another. Here's a hunger hurt, and here's a pain pinch, and here's a scare scar, and a selfishness scrape, and here's a booboo of badness. Why, all the people who live on this world are in danger, and they ache! Look out! Oh, my, this world is sick with sin and sorrow. Uh-oh! Poor world!

(*If desired, a SECOND STORYTELLER or READER may begin here, or THE STORYTELLER continues.*) But God said, "O World, you are my world. I made you, World, and all the people on you. And I love you. I want to make you all better." First, God tried to cool the world's fever with cool water (*dipping fingers in water and touching the balloon or globe*), and the world got a little better; (*manipulating globe, perhaps inflating-deflating, the balloon*) but then it got sicker again. So God sent some doctors called prophets—Dr. Amos and Dr. Isaiah, Dr. Jeremiah, Dr. Hosea, and even Dr. Ezekiel (Dr. Ezekiel is the bone specialist). And the world got a little better again; but then it got sicker again. So God said, "I'd better go save the world myself in Jesus." (*Claxon.*) Problem! After Adam and Eve, God had decided that having earthly parents was so good for little people that ever after no one would be allowed into the world without big people to take care of them. So God looked around to see if he could find some parents for Jesus.

(*If desired, another READER might take up the story here.*) Where do you think we could help God find a Mommy for Jesus? Maybe some people were too busy. Maybe some people didn't want to be bothered. Will you be Mary, the mother of Jesus? Thank you! Why don't you kneel right here? So God chose Mary because she was willing.

And God sent an angel to Mary with the good news. Where do you think we could find an angel to bring Mary good news? Will you be the angel to bring the good news to Mary? Thank you! (*Guides the angel-child to give Mary an "It's a Boy!" balloon.*) And when she heard the good news, Mary sang a song. I need

THE STAR THROWER

you to hum while I sing the words that Mary sang. (*Gives them a note to start them humming, and then sings to the tune of "Away in a Manger"*)

> Our dear God appoints me to carry his Son,
> And after I'll be called the most blessed one;
> I'll carry his baby and bring him to birth,
> And then he will grow up to save our sick earth.

(*If desired, another Reader may begin here.*) Where do you think we could help God to find a Daddy for the baby Jesus? Will you be Joseph? Thank you. (*claxon.*) Problem! It's tax time! Caesar Augustus said to Joseph, "Joseph, you go up to Bethlehem and pay your taxes!" And Joseph said, "But I can't go, because Mary's going to have a baby." Caesar said, "Do what I tell you! Go!"

So, they started out for Bethlehem, along with a whole lot of other people. Shall we go with them? (*Leads MARY and JOSEPH and CHILDREN about the area.*) Oh! Poor Mary! She's so tired! If only we had a donkey, she could ride. Will you be our donkey? What does a donkey say? You're such a little donkey, maybe Mary could walk along beside you and just hang on, and that would help her along the way.

(*If desired, a different Reader may begin here.*) And so they walked and walked and walked. It was a long way to Bethlehem. They got tired. How do you walk when you get tired? They got cold. What do you do when you get cold? And when they got to Bethlehem, it was late. Joseph looked for a place to stay. Could they stay with an uncle or an aunt? (*claxon*) They didn't have any aunts or uncles in Bethlehem. Could they stay in a motel? (*claxon*) No motels in Bethlehem. What about a hotel? (*claxon*) No hotels in Bethlehem. They got so tired. They got so cold. What to do? I know! An inn! There's an inn! Where's the door? We need a door. Who will be the door to the inn? And Joseph knocked on the door . . . . The innkeeper opened the door. We need an innkeeper. Who will be the innkeeper? The innkeeper opened the door . . . . And Joseph said to the innkeeper—you can help me if you want to hum—Joseph said (*giving the children a note to start humming, and then singing to the tune of "Jesus Loves Me"*)

> We have come a long, long way
> And we need a place to stay.
> Can you let us stay with you?
> Any room you've got will do.

(*A different Reader may take up here.*)

> But the innkeeper said, (*singing*)
> I don't have a room for you.
> Can you make the stable do?
> Since you have no place to stay,
> I will let you sleep on hay.

So Mary and Joseph went out to the stable where Joseph made some beds of straw, and the donkey ate a big dinner of hay. (*Allow the action.*)

And that night happened God's great miracle of birth and the baby Jesus was born. Mary and Joseph held their baby.

(*claxon*) Problem! (*A mock search and inspection of the children.*) None of you is tiny enough to be the newborn baby. Maybe you were once upon a time, but now you're too big. What can we do? Sometimes we use a doll to be the baby, but Jesus was a real, live baby, and I don't want you to think he was only a doll. And Jesus wasn't just any baby, but God's special baby. All babies are special, but the baby Jesus was extra-extra special. The baby Jesus is so special that even though we can't see him with our eyes anymore, we can still see him with our eyes of faith. Sing with me:

> Silent night, holy night,
> All is calm, all is bright.

THE STAR THROWER

'Round yon virgin mother and child,
Holy infant, so tender and mild,
Sleep in heavenly peace,
Sleep in heavenly peace.

(*A different Reader may resume here.*) And then the angels
sang! Where do you think we could find some angels? Angels are
God's messengers. Who will be an angel? Who else would like to
be angels? We can have a whole host (that means "a whole lot").
Can you glow? Angels glow with the light of God. I just happen
to have a flashlight, and if I shine the light on the angels, we can
pretend they glow. Now our cast gets bigger. There were sheep
out in the fields. Where do you think we might find some sheep?
(If some angels decide they'd rather be sheep, that's OK—we
need some of both.) (*Sets sheep in place.*) Who knows what a
sheep is? That's right; a sheep is a warm, wooly animal. What do
sheep say? . . . Who takes care of the sheep? Shepherds! Why,
sheep without shepherds to take care of them would be as lost as
little children without caregivers. Where do you think we could
find some shepherds? Who will be shepherds? How are you going
to take care of your sheep? Show me. Let's hum some more. I
think shepherds hummed or played flutes to pass the time in the
middle of the night.

(*Another possible spot to rotate Readers.*) Now where are our
angels? (*Setting the angels before the shepherds.*) So the angels
came to the shepherds and the angels sang (*giving them a note to
hum and singing to the tune of "Away in a Manger"*)

I bring you all great news of wonderful joy,
For to you this day is born a new boy—
A Savior to save you from all of your sins,
And so God's new kingdom among us begins.

And then God set in the sky a new star. (*claxon*) Problem!
This show doesn't have a star. Hold on! We can use this. It's not

a real star, but on our budget . . . . Who will hold the star up over the baby Jesus? Maybe we need a couple of people to help in case your arms get tired; you can take turns. Now where do you think we could find some Wise Men? How many Wise Men do you think we should have? That's right, the three kings. Maybe we can use a few more or less. Inflation; deflation. Do you have a present? How about you? Well, the Wise Men have to bring presents. After all, it's Jesus's birthday. Well, what counts is the thought. Suppose you *think* of something you could give Jesus.

(*Reader rotation, if desired.*) Oops! We almost forgot! Camels! Where do you think we could find some camels for the Wise Men? Who will be a camel? I think it takes two people to make a really good camel—if you hold onto the person in front . . . . What do camels say? Are you a one-hump camel or a two-hump camel? I'm afraid these kings are still too big for these camels to carry, so why don't we just lead the camels along—royally? (*Allowing time for the children to act out the story.*) How do kings walk? How do camels walk? And the Wise Men and the camels followed the star (is the star still shining up there? Good!) until they came to where the baby Jesus was. And the Wise Men went near. And the Wise Men knelt down. And the Wise Men gave the baby Jesus their gifts. One had gold. One had frankincense. One had myrrh.

(*Possible Reader rotation.*) And then they sang. Hum when you think you know the tune. (*Singing*)

> Twinkle, twinkle, little star,
> How I wonder what you are.
> Up above the world so high,
> Like a diamond in the sky.

(*Abruptly stopping the children so those who have begun singing the words don't sing ahead, and then finishing the song with these words:*)

THE STAR THROWER

Jesus shines still brighter far,
Jesus is the morning star!

And that's how God came in Jesus to save his sin-sick world with his great love. The baby Jesus grew up to be a person who lives and loves us still today, and it makes him happy to hear us sing to him. Where do you think we could find some children to sing about how Jesus loves us? Who will sing with me?

Jesus loves me!
This I know, for the Bible tells me so.
Little ones to him belong; they are weak, but he
    is strong.
Yes, Jesus loves me! Yes, Jesus loves me!
Yes, Jesus loves me! The Bible tells me so.

And that's the story of Christmas. Where do you think I could find some children to pray with me? Will you pray with me? Dear God, thank you for giving us the Christmas gift of our Savior Jesus. Amen.

CURTAIN

BOXES

Preface

Greatly talented, greatly loving, and greatly loved Cassandra Lee was an exceptional young actress, a star. Twice while she was only a high school student playing with our college-based community theatre at state drama festivals, she brought our theatre group top honors for production and first awards as actress. I had the privilege of directing her in many major roles. She portrayed Juliet, Isabella, Rosalind, Saint Joan, and Dorine, as well as minor roles which she played with equal dedication and distinction. She in turn directed me in a production of my *The Browning Show* for stage and television.

In her senior year in college, Sandi was an intern with The Bread and Puppet Theatre. After college she toured with a repertory theatre sponsored by The North Carolina State Department of Public Instruction. She completed her class work for a Master's Degree in Theatre at the University of North Carolina at Chapel Hill. Then Sandi became interested in theatre for the deaf. She developed proficiency in American Sign Language, earned a Master's Degree in Counseling from North Carolina State University, and dedicated herself to counseling persons with disabilities. She served as School Counselor for the Governor Morehead School for the Blind in Raleigh, North Carolina, and then as Operations Manager of the National AIDS Hotline for the Deaf at the Research Triangle. She was interested in using the arts, especially drama, as therapy. One month before

THE STAR THROWER

137

completing her class work as a doctoral candidate in Counselor Education at North Carolina State University, she was murdered by her sociopath son.

Sandi was my eldest child and only daughter. Her death plunged me into a depth of sorrow I had never known before. My brother, the Reverend Virgil N. Versteeg, ministered to me powerfully, encouraging me to "do for others what you would have wanted to do for Sandi, and to do the things you know Sandi would have wanted to do."

A bereavement group at the Hospice of Northwest Ohio also helped guide me in the grieving process, eventually offering me the opportunity to write and perform a play—*Boxes*—for their Living Through Loss series in Toledo, Ohio. In turn, this experience led me to found the Playback Theatre of Northwest Ohio with the primary mission of serving bereaved persons—a mission I know Sandi would have been glad to be part of.

During the fruitful discussion that followed the Living Through Loss production of *Boxes*, our audience bruited the question of which box each person felt would be the biggest and/or the heaviest. Some said the box of loneliness, some said anger, some guilt. Another way of ranking and discussing the boxes might be to ask what colors, shapes, or degrees of attractiveness/unattractiveness the boxes might have.

A cast comfortable with improvisation or interactive acting might try this variation: after the first two or three boxes have been described by the WOMAN, and the audience has caught on to the idea, let audience members decide what might be in the other boxes. The actors could show the boxes to random audience members under the pretext of not being able to read the label, and act out the audience member's answer.

However, we were pleased that even in a traditional script format the play connected effectively with its audience. The Hospice staff prepared small empty boxes. At the end of the evening, they distributed the boxes to the audience members. They invited each person to consider what he or she would place into this personal grief box. Some eight months later one audience member reported that she had placed special mementos of her loved one in her box, and that it had become part of her healing.

In our society, we put the physical remains of our loved ones in boxes—caskets or crematory containers. But their spiritual remains—"memories that bless and burn"—we keep in the treasure chests of memory and heart. As we would sprinkle pure ashes, so we would scatter on the world the stardust of their lives.

BOXES

A Play in One Act

CAST OF CHARACTERS
ATTENDANT
WOMAN

(*An airline terminal departure gate. ATTENDANT reads a newspaper, presumably the Obituaries. ENTER WOMAN staggering crazily under an impossible stack of boxes [not really: there are seventeen boxes in her load; one more is pre-set on stage—assuming, of course, that she uses actual boxes] and reels toward the gate.*)

ATTENDANT: Whoa! Hold it, ma'am!
WOMAN: Gate seven?
ATTENDANT: Right! Here, let me help you.
WOMAN: I've got to catch that flight!
ATTENDANT: Thirteen-thirteen?
WOMAN: Yes. Hurry!
ATTENDANT: Ma'am! Ma'am! Thirteen-thirteen's already gone.
WOMAN: Gone? My husband's on that flight.
ATTENDANT: Yes, ma'am, departed. Five minutes ago.
WOMAN: Oh, no. No! Gone? I didn't even get to say goodbye.
ATTENDANT: Sorry.
WOMAN: But these boxes! He left these boxes!

ATTENDANT: Yes, ma'am.

WOMAN: What am I going to do with them?

ATTENDANT: We can send them out on the next flight.

WOMAN: Oh, darn! The next flight? I suppose that's what we'll have to do.

ATTENDANT: No problem. Really.

WOMAN: I suppose that's best.

ATTENDANT: I can check them through for you right here, if you'd like.

WOMAN: What?

ATTENDANT: The boxes. I can check them through.

WOMAN: Here?

ATTENDANT: Everything's got to be inspected. Security.

WOMAN: Now?

ATTENDANT: If you'd like.

WOMAN: Yes. All right.

ATTENDANT: OK. (*surveying the pile of boxes and picking one up*) This?

WOMAN: Yes.

ATTENDANT: I mean, what's in it?

WOMAN: You have to know? Oh. Let's see. That one's promises.

ATTENDANT: Pardon?

WOMAN: Promises. Some of them are broken. Couldn't keep them all. But they're promises we made to each other, my husband and I.

ATTENDANT: I see. Promises. For example . . . ?

WOMAN: Oh, you know. The usual kind. "You can count on me." "I'll always be there for you." "I'll be at your side." "Love. Cherish. Honor. Till death do us part." Promises.

ATTENDANT: (*putting label on box and setting it on the counter*) Wedding gifts. How 'bout this one?

WOMAN: Same kind of things. Plans. Some of them are broken, too, or changed. But they were precious, once.

ATTENDANT: You mean like house plans?

WOMAN: Yeah, some of them. We were going to build. The children needed more room. And trips—to Bali.

THE STAR THROWER

ATTENDANT: Bali? Bali, Indiana?

WOMAN: That island. You know, in *South Pacific*. He never wanted to go to Hawaii. Said it was a rip-off.

ATTENDANT: Ah! Travel plans.

WOMAN: And, oh, yes—garden. We had plans for a garden, a new one. Wild flowers, daisies, and herbs. Day lilies. And our anniversary plans. We've got dates at the lodge. All our friends. In June.

ATTENDANT: OK. These are going to have to go on hold. (*setting it aside and picking up a small box*) This one?

WOMAN: Oh, Lord! That one's full of unanswered prayers. Prayers for health. Prayers for safety . . . protection . . . happiness. All kinds of prayers. Unanswered.

ATTENDANT: There's no address.

WOMAN: Well, you know. Just "To Whom It May Concern." I suppose there's no sense sending them on now.

ATTENDANT: Why don't you send 'em through and see what happens. I've seen answers to these things come back in some, well, unusual, unexpected ways. Never can tell.

WOMAN: I suppose it can't hurt.

ATTENDANT: OK. Hey! This one's hot! What is this—some kind of fire-proof box?

WOMAN: Memories. They burn.

ATTENDANT: No kidding. These things could ignite the whole cargo.

WOMAN: That's why it's a steel box.

ATTENDANT: (*suspicious*) Can you be a little more specific about the contents?

WOMAN: They're private.

ATTENDANT: Ma'am, I respect that. This isn't personal. I'm a professional. Security regulations. Health and safety.

WOMAN: The day we met. First date. Wedding. Honeymoon.

ATTENDANT: (*hurriedly*) I don't need the details.

WOMAN: Our first apartment. First promotion. Kids. School. Little league, graduations, proms, trips, birthdays, holidays. Funny things. Jokes. Songs.

ATTENDANT: Lady, you want some advice? You keep these.

WOMAN: But . . .

ATTENDANT: Yeah, I know. Right now they burn. But sometimes, after a while, after they burn down, these things can make glowing embers. A box like that can keep you warm.

WOMAN: You think so?

ATTENDANT: Trust me on this one.

WOMAN: (*After taking the box back hesitatingly, she turns her attention to the next box the ATTENDANT is holding.*) That one's loaded down with sadness and depression.

ATTENDANT: Sorrow.

WOMAN: You bet.

ATTENDANT: (*holding the box to his ear and shaking it*) Can't hear anything in there.

WOMAN: It's silent.

ATTENDANT: Oh. (*hoisting a heavy box*) What've you *got* in *here*?

WOMAN: Nothing.

ATTENDANT: What!

WOMAN: Nothing. It's empty.

ATTENDANT: You're trying to tell me this box is full of emptiness?

WOMAN: The emptiness is the heaviest. "A telephone that rings, but who's to answer?" . . . The empty supper table . . . empty laundry basket . . . the empty bed . . . the empty house.

ATTENDANT: All that's enough to break your back.

WOMAN: Uh-huh.

ATTENDANT: What's over here?

WOMAN: I forget. Oh! Loneliness. Invitations that never come. Visits and phone calls that petered out. Couples lists with our names scratched out. I guess it was him they liked; they don't call me. A sea of silence. A desert island.

ATTENDANT: I'm afraid we're going to have to leave that one out.

WOMAN: Figures.

ATTENDANT: Here?

WOMAN: That's not worth anything at all.

ATTENDANT: No value? Feels like a bunch of worn-out stuff.

WOMAN: Uh-huh. Clichés. My attic is full of them. You wouldn't believe it.

ATTENDANT: Clichés?

WOMAN: Yeah. Like this: "He's in a better place." "It's God's will." "Time heals all things." "You have to be strong." "You have to go on living." Honestly, when I've got the house, the bills, the paper work, the children are all upset about their Daddy leaving—when I've got all this stuff to take care of, why do people unload all their platitudes on me?

ATTENDANT: I know just how you feel.

WOMAN: Oh, my God! I've got a closet full of that one alone!

ATTENDANT: Sorry. (*hefting another box and looking questioningly*)

WOMAN: (*wearily*) Those are the "What Ifs?" "What if we'd found out sooner?" "What if we'd moved to Florida?" "What if we'd been better people?" "What if we'd had a better doctor?"

ATTENDANT: I'm sorry, Ma'am. That's toxic waste and it's not allowed. (*He casts it onto the reject pile.*) Now what's this?

WOMAN: Those are the "What Nows?" "What's going to happen now?" "What am I supposed to do now?" "What happens to the rest of my life now?" Worse than that, what do I do *right* now?

ATTENDANT: (*shrugging*) I don't know about all that. This here looks like a toolbox.

WOMAN: He left behind a garage full of them—screwdrivers, hammers, pliers, and scads of things I haven't any idea what it's all for. Now *I've* got to cut the lawn. And there's the vise.

ATTENDANT: Vice?

WOMAN: That thing on the workbench. It holds things.

ATTENDANT: Oh, yeah. A vise.

WOMAN: It wants to clamp down on me. Sometimes I can't move. Paralyzed.

ATTENDANT: (*making a joke*) You've got to unwind! (*labeling the box*) Toys. (*tugging at another box*) Let me guess. Bricks.

WOMAN: Regrets. I shouldn't have brought them. Things I wish I'd said, wish I'd done, hadn't done, hadn't said. A few resentments, too: things *he* didn't do, didn't say. I shouldn't have brought them.

ATTENDANT: (*setting the box aside*) No use, maybe, but they show what you value. This?

WOMAN: (*shuddering*) Guilt. It goes with the regrets.

ATTENDANT: I don't know—that's the kind of things people usually carry on with them.

WOMAN: That's *his* guilt. I've got my own.

ATTENDANT: OK . . . . That's funny—I almost asked you about *this* box, and this one belongs to *us*.

WOMAN: You've got boxes, too?

ATTENDANT: Kind of. This is our lost and found.

WOMAN: Lost and found!

ATTENDANT: Um-hmm. (*Turning to another box*) I guess this is next.

WOMAN: It's just what it says—Ys.

ATTENDANT: Wise? Uh, you mean like wisdom?

WOMAN: No; Why's. "Why did it happen?" "Why now?' "Why did he leave?" "Why couldn't he stay longer?" "Why us?" "Why me?" Why's.

ATTENDANT: You know, I've never yet seen one of these things get answered.

WOMAN: About that box of yours, the lost and found. Can I look at it?

ATTENDANT: Why? You lose something?

WOMAN: I've lost everything. (*rummaging through the box*) My appetite . . . my sleep . . . warmth . . . comfort . . . support . . . (*coming up with a hand puppet on her hand*) . . . even my laughter.

THE STAR THROWER
145

ATTENDANT: You know, lots of folks lose those kinds of things here. Sometimes takes a long time to find them again. Better leave your name and number. (*turning his attention to another box*) This one's pretty beat up.

WOMAN: Yeah, well, that's my life.

ATTENDANT: Your life!

WOMAN: Such as it is—broken, shattered. It's all in pieces.

ATTENDANT: Ma'am, I think maybe you better keep these pieces.

WOMAN: Why? What good are they now?

ATTENDANT: Maybe you can glue 'em back together.

WOMAN: It wouldn't be the same. It'd still be broken.

ATTENDANT: Yeah. Different, maybe. Kind of like a patched-up pitcher. But it could still carry water.

WOMAN: Not with pieces missing.

ATTENDANT (*holding another box*): And this would be what?

WOMAN: I can't tell you.

ATTENDANT: (*frustrated*) Ma'am, once again: this isn't personal . . . . I flat out have to know.

WOMAN: Well I flat out can't tell you.

ATTENDANT: Then we flat out can't send it . . . . (*feeling the box*) Is it alive? (*listens to it*) Lady, this thing is ticking! (*looking at her*) I think we'd better open this up.

WOMAN: No! Don't! Don't open it.

ATTENDANT: Why not?

WOMAN: Once you take the lid off, I don't know if I can ever get it back on.

ATTENDANT: Lady, I've got to know what's in this box.

WOMAN: All right. I confess. Dynamite.

ATTENDANT: What! Dynamite?

WOMAN: It's packed with emotions. I've got to get rid of them. I know they're going to explode.

ATTENDANT: You're telling me this is a time bomb and you expect me to let it pass?

WOMAN: I can't handle it.

ATTENDANT: Looky here, Ma'am. We open this box—ver-r-r-ry carefully, like so. Now look. What a mess of wires!

WOMAN: See what I mean? I couldn't begin to untangle all that.

ATTENDANT: Yeah, that'd be something. But you don't have to untangle it all—at least, not all at once.

WOMAN: That's a relief.

ATTENDANT: But what you do have to do is to get to the detonator.

WOMAN: The thing that sets it off.

ATTENDANT: Right.

WOMAN: I don't know which one it is.

ATTENDANT: It's this little gizmo here. See? The one with the little red flag. That's the detonator. We just ease that apart—like so!—and *voila*! There! It's defused. Here. You keep it.

WOMAN: What do I do with what's left?

ATTENDANT: Well, these emotions are under a lot of pressure. You're going to have to go through this box. Take your time. Take each one of them out. Feel them. Examine them. Put your name on them, so you know they belong to you. Then put them someplace safe. Take them out and look at them from time to time. Here. How's it feel now?

WOMAN: Heavy. But maybe it'll be OK.

ATTENDANT: Try it.

WOMAN: I'll try. (*sets the box aside*)

ATTENDANT: (*picking up another box and recoiling in alarm*) What've you got in here? Sounds like a nest of hornets.

WOMAN: (*drawing back*) That's exactly what it is, bees, wasps, yellow jackets, killer bees—everything that stings. That's my anger. I've got so much of that it wouldn't fit in the box with the other emotions.

ATTENDANT: Hey! What are you mad at?

WOMAN: Are you kidding? I'm mad at everything—the whole world, God, him! He should have booked a later flight.

THE STAR THROWER 147

What's his hurry? Why'd he go off and leave me alone? I
begged him to stay. They said there was nothing they could
do. I'll tell you, I am so mad. I've got to get rid of that
box. Killer bees! They're going to sting me to death. He
thinks he can just leave me stuck with it, he's got another
think coming!

ATTENDANT: And what's this plastic jar that's taped to it. Is it
honey?

WOMAN: I wish! Those are tears. Tears! I've got gallons of them
at home! Start coming at the lousiest times; no reason. All of
a sudden, *whoosh*! I'm gushing tears. Just like that.

ATTENDANT: This?

WOMAN: Oh . . . I'm sorry. Never mind that one. Just forget
it.

ATTENDANT: Why?

WOMAN: To tell you the truth, it's personal. I'm embarrassed.

ATTENDANT: Lady, like I said, I'm a professional.

WOMAN: If you must know, it's—(*more confidentially*) it's birth
control things.

ATTENDANT: Oh! Say no more. Sorry.

WOMAN: What am I supposed to do with them now? He's
gone.

ATTENDANT: Now I'm embarrassed. He's not going to need
them, either, is he? I mean, since you're *here* and he's *there* . . .

WOMAN: That's just the point. He's taken off and left me
with all this stuff. I want it, but what's the use?

ATTENDANT: Well, OK, I'll send it through, but I'm not
sure they use this stuff there. Now what about this here
package?

WOMAN: It's a pressure pump.

ATTENDANT: (*puzzled*) Like for bicycle tires?

WOMAN: No, it's a circulation pump. My family pumps up
this pressure for me to get back in circulation.

ATTENDANT: So?

WOMAN: So even if I wanted to get back in circulation, I wouldn't know how.

ATTENDANT: You know, it really is a shame. Look at you. You're still an attractive woman. Very attractive.

WOMAN (*uncertain*): Thank you . . .

ATTENDANT: I'll tell you what: I'm off work here in an hour. Maybe you'd like to talk about it over a drink somewhere.

WOMAN: I promised the children I'd be home to fix dinner.

ATTENDANT: Maybe some other time.

WOMAN: I thought you were a professional.

ATTENDANT: All work and no play . . .

WOMAN: (*not angry, but in control*) You're going to have to find someone else to play with.

ATTENDANT: Clear enough. No offense.

WOMAN: No.

ATTENDANT: . . . Well, I guess that's about all, huh?

WOMAN: Oh, no; I've got a rental truck parked outside.

ATTENDANT: Right. Then we'll need this. (*He produces a handcart, labeled "Resources."*) Helps carry the load.

WOMAN: (*looking around as they start out*) This is a strange terminal. Only one gate.

ATTENDANT: Yeah, that's the way the architect designed it. Whole building's box-shaped. I spend so much of my life here, it's like living in a box. Sometimes I almost forget about the outside.

WOMAN: I feel the same way about going home. Going home is like walking into an empty box.

ATTENDANT: Lady, that's what I'm trying to tell you—every box has got an inside and an outside. For every inside of a box, there's an outside.

WOMAN: But if you're in a box, you don't know that until you get on the other side. (*EXEUNT.*)

CURTAIN

PART TWO:

SOLO PLAYS AND MONOLOGUES

INTRODUCTION

For the past twenty years I have used solo performances as a vital part of my ministry. Often I have been the performer. Other times I have enlisted laity and non-church members to perform.

It has been an effective ministry. Drama engages people in intense ways. It reaches them at other levels than those touched by the traditional sermon. I call it preaching to the right brain.

Here I share some of my favorite scripts.

All of them have been used in worship settings. Some are clearly more at home in a church setting. However, the life and work of John Donne (*Donne to Death*), the story of the Garden of Eden (*Four Fathers*), and the story of The Prodigal Son (*The Prodigals*) transcend any parochialism.

The following section, "Developing and Presenting Solo Plays and Dramatic Monologues," shows you, step by step, how to find other worthy material or create and perform your own powerful dramatic monologues and solo dramas.

DEVELOPING AND PRESENTING SOLO PLAYS AND DRAMATIC MONOLOGUES: A SHORT COURSE IN THE ART OF DRAMATIC MONOLOGUE

A Forerunner

Scene: Judea, a wilderness. Twenty-eight AD. Throngs stream out to the Judean wilderness to see a sensational attraction—John the Baptizer.

Some of the multitude believe (and Jesus may have confirmed in Matthew 17:12) that John is the reborn prophet Elijah last seen in these parts some eight centuries earlier. They remember that Malachi had prophesied Elijah's return before the day of the Lord (Malachi 4:5).

However, with equal plausibility—at least when it comes to sheer dramatic flair—those crowds might have matched up John the Baptizer with yet other prophets—say, Jeremiah and his yoke (Jeremiah 27), or Isaiah and his startling costume—or lack thereof

THE STAR THROWER   153

(Isaiah 20:2-4—"some nudity required"). If any of these prophets—John, Jeremiah, or Isaiah—were to appear in New York today, Manhattan cognoscenti might call them "performance artists."

But back in 28 AD when the Jerusalem authorities dispatched a delegation to interrogate John the Baptizer, that Wilderness Wonder did not identify himself as Elijah, nor as "the prophet" foretold in Deuteronomy 18:15-19. He did not compare himself with Jeremiah or Isaiah. Instead, John borrowed from Isaiah a blurb that billed him simply as "the voice of one crying out in the wilderness, / Make straight the way of the Lord" (John 1:23).

Just as Baptizer John disclaimed any pretension of reincarnation or reenactment, he surely did not consider the title of "performance artist" a thing to be grasped. For, unlike his secular contemporaries in the Hellenistic world, John the Baptizer owned no dramatic tradition.

Of course, like any other subject of the Roman Empire, John conceivably might have had some hearsay knowledge of the great Graeco-Roman theatrical heritage that flaunted itself all around him. That heritage, in John's day, was putrefying—becoming "little more than a vulgar form of popular entertainment."[9] Genuine actors were being replaced by gladiators. Artistic, offstage death scenes were being supplanted by brutal and actual onstage butchery (a major reason why the early church father Tertullian demanded the closing of the theatres). Thus when a wrathful mob will drag St. Paul's companions into the theatre at Ephesus (Acts 19:29) it will be an ominous moment.

But the Kingdom of Baptizer John's real loyalty possessed no theatrical legacy at all, noble or corrupt. Therefore, very likely John—whose Jordan performance was clearly dramatic— nevertheless had no concept of dramatic performance.

All the same, and notwithstanding that he probably never could have thought of himself that way, John was in effect a one-person show.

But suppose John had possessed a heritage of drama. Suppose

John had known what an actor was. Suppose John had even been an actor (and in a sense aren't we all?). Then might we not imagine John enacting the role of Elijah the Forerunner? As it was, and non-actor though he was, John certainly did faithfully embody Elijah's essence.

Unlike John, you and I, as well as the world we live in, do in fact inherit dual treasures. We inherit the Judeo-Christian spiritual birthright and we inherit the Graeco-Roman culture, not the least valuable component of which is its theatrical tradition.

Very well, then; suppose that we, thus doubly endowed, recreate John's act for audiences today. Suppose we dramatize this Biblical scene. Suppose we let an actor impersonate John. Suppose our actor *re*enacts what John enacted, and tries to bring the New Testament past to life for today's people.

Whatever we may imagine, this much we know—whether or not we are actors, we may in our own faithfulness take John as the prototype for our own action. In harmony with John's spirit, we may do in our context what John did in his. We, too—either in our own persons or as *personae dramatis*—may explore and use the power of a solo voice—"the voice of one"—dedicated to proclaiming the word of God dramatically. The word *drama* originally meant "doing."

A Follower

Scene: A sanctuary. Sunday morning. The present. Something special is about to happen.

Our congregation is made up of both experienced disciples and new Christians. There are some lukewarm spouses, some fidgeting children, and some rebellious or compliant youth. We have out-of-town guests, even a few seekers. We are a rich, at times inchoate, but exciting mixture of God's people. We gather in an aura pregnant with vague but palpable expectation.

Now the worship service progresses to that point where

habitual worshipers expect a preacher to come to the podium and deliver a message. Our church has an excellent preacher whose sermons are a source of comfort, challenge, instruction, and inspiration.

However, on this particular Sunday, instead of the preacher (or could that be our preacher in disguise?) a disheveled figure swathed in some kind of faux animal skin stamps to the dais. He stabs his hand into the air: "Repent!" In a voice of alarm, he lets us know exactly what we need to repent. He accuses us of smugness, selfishness, lukewarmness.

Now, perhaps to conceal our chagrin, we smile tentatively. We have located the proper frame for this event. We understand that this person before us is playing a role—even if he plays a bit roughly. Also he implicitly invites us to risk playing, too. He prods our imaginations. He dares us to *pretend*—the word derives from "to stretch forward"—to pretend that we are among those who once upon a time thronged to the Jordan to see the wilderness prophet, John the Baptizer.

The children in our congregation are mesmerized. There are some open mouths. Casual attendees lean forward. Mature Christians apprehend Christian hope in a new way. Disgruntled parishioners murmur that the preacher is too innovative to suit their tastes.[10] For the majority of us, this moment of consecrated make-believe produces real and lasting effect.

What is this we are experiencing? Different people call it different names. Call it a first-person sermon, an illustrated sermon, a dramatic monologue, or a solo play. Or call it what John called it: "the voice of one crying, 'Prepare the way of the Lord.'" I like to think of it as preaching to the right brain.

My purpose statement for this kind of right-brain preaching is this: By the use of solo dramatic art, to proclaim the abounding grace of God in Christ so as to awaken, call, nourish, and sustain God's people for their spiritual life, growth, and maturity in Kingdom life.

Except for the first phrase, this might serve as a purpose

statement for any kind of preaching. That first phrase, "by the use of solo dramatic art," simply makes it preaching by monologue.

Understanding the Monologue Form

In our Western tradition, monologues—that is, one-person performances—appeared at the very dawn of drama.

It happened, according to one widely accepted theory, something like this. One day—an unrecorded day, but probably a day in at least the seventh-century BC (give or take a century!)—somewhere in Greece a certain anonymous but enthusiastic individual broke away from a chanting, dancing chorus of Dionysian worshipers. Then, like some primitive cheerleader or drill instructor perhaps, he or she spoke or sang a speech or a stanza of poetry to prompt, to encourage, or to echo the writhing, ululating chorus.

Inspired or inebriated, who can tell? Ancient Greeks made small beer of fine distinctions in these matters. But this Dionysian person eventually evolved to become the first—and solo—actor, a thespian named Thespis who was also, by 534 BC, the first winner of ancient Athens' version of an Oscar—which, instead of a twelve-inch, gold-plated statuette, turned out to be one live goat! We aren't told whether Thespis put it on his mantel.

Or, if you don't like that capricious theory, J. Michael Walton[11] reconstructs the birth of drama and monologue slightly differently. Walton doubts that Thespis descended from someone who spontaneously split off from a group of worshipers. Rather, Walton hypothesizes that Thespis derived his act from the role of those proto-monologists par excellence, the epic bards, of whom Homer (if there was a Homer) was the exemplar. In Walton's scenario, Thespis merely makes the transition from narration to impersonation, and thus transforms himself from bard to actor, from poet to player. All of these were monologists.

THE STAR THROWER

Whichever theory you prefer, Professor Oscar Brockett teaches theatre students:

> The drama of Thespis was relatively simple, since it involved only one actor and a chorus. This does not mean that there was only one speaking character in each play, but rather that all characters were played by the same actor. This single actor used masks in shifting his identity . . . . Face-to-face conflict between opposing characters, which most later periods have considered a necessary feature of drama, was impossible so long as there was only one actor.[12]

This means that until some thirty years later when that great and innovative playwright, Aeschylus, came along to add a second actor and dialogue, all dramatic acting (other than that performed between the single actor and the all-chanting, all-dancing choruses) was the acting of monologues.

And ever since, monologue has remained a vital part of drama. It has persisted through all those one-person chorus speeches, prologues, and epilogues, and the towering soliloquies of Shakespeare's plays. It continues in contemporary drama in the work of Mamet, Shepard, Beckett, Spaulding Grey, and others. In fact, so enduringly rich is the monologue form that dramatists such as Chekov (*The Harmfulness of Tobacco*), Strindberg (*The Stronger*), again Beckett (*Krapp's Last Tape*) and others have created entire plays for a solo performer. Thus in our day one-person shows constitute a thriving niche in world drama.[13]

Why? Why does the monologue continue to command our attention? What riches does the monologue form offer to authors, performers, and audiences? Attractive answers flock to mind: heightened actor-audience contact . . . intimacy . . . depth of character exploration . . . intensity . . . focus . . . affordability . . . freedom to experiment . . . .

Salvation Army founder William Booth once volunteered that he was willing to stand on his head on street corners if by doing so he could gain an audience for his preaching. Saying this, General Booth demonstrated the spirit of a spiritual strolling player, an evangelical *saltimbanque*—or, if such an oxymoron is permissible, a spiritual carnival barker.

And Booth's spirit descended directly from the spirit that powered John the Baptizer and the other prophets and preachers. It's the same spirit that motivates today's religious performer who sets out to enact the voice of one preparing the way of the Lord— our Lord who was willing to be lifted up on a cross in order to draw all persons to himself.

Furthermore, scripture demonstrates that narrative is a particularly effective instrument for communicating the active, dynamic nature of God. Narrative is the Bible's native language. Jesus tells stories. And no wonder! Story is made up of development—from beginning to middle to end ("But not necessarily in that order," as film director Jean-Luc Godard insisted). This dynamism of development is what makes a story. Therefore, because spirit, too, is dynamic, stories and drama communicate—"embody"—spirit well. They are the right form for the content. Eric Bentley reminds us that to a large extent "form is meaning." McLuhan put it: "The medium is the message."

At the same time that the dramatic monologue form perfectly fits the message of God's drama in history, and offers freshness and diversity to a preaching program, it also opens an infinite variety of angles of approach to and contact with listeners and spectators.

Perhaps best of all, the monologue contributes its own special vividness. The word *vivid* implies "lively, full of life, striking, strong, distinctive." Vividness makes the difference between hearing reports about John and seeing John himself in person and in live action (well, in the live person and action of a performer).

Paul Ricoeur tells us that the human condition embraces "the conflict between judging consciousness and acting man."[14]

Dramatic presentation may address the human being in action as well as the judging consciousness.

A member of a search committee who was interviewing a colleague of mine made a point of noting that, since the church was a university church, she expected the sermons to be intellectual. My colleague replied that she preached to the whole person, and not only to the person's brain. Keith Johnstone nails this portrait of "intellectual" listeners: "leaning back away . . . , and crossing their arms tightly, and tilting their heads back. Such postures help them to feel less 'involved', less 'subjective.'"[15]

I think people listen in church with a different quality of attention than they listen with anywhere else. I know I do. Still, the person listening to a traditional sermon may evaluate the sermon and accept it or reject it. And of course that's good. But is it always good enough? On the other hand, that same person experiencing a right-brain sermon, a dramatic-monologue sermon, may for a time achieve escape velocity and leave the realm of "judging consciousness." By entering into an open spirit of imaginative participation, the person may journey to that realm of the "acting [person]." We are saying that this adventure need not exclude, but may include more—go deeper than—left-brain-only judgment of and response to a discourse. Dramatic presentation can entice the listeners to lean forward from the edges of their pews.

Aligning himself with John, and describing his and John's relationship to some strait-laced members of their generation, Jesus said,

> They are like children sitting in the marketplace and calling to one another,
> 'We played the flute for you, and you did not dance; we wailed, and you did not weep.' (Luke 7:32}

That wet-blanket audience that Jesus and John encountered ("a tough house," in actor parlance) has not vanished from the earth. Even in our own generation, some people seem unable to play. Some people must act (!) their age (even if they subconsciously resent doing so).

Other people, however, may be freer to own and integrate their feelings as valuable parts of themselves. Whole persons can respond to life's invitations to dance or to mourn, and to enter the Kingdom as children.

But how shall the frozen ever become the chosen unless we at least invite them and offer them opportunities to enter into the holy child spirit? First-person preaching can help us do that.

Monologues also hold out the potential for sharing more widely among God's people the privilege and responsibility of proclaiming the Good News. Actors and non-actors alike who might balk, not to say panic, at being invited to preach a sermon may be eagerly excited to present a monologue. Unlike the traditional sermon, the monologue offers its presenter the protection of a literal or figurative mask. Non-actors often seem surprised to learn that many actors are shy. The performed persona confers personal anonymity and therefore seeming safety. The mask frees. Not for nothing did Luigi Pirandello call his plays "Naked Masks." Give the mask of monologue to a shy person, and you may confer the gift of freedom of expression.

And in this way others may nurture and employ their personal and spiritual talents, gifts, and potential. You may want to take the opportunity to reach out to actors beyond your walls and encourage their growth, too. In short, this stewardship may be significant ministry.[16]

Looking for Monologues

There are plenty of monologues waiting at booksellers and libraries. Many of them should stay there. Often you have to sift through an enormous amount of chaff to find some wheat. I have a friend who searches for church music by going to music stores, plopping herself down on the floor, and leafing through music books, reading the lyrics and humming the tunes. I would covet that same smorgasbord system for the monologist who goes looking for material. Therefore, a library (presided over by a deaf librarian, perhaps) seems a good place to start, or a bookstore with comfortable seating, or a publisher willing to let you order on approval.

If these searches prove impractical or fruitless, what other alternatives do you have? As Mickey Rooney might have enthused to Judy Garland, "We can write our own show!" And if we can't find an actor to perform it, we can do that ourselves, too. After all, it wasn't just Andy and Judy who did it. The earliest Greek playwrights played the role of protagonist/monologist in their own productions, too.

Or you can call on a talented friend or church member (it doesn't always have to be a church member!) to create your monologue. This way you can even custom-tailor the monologue to the specific requirements of the audience in its situation. Also, this do-it-yourself option offers authors opportunities to grow through research and writing. It fully engages the monologist's unique personality and viewpoint. Furthermore, the monologues you generate this way may eventually find publishers who will make these quality pieces available to a waiting but under-served market. Perhaps the wave of the future will bring sharing of such resources via the Internet.

Recognizing the "Right" Monologues

How do you know when you have found or composed the monologue you're looking for?

1. The first consideration is your audience. To whom are you

going to present the monologue? (Note the language of gift underlying the activity: *present*.)

Do not choose material out of narcissism or romanticism— "I want to do that! I could do that really well!" If you start from such a selfish standpoint, chances are a discerning audience will sense and resent that. On the other hand, audiences will often respond positively to the performer's sincere desire to share something of value.[17]

So you present the monologue for the sake of the audience. Their requirements rule. Real actors accept roles that need to be played for the sake of the play and the audience, rather than merely looking for roles that please those actors or make them look good.

And it goes without saying that once he or she undertakes a role or a piece, the monologist wholeheartedly accepts responsibility to perform it as well as possible. The performer should have, or be able to build, enthusiasm for and commitment to the work.

Potential benefits for the audience may be as many and varied as monologues themselves, ranging from entertainment to conversion and sanctification.

And please note that there is nothing wrong with doing a piece solely for entertainment. It comes under the rubric of "Consider the lilies." Entertainment in the sense of "amusement" is appropriate to fellowship occasions. I remember my youthful delight in being entertained by a preacher at church camp who impersonated a preacher delivering a sermon on the "text" of "Little Jack Horner." His humor, and his demonstration that a preacher could poke fun at himself and the serious business of preaching, charmed me! That entertainment may have been one of those Holy-Spirit nudges that moved me towards the ministry.

Professor Jennifer McMahon writes: "Whether it offends one's intellectual taste or not, humor is an incredible pedagogical tool." She reminds us that "people have been using stories as a means to educate for hundreds—indeed thousands—of years."[18] We can go further and assert that entertainment, in the sense of "to hold attention," is essential to any effective communication. To entertain is "to receive as a guest," "to engage the attention agreeably," "to entertain friends with conversation," and "to entertain strangers" as in Hebrews 13:2. The monologist who thinks of him/herself as a host entertaining company has the foundation for a meaningful encounter.

Often the performer in a church setting will also be looking to share spiritual values such as conviction, heightened and deepened commitment, increased understanding and awareness, comfort and challenge.

You can also use a monologue to promote mundane but important Kingdom enterprises, for example, mission support and recruitment or fund raising. God's people are no fonder of bitter waters today than they were in the time of Moses. Therefore, if you can sweeten the waters a bit and make them more palatable, that may be a positive contribution. However, when you use monologues this way, beware of going overboard with propaganda to the point of drowning the goose that lays the golden eggs.

If the audience feel that they are being manipulated, if they suspect rightly or wrongly that the event is being distorted in order to disguise or put over something that cannot stand on its own merits in the open light of day, or if the audience conclude that the sugar coating is merely deceptive rather than pleasant sweetening, then they may reject the piece altogether. With artistic integrity maintained, a monologue may be good entertainment, good art, and good propaganda all at once.

2. This leads to the second criterion for choosing a monologue, namely, the inherent excellence of the monologue as a performance piece. We grow impatient with mere good intentions in church (probably we ought to rejoice for them!). Good intentions may be the ethical gold standard in heaven, but in the church militant (as in the theatre where "It works" or "It doesn't work" are often final judgments), good intentions need to be transformed into good works by effectiveness.

If, as is too often the case, a monologue comes across as the work of an author who means well but who lacks either instinct for, or knowledge or experience of what works for an audience, we should regard that monologue with the same jaundiced eye that a Biblical priest might have cast upon a blemished animal offered for sacrifice. The unfortunate actor who tries to perform such a monologue, becomes the one offered up as a sacrifice.

Also unfortunately, if perhaps unintentionally, the church's hospitality to dramatic artists has been so lukewarm for so long[19] that by now we suffer a shortage of competent dramatists willing to write for the church. And thus it comes about that much of the material available to us tends to be precisely that well intentioned but ineffective stuff. It is compounded of shallow theology and sophomoric theatre. Good intentions notwithstanding, and calling a spade a spade, it reeks of amateurism in the pejorative sense of that word. It is inept, clumsy, shallow, crude, and maudlin. In case I'm not making myself clear, lots of church monologues are just plain bad.

Some publishers share the blame. They exacerbate the situation by tunnel vision focused only on the bottom line. They sacrifice the prophetic for the profitable. They are understandably interested in selling. And they think that what sells is what is perceived to be "easy." (They are liable to call this, "Considering our audience.") Trouble is, what they mean by "easy" turns out to be what most theatre people mean by "flop."

Take this as a maxim: A weak script, the actor has to carry; a strong script carries the actor.

It's "easier" to ride a kiddie car than to handle (let alone acquire!) a Land Rover. A kiddie car won't get you far. A Land Rover (I know because I've seen the commercials!) will take you to the mountain top.

3. After considering the needs of the audience and the dramatic effectiveness—the "stage worthiness"—of the material, the third criterion for selecting or creating a monologue is the monologue's suitability to the available performer.

So-called typecasting (that usually means "stereotype casting") tends to be unimaginative and self-limiting. At one community Good Friday service, a male and manly pastor dressed in his customary business suit had the courage to present a first-person sermon of Mary, the mother of Jesus. He succeeded, one audience member observed, "masterfully." That man must be a talented actor.

Perhaps not everyone can do what he did. If a particular actor's range really is limited, say, to ethereality, then that actor perhaps might play a Mary but not a convincing Barabbas. Likewise, some young actors can portray age. Some can't. If you cast one who can't as old Father Abraham, you put that perhaps otherwise fine actor at a disadvantage.

But I have seen casting against type turn out to look like genius. I have seen directors cause arid actors to blossom like the rose. I have seen unpromising actors, when challenged, break through. Therefore, I lean toward the view that most of us can stretch ourselves, and we should. You can afford to challenge the stereotypes and assumptions, and you should.

Creating the Monologue

Selecting the Topic. It is possible and preferable to begin to create a monologue by asking, "What do the persons in my potential audience need to experience? What will benefit them?"

This is not to say that you may not also follow your personal fascinations. You should. Those are your "energy centers." What fascinates you will likely fascinate others.

Maybe you are entranced with (1) a real or imagined character—St. Paul, say, or—who?—The Lone Ranger (why not?). Or you feel fascinated by (2) some striking situation or premise— say, the mysterious disappearance from scripture of Jesus' earthly father, Joseph the carpenter. Or maybe you are drawn to (3) a certain theme such as Christian teaching about heaven, perhaps, or the theme of bereavement, or racial justice, or forgiveness, and so on. Any of these might be a great topic for a monologue.

Nonetheless, once you select a topic, the primary concern reasserts itself, namely, "What is in this for my audience?" Answer that first. Don't skip this step; or you may trip over it.

Researching the Topic. When it comes to research materials about some subjects—the Apostle Paul for example—you're overwhelmed with an embarrassment of riches. The Apostle himself has bequeathed us a treasury of writings. Years of study have familiarized us with Paul. But once you choose him as the subject of your monologue, reread all his words afresh. Consult commentaries and other materials. Focus on Paul's *story* and its most typical and powerful expressions.

But research material is not always so abundant. Consider the case of, say, carpenter Joseph's disappearance, or some even more obscure Biblical character such as Sceva (Acts 19:14), or, to take one who excites my own interest, Justus (Acts 1:23). Or consider the case of a monologue centering on a theme of social justice. In such instances, your research may once again delve into primary documents and scholarly tomes. It may also include current events, literature, and other arts. And you can look, too, into your personal vaults of random primary and secondary experience that each of us accumulates in the process of living and learning.

The richest resource of all may be your consecrated imagination through which the Holy Spirit may brood upon the face of the deep—the chaos of accumulated research—until God's clear word creates. At some point, you need to discipline and even check mere speculation. The rule is: first create, then critique.

Locating the Dramatic Moment. The monologist is a spiritual surfer (notice you left your Land Rover on the mountain, the Holy Spirit brooding on the deep, and now you find yourself paddling a surfboard off the shore!). The monologist is a surfer trying to catch the right wave at the right moment. The surfer wants to mount the wave just as it begins to gather momentum and build toward full ripeness. Then the surfer rides the crest as it peaks, plunges, and subsides. This spiritual surfer pays attention to such theatre axioms as, "begin in the midst of things," and "the higher the stakes, the higher the dramatic tension." Thus in the monologue about Paul, Paul is in a Roman prison awaiting beheading—a life-or-death outcome considerably more serious than wiping out on a bad wave.

Determining the Narratee(s). This brings you to a crucial decision in the shaping of the monologue, namely, to whom shall the monologue be addressed? To whom is the solo performer supposed to be speaking, to the audience as audience, or to the audience as character? In the study of narratology, this addressee is known as the "narratee."[20]

As you determine your narratee, you in effect designate the role which you ask your audience imaginatively to assume—either to play themselves (that is, to be the literal audience they factually are—with all the socially conditioned conventions implied by their particular idea(s) of "audience") or some imagined other. At the same time, you are selecting the particular frame through which, or the mirror in which, your audience will experience your monologue.

Furthermore, if, as some maintain, the self is known relationally, then the character you are portraying will reveal him/herself by your character's (1) relationships with him/herself, (2) reports of relationships with others, and (3) relationships with the audience or narratee.

In our example of a monologue with Paul as protagonist, if you ask your audience to imagine themselves in a narratee role, to whom should Paul speak? Fellow prisoners? Guards? Possibly. You know he did indeed speak to them, even converted them. You know also that the imprisoned Paul wrote letters to churches, friends, and proteges (in fact the pseudopigraphical letters of Paul may be exact equivalents to our monologues!). You know, too, that he received visitors. Ah ha! You feel your heart stirred by the warmth and poignancy of that scene. Follow your heart. This will be the moment—when faithful friends visit Paul in prison where he awaits death. The scene is reminiscent of Plato's *Phaedo* dialogue on the death of Socrates. You will invite your audience—the "narratees"—to play the role of Paul's visiting friends.

Crafting the Monologue. Many principles for shaping dramatic material are obvious and well known. Libraries have books on playwriting and directing, and colleges teach courses. Play-going and practical stage experience are great teachers. From such resources each monologist will assemble a group of favorite guidelines expressing her or his personal dramatic style and voice. Your selected list of monologue-creating "rules of thumb" (which, like Peer Gynt's thumb, sometimes need to be amputated) might include the following.

- Win attention at the start (but don't do anything that is not justified by your vision or integral to the character in the situation).
- Work in "beats" or "units of action"[21] each with its own fresh beginning, development, and destination.
- Let units grow out of one another the way sections slide out of a telescope. Principles of such growth include the chronological, logical, and psychological.
- Regain attention at the start of each new beat; build each beat to its climax.
- Plan variety—"a laugh, followed by a tear;" alternate fast segments with slow, intense with relaxed, serious with light.
- Let your audience release tension between beats.
- But stay on track—keep advancing your story.
- Build the beats themselves to one overall climax.
- As George Orwell might advise, break or ignore any of these "rules" if doing so helps the piece to "work."

Finding the Performer

Where can you find competent performers to present your

monologue? They are in every congregation—again, not that you should limit yourself to members of the congregation. Actors are everywhere—and available! Finding them can be an outreach—if not necessarily a proselytizing—opportunity. Don't be shy about asking. Performers are eager to perform. It's not always about money (although money can be nice). It's also about the sheer joy of performing. It's about experience, growth, and showcasing one's abilities (no, that is not the same thing as "showing off"—well, not *exactly* the same thing). And it's about art.

Immediately after his success in the film, *The Godfather*, Al Pacino appeared in Boston in David Rabe's *The Basic Training of Pavlo Hummel*. Someone asked him, "Now that you've made it big in *The Godfather*, why are you doing seven shows a week in this tiny theatre?" Pacino replied, "I'm an actor. This is what I do." You may not get Al Pacino to do your monologue. But then again, have you asked him?

Rehearsing the Dramatic Monologue

In at least one way, rehearsing a monologue is more difficult than rehearsing a multi-character play. When you rehearse solo you don't enjoy the continuous back-and-forth of lines and actions to help motivate and guide you. You don't have the inspiration of responding to, of "playing off of" other actors. And you don't have the structured environment of group rehearsal schedules. Your discipline has to be self-discipline.

But in at least one sense, solo rehearsal is more convenient. The flip side of not having a director-posted rehearsal schedule is that you can rehearse wherever and whenever you want. I enjoy rehearsing when I need a break from other work—writing this book, for example. You may find undisturbed rehearsal space in a church. In good weather, I like to rehearse out of doors. I have rehearsed at the seashore in Kitty Hawk, North Carolina, in the front lawn of a hospital in Toledo, Ohio, and in the mountains overlooking Telluride, Colorado. In bad weather, I retreat to my garage.

How much rehearsal do you need? No one rule fits all monologues and all actors. Generally speaking, you will want to rehearse a monologue more than you would a straight play—certainly never less than an hour of rehearsal for every minute of performance. An hour of solo rehearsal at a time is efficient. Space your rehearsals. One hour on two days beats two hours on one day. Your subconscious rehearses during the off time.

Rehearse creatively.[22] Sing the lines. Dance the lines. Rehearse in incongruous settings. Try a variety of dialects. Do the piece as different actors might do it. How would a Shakespearean actor do it? A TV cop? A Lilliputian? A Brobdingnagian? A Yahoo? Try it as comedy. Try it as tragedy. Play with rhythms and inflections. Let your imagination run free. Experiment. Explore.

Give yourself, or whoever the performer is, plenty of lead time. A director—another set of eyes and neurons, a co-creator—can be a priceless resource. There are actors who can direct themselves, but not every actor can or should. Videotape and audio tape can help. In extreme conditions, even a spouse can help. This, however, should be attempted only by couples in secure marriages.

Performing the Monologue

Seize the Moment. Curtain up! Light the lights! No curtain? No lighting board? OK, just enter! It's show time!

The moment of performance! The live, lively, living energy-exchange between performer and audience! Gifts given and gifts received!

This is the dramatic moment that has nourished human souls for millennia. This is the transaction that keeps audiences coming back to the theatre in spite of weather, traffic, disappointment,

THE STAR THROWER

germs, even in spite of audiences themselves! Likewise, this exchange continuously enthralls performers regardless of its arduous apprenticeship, sometimes-tedious rehearsals, miserable working conditions, and daunting obstacles. Performance is powerful!

Since the monologue is a piece of drama, the same considerations that apply to other dramatic events also apply to the performance of dramatic monologues.

Play with your audience. Don't bully them. Some audiences are like some cats—the surest way to drive them away is to appear to go after them. Concentrate instead on what your character is doing, and the audience's unthreatened curiosity may bring them around. You can invite the audience, but "capture" is probably not the best image for the best relationship. A captive audience may not be a cooperative audience, while a captivated audience may be a creative audience.

On the other hand, in the excitement of the performance exchange, you want to maintain the kind of control that a sailor exercises in managing powerful winds to propel his or her craft.

Performer and audience create the performance together.[23] They work in a spirit of give and take. This feedback loop—this reciprocal dynamic—is immediate and continuous as the performer adjusts to the audience(s) and the audience adjust to the performer and to one another. And should the performer, as in most monologues, address the audience directly, this element of interaction is heightened.

Audiences differ, as do performers. Some audiences seem more responsive and demonstrative than others. Some performers seem more sensitive and communicative than others. Factors governing these differences may be both infinite and obscure. The weather, the day of the week or month, the time of the year, biorhythms, the mix of persons present, hidden agendas, debris of domestic disputes, digestions—who knows what gives a person or a group of persons a particular personality profile at any given moment? Exploring those personality factors and the interplay among them is part of the fascination and frustration—and fun!—of live performance.

A quiet audience is not necessarily a "dead" audience. Audience members may be so absorbed in a dramatic exchange that they collectively hold their breath for fear of missing anything or breaking the spell. Contrariwise, a demonstrative audience may in fact be a disappointed audience, its members attempting to jump-start a stalled performance. Or the demonstrative audience may be, as we would hope, demonstrating its enthusiastic participation!

Do the work of an actor. Most of the solo actor's tasks are the same as the ensemble actor's tasks including the following:

- know your character
- know what your character wants in life and what he or she wants in this particular exchange or beat
- know what the character is trying to accomplish both overall (the super-objective) and in this particular moment
- allow your character to be at home in your body, your mind, and your voice
- know your script and its structure
- know your beats, each fresh tack and attack your character takes to work toward his or her objectives
- know your obstacles, the internal and external factors which impede your character
- know what is at stake for your character, what consequences hang on success or failure to achieve his or her objectives
- know what your character is doing with each paragraph, each sentence, perhaps each word, stress, pause, and inflection
- know how your character looks, moves, and sounds

Add Production Values. How can you make full use of the

THE STAR THROWER

playing space? What are possible places and positions? How many different ways can you stand, sit, move?

Visualize costumes, properties, makeup, setting, and other technical elements. Will there be effects? Lights? Scenery? Props? Or will the audience be asked to supply these imaginatively? If imaginary, does your mime verify their existence? Or did you let the "cup" you were holding vanish into thin air as you proceeded to walk through a "table"?

Will effects clutter or clarify? Will spotlights steal the spotlight from the central exchange? I have seen complex lighting plots spoil professional solo performances that might have succeeded if the lighting designer's directions had been simply, "Turn on the lights." Perhaps because of their intimate nature and appeal to the imagination, solo performances often seem to benefit from a "less-is-more" approach.

We can imagine a monologue performed in total darkness—as long as we can hear the speaker. We love mime, as long as we can see it. But if you're using both body and voice, make sure the audience can hear and see you. This is absolutely necessary. Without this, nothing. Lighting and sight lines need to guarantee the audience's view of the performer in the theatre (*theatre* means "seeing place"). Also, if the performer's voice and articulation are inadequate to the acoustic demands of the playing space and auditorium (*auditorium* means "hearing place"), then amplify.

To Prompt or Not to Prompt? Alec McCowen used to begin his great performances of *The Gospel According to Mark* by very deliberately placing an opened Bible on a small table stage right. Then he would look up at his audience with a twinkle and explain, "Just in case!" Of course he knew the words and did not need his "script" (on the other hand, almost anyone, maybe even Alec McCowen, could once in a lifetime momentarily forget even what one "knows" best—what preacher has not lost the next phrase in The Lord's Prayer?

But McCowen's humorous and humble gesture started his performance off with a delightfully human moment of audience contact. It was an icebreaker that instantly won the hearts and support of the audience. Not only did he acknowledge his audience's vicarious anxiety about an actor balancing on memory's high wire, and thereby set us at ease. With that gesture McCowen figuratively invited us into his backstage dressing room and confided his humanity with us. We bonded.

Another of England's finest actor/directors, Simon Callow, writes in similar vein, "[D]uring the longest five minutes in the world, the five minutes before a one-man show hits the stage . . . you think: 'Please let there be a bomb scare. Please nobody have bought tickets' . . . ."[24] Solo performance may seem about as lonely as a performer can get—"Alone, alone, all, all alone, / Alone on a wide, wide" stage. And there is no fellow cast member to rescue you from a jam.

Yet, paradoxically, the solo performer is not alone—the audience is right there with you. Like the infants Romulus and Remus, you may find the seemingly ravenous wolf to be a nourishing mother. The audience want you to succeed. They want to be part of a great experience. Therefore they want to support you. And if/when that audience embrace you, you experience a spiritual fellowship, a bond of terrific, bracing power.

I like the emotional security that a prompter provides. However, you don't want to be lulled into a false sense of security as I once was. I tried to perform a script I had written myself but had not adequately rehearsed. I drafted my spouse, a fine person, but a reluctant and then inexperienced prompter, to help me.

And of course I went up in my lines. So far gone was I that my novice prompter did not know how to find my place. Worse, I was so rattled at being thus adrift and apparently abandoned that I did not have the sense to stop, as Alec McCowen might have done and as I ought to have done, walk over to the prompter, and ask to look at the script. Instead, I treaded water. I faked it. I adlibbed for twenty-five minutes—a whole lot longer than Simon Callow's five fearsome minutes before curtain—and the worst twenty-five minutes, I promise you, that ever I endured on stage. I don't imagine it was much fun for the audience, either.

But by this time, you understand, the audience no longer consisted of human beings. Instead, I distinctly remember seeing that the auditorium seats had become, not dens of nurturing wolves, but branches where sanguine vultures craned and watched me dying. My folly, of course, merely points to the basic necessity for sufficient rehearsal.

The crisis and opportunity of performance emphasizes again the importance of the initial decision to present a piece packed with intrinsic value for the audience. The prepared performer who knows that he or she brings the audience a quality experience can enter into the exchange with confidence.

Ending

Shall there be some acknowledgment that an exchange of gifts has taken place? Shall there be a curtain call? Will the curtain call enhance or diminish the event? If there is a curtain call, how can we do it simply, sincerely, and graciously?

The performance completed, you devoutly wish that it may not be over. It has released energies in human lives. That energy will go on. How can you foresee all the ways the vibrations may reverberate consciously and unconsciously in the lives of performer and audience members? Repercussions may roll on even into lives of contingent others who were not part of the originating event. The continuance and effects of the energy you release are incalculable.

Theatre is the most lifelike of the arts. Not that it must mimic life in a naturalistic style. But drama is made up of the very stuff of life itself. Drama is human beings in time and space being human (including at times being inhumanly human).

The "poor player / That struts and frets his hour upon the stage / And then is heard no more" represents life's evanescent but divine spark as a "brief candle." Now the candle shines, now it flares, now it flickers, now it glows, now it smolders, now it rekindles. Is all this a mere "tale / Told by an idiot, full of sound and fury, / Signifying nothing"? So Macbeth. But illuminated by God's Spirit, walking shadows may be transformed to *shekinah*—"the visible dwelling of the divine."

The monologue ends. Applause fades. Humanly speaking, the rest may be silence. But listen! In the sounds of that silence you can hear flights of angels. Once all of them were soloists, too, singular voices crying out in the wilderness. But now they have become a chorus swelling praise to God on high.

MEN OF FAITH

I had longed long to perform a solo play about Simon Peter. It would be a fantasy in which Saint Peter welcomes newcomers to heaven. At last I found my longing matched in a whimsical book, *Heaven: A Guide*.[25] That provided my key to the Keeper of the Keys.

As an actor, I listened long, too, for Peter's voice. The King James translation of Mark 14:70 tells us that Peter spoke with a noticeable Galilean accent, and John 1:46 reveals that the Galilean town of Nazareth, for example, was proverbially a place that, in Rodney Dangerfield's translation, "got no respect."

And I mean no disrespect for the birthplace of many wonderful people, including my sister and brother, in deciding that a serviceable modern American equivalent for Saint Peter's unrespectable Galilean accent might be a Brooklyn accent. And so it is.

One audience member referred to the play as "The Gospel According to Robert de Niro"—not quite what I was aiming for, but I can live with it. The actor who wishes to dispense with this colorful if non-prestigious American dialect is free to adjust the idiom to suit that actor's own dialect style or preference.

Is it "sacrilegious" or at least "disrespectful" to portray St. Peter as a humorous or even comic character? In her *Clowns and Tricksters* encyclopedia,[26] Kimberley A. Christen reminds us that the popular Christianity of other cultures—especially Mexican, Hispanic, and Yaqui—has taken a lighthearted view of St. Peter. They see "San Pedro" as a trickster, prankster, and taboo-breaker quite capable of foolery and (for those who take their fun seriously) a representative of the chaos and disorder we find in this world). I see "Rocky" as good-hearted, humorous, and human.

In performance, I have often had fun addressing the line, "*You* might want to get in a little extra repenting before it's too late," to a host pastor.

But the well known problem with comedy is that it dates. At the time of the writing of *Welcome to Heaven,* "Air Jordans" were a popular brand of basketball shoe named, not for the Jordan River, but for basketball superstar Michael Jordan. Likewise, Birkenstocks were a brand of upscale sandal-style footwear. And *Baywatch* was a popular television program whose well built protagonists disported themselves in skimpy beachwear. I anticipate that such topical references will need to be brought up to date regularly.

Paul, A Prisoner was my first solo play, conceived immediately on my return from teaching to pastoral ministry, but not completed and performed until nine years later, and subsequently performed live some 200 times and broadcast in two televised versions.

It is a patchwork quilt of Pauline writings stitched together with only a few added words of transition.

Although I had *The Browning Show* with its dramatic monologues under my belt, *Paul, A Prisoner* became my laboratory for learning about monologues and solo plays.

Donne to Death is in many ways my favorite project. John Donne (1572-1631)—by consensus England's, and arguably the world's, greatest preacher, not to mention one of the world's greatest poets—is such a towering and complex figure as to compel enthusiastic interest.

Donne's poetry will survive at least as long as English remains a recognizable language, and even afterwards we may imagine that much of his prose, at least, will live on in translation. This play is a vehicle for sharing the glorious power of Donne's spirit.

Donne to Death is a solo play for two characters. This apparent contradiction is easily explained. One actor plays both characters. This is fitting. Donne was (like most of us) at least two persons. Donne was both priest and poet, John Donne and Jack Donne. I designed and have performed the play along the fault line of this dichotomy. The "contemporary" technique of one actor playing multiple roles comes to us through the French avant-garde theatre, but, as we have seen, it simply revives the everyday practice of golden-age Greek theatre. Of course two (or more) separate actors could perform the roles, the Narrator(s) speaking chorus-like commentary to the audience.

Also as in Greek theatre, a mask or masks may be used with good effect—the Narrator's mask being a death's head which the Performer appropriates for his scene atop the urn. (The illusion was created by Donne standing on a black cube containing an urn.)

As I played him, the Narrator was a bit manic; mad, perhaps. The Performer, as I performed him, performed Donne, and Donne, according to reports, was a dramatic figure. (Donne's daughter, Freudians may take note, married the actor-manager Edward Alleyn, six years Donne's junior.) In keeping with a presentational style, Brechtian title cards or projections may announce scene and poem titles.

I had costume pieces built to permit the Narrator to transform to Donne by the onstage addition of a cassock skirt (doubling as a cape for the soldier Donne), and then surplice and stole.

Featuring some of the world's best poetry and prose, the play is a romp for an oral interpreter. It places exquisite demands on both actor and audience and rewards the effort. My best success with the play came with an audience composed mostly of attorneys.

A word about the most famous of all Donne passages, "For Whom the Bell Tolls." It is prose, not poetry. It comes from

"Meditation XVII" in *Devotions Upon Emergent Occasions* (1624), the emergency being that Donne was quite ill. Properly to set it in the scene of London plagues, I have added to Donne's own plague descriptions from elsewhere in the *Devotions* a passage I imported from Daniel Defoe's *A Journal of the Plague Year* (1722). Chaucer (1342-1400) gives us a no less precise picture of the thing Donne refers to (but using another bell than the church's tolling bell) when in *The Pardoner's Tale* he describes "three young roisterers . . . seated in a tavern at their drinking":

> And as they sat, they heard a bell go clinking
> Before a corpse being carried to his grave.
> One of these roisterers, when he had heard it, gave
> An order to his boy: "Go out and try
> To learn whose corpse is being carried by.
> Get me his name, and get it right. Take heed."

Those producing this play may be glad to know of the availability of the recording of *Seven Settings of Donne Lyrics by Seventeenth-Century Composers*, edited by Andre Souris and Jean Jaquot.

WELCOME TO HEAVEN

(ENTER PETER *singing*) Heaven! Heaven! Gonna walk all over God's Heaven!

Hey! How'ya doin'? I'm very glad to see you! Actually, I was expecting you a little sooner. You didn't have any trouble getting here, did you? Well, allow me to be the first to welcome you to heaven—with all due condolences, of course. I trust that your journey here was uneventful, and that you will be staying with us for some time now.

Of course, this here is only a waiting room. Heaven lies just beyond them golden gates. Some folks, when they first arrive where you are and see them golden gates, they're overcome with nostalgia and they feel like singing, (*singing*) "I Left My Heart in San Francisco." You were expecting maybe Tony Bennett? I can understand how they feel, but that's a different kind of golden gate, and that kind of heaven don't even begin to compare with what lies beyond *them* gates. So, look, you want to sing here, you feel like busting out in song, go right ahead. (*Singing*) "Gonna sing all over God's heaven!" And you don't got to sing only hymns or chants, either—very popular with some of the population— but any kind of music lifts your heart, or eases your heart, that's good music, and all good music is OK here. Rock'n'roll? Sure! We use it to celebrate the rock being rolled away from the tomb. 'Course, there's an awful lot of harp music, too. Hey, it all belongs to God and his angels. And you don't got to be embarrassed account of your singing voice, neither. We got no critics here. We invited a few, but they seem to feel more at home in the other place.

What's the matter? Some of you looking so sad, you look like *you* about to sing a *dirge*, you know, something like, "I left my folks, and now I'm feeling low." Aw! You're anxious about those you have left behind, hmm? Sure enough, those you have left behind—we call them the dear undeparted—they're upset about your leaving. Just think how you'd feel if they was doing cartwheels! Tell the truth, I can't promise you they're ever really going to get over it, but they probably going to get through it.

Still, some of you are worrying about how they're going to get along without you there. They're going to get along about the way human beings have always got along—good times, bad times. You ought to be thankful for all the good things you put into their lives to help them on their way. The fact you care about those you've left behind, that's good, maybe one of the reasons you've gotten this far, but you don't want to let it get out of control. They're in our Father's hands, just like they always been, same as you and me. No matter what we had to go through down there, his hand was holding us and leading us, and it's always going to be that way. Same way with them until they come to join us. You got to commit them, just like they committed you, to the Lord's care. He is able to keep that which we entrust to him. They got to go on, just like we got to go on. Believe me, there's plenty of souls up here put up with the same or even worse troubles than those you have left behind are going to have to face, and these, having worn the crown of thorns, now wear the crown of life! Actually, they don't wear them crowns— they keep casting them down before the Lamb on the throne.

And I know that some of you feel like singing the Unfinished Symphony. By the way, he finished it just the other night— terrific! But you're worrying about *your* unfinished business— interrupted plans, dreams deferred. Please have no regrets. Ain't no good work the Lord's begun through you or anybody else he ain't going to finish in his own good eternity. Think of it this way: you have acted your part upon the world's stage, the part which the Lord give you to play, and now it is time for that character you played to exit the drama of earth. But the play goes on to the final curtain. Meanwhile the Lord, he's going to cast you in yet another drama, the drama of celebration and continuing growth here on the stage of heaven.

I can see some of you chomping at the bit. You're ready to

THE STAR THROWER

183

sing, (*singing*) "Open up them golden gates, hello heaven, here I come!" You'd like me to stop talking so's you can leave this here waiting room and go ahead and make your entrance, huh? Hey, you got to learn to be patient. We got all eternity here, and we don't think of it so much as waiting as growing. Besides, processing all these new people takes some time. I mean, you can't wait in eternity, it's just going to seem even longer, right?

Did you get your number? You're supposed to take a number at the door. That way, we can take care of you in the order of your arrival. Well, don't worry about it. We don't miss nobody.

While you are waiting, we will put you up in a guestroom in one of the outer courts. We got motor courts, and Pharaoh's courts, and hotels, and Bed and Fasts, and you can stay there until, well, you know—until some final decision is made in your case. Naturally, until we know which way things are going to turn out for you, there's no way we can go ahead and give you your own permanent place. But all the accommodations are swell, even, well, Lordly. You're going to love it. And, you looking a little nightlife tonight, you might want to slip on over to Noah's place. Can't miss it—it's the one shaped like a . . . you know. Take it from me, that Noah, he shakes a mean milk-and-honey cocktail. But if I was you, I would take a pass on the Sailor's Slow Boat to Ararat Slugger. You going to want to have your wits about you tomorrow.

My name is Peter. Aw, that "Saint" stuff, that's kind of like what you call a honorific title. You can just call me Pete, or Simon, or if you want to you can call me Rocky. That's what the Lord calls me, Rocky. Sometimes he used to call me Blockhead. You know, when I disappointed him or said something or done something without thinking, then it was Blockhead. Guess I always was kind of hardheaded. But not hardhearted. Sometimes I had to be hard-nosed. Didn't we all?

No need to introduce yourselves. You notice we got no name tags here. Most the time we call each other Friend, like the Lord calls us. So you run into somebody and you can't think of the name, Friend'll do it.

Let me give you a couple more tips how to get along up here. We do a lot of blessing here. Like joining the army; when in doubt, salute. Here, when in doubt, bless. Can't go wrong. So, you meet this friend in the street, you just kind of bat blessings back and forth like a game of pepper, you know? Maybe he says, "Bless you, Friend." And so you say, "God bless *you*, Friend." And then maybe he'll say something like, "May you know the fullness of the Lord's blessings!" And then you want to come back with something like, "May the blessing of God Almighty rest upon you from this day forward!" And so forth. But if you're in a group of people, and you happen to meet another group of people, hang it up, Baby, because that's it for the rest of the day.

Naturally, therefore, most of the folks here, they go around looking very blessed and happy. You know, kind of a bounce to the walk, a song in the heart, and a smile on the face. And if you don't always feel like smiling, at least try to look reverent, OK? After all, this is heaven. On the other hand, I would not try to force too much reverence on others just to make yourself feel better. Ain't nothing worse than a pushy reverer, you know what I mean. Any doubts, just hang back a little and let the others revere *you*.

Now let me tell you a little bit about what you're going to find inside here.

First, getting around. It's a cinch. We got maps and directories all over the place. The main road into town, that is called The Highway of the Lord. Downtown, just past The Plaza of the Saints, is the main Cross Roads with The Holy Way. We got the Dead Sea Passage and we got the Strait and Narrow Path. You want to be alone, we got a Wilderness Trail. And you want to travel fast, you just hop on the belt line—we call it the Bible Belt Way. We got all kinds of gardens: the Garden of Eden, the Garden of Gethsemane—you go to the Garden of Eden, you got to look out for the snakes, all right? You want to look at different sections of town, we got Capernaum on the Sea, we got Genessaret on the Lake, and we got Walking on the Water. That's a little joke,

THE STAR THROWER

Walking on the Water; a little bit of humor. You got to lighten up, or else you going to sink right through.

For your mode of transportation. Most folks, they like to walk. Some people, they like to ride . . . on clouds. I got to tell you, for riding on, clouds are not all they are cracked up to be. For one thing, they are damp. And they are slow—you ever seen a aerodynamic cloud? 'Course, we got no speeding tickets. Everybody here drives on the theory that the first shall be last, and traffic don't even creep along. I mean it's like moribund, you know? Everybody's always letting everybody else go first. And parking? Forget it. You park your cloud, you come back and it's evaporated. So like I said, most folks, they prefer to walk. Now, the ones that you will see flying, them is angels, and they got to fly account of they are on the Lord's business, you know, missions of mercy and stuff like that. You're better off not to bother them; just try to stay out of the way, all right?

Clothes. Almost everybody up here wears just the simple, standard white robe. Some of the kids, they like to jazz them up, you know, tie-dye them and stuff like that. They like them T-shirt models with the brand names. Same goes for the shoes. All the kids here wear Air Jordans. Is this heaven or what? Old timers, they mostly stick with the sandals. A few of them always wanted Birkenstocks, so they get them, too. Hey, we even got nudists here. Yeah, they figure what was good enough for Adam and Eve is good enough for them. But lots of us, we find it is difficult to look reverent in the nude, so we're content just to bare our souls, you know what I mean. But it's like a matter of personal preference.

Food. First-class restaurants. Myself, I frequent The Loaves and Fishes. That's a little seafood place down by the lake with room to seat a surprising 5,000 souls. Deuteronomy's Barbecue, that's OK, but they don't serve no pork there. Same goes for Chez Leviticus. All the food here is home cooking, and of course it's non-fat, non-cholesterol, and non-caloric. Just to be on the safe side, go easy on the manna at first, OK? Fast food? Very popular. Lots of folks here *like* to fast. Average fast here will last you a couple days, usually toward the end of the week. Also a great favorite is the part-time fast, which lasts only between meals. But fasting on a empty stomach is not good for you.

For your entertainment, you will find that the Heavenly Choirs are simply superlative. They got singers like Bing Crosby and Ella Fitzgerald. They got sopranos, and altos, and tenors, and basses, and a whole section of Elvises. And, like I say, they sing every kind of music. The Lord, he seems to prefer Bach; the angels, they go in for Mozart; but it turns out that when the Heavenly Choirs sing, you *hear* whatever you like best. Also, like I said, harps are much in demand. We got a couple fellows here name of Freddie Chopin and Jelly Roll Morton, they get into jam sessions banging on the piano and keep the neighbors awake all night. Can't stop them.

But the most of your time in heaven is going to be taken up with praying, and praying, and still more praying. All the same, there may be times when you'd like to just relax and consequently *not* enjoy yourself.

Then you might like to read a little. Poets, they got their own special quarter here, kind of like the Quebec of heaven, where they speak their own special language, the tongues of angels. But we got next to no playwrights and novelists within the precincts of the city proper. They like to create their own worlds and they prefer living there, in kind of like what you might call the outlying suburbs. But you can see their plays performed by the finest actors of every age, and you got time to read all the greatest books ever written.

Sports here, we got some problems, mainly on account of sportsmanship. Ain't nobody up here got that killer instinct, you know? I mean, before a ball game, the teams are liable to give the ball away to somebody needs it more than they do. The worst ones are the Presbyterians; in the dressing room, they like to predestinate how the game is going to go and how it's going to come out. OK for them, maybe, but for the fans it ruins the suspense.

One sport which is very big here is theological wrestling. We got heavyweights like Paul the Punisher Tillich versus Rassling Reinie Niebuhr. We got tag teams like Crusher Kierkegaard and Bonhoffer the Basher. And they like to grapple with these moral and theological issues, best two out of three falls, or until the referee, which is Jacob, calls the match a draw, which he always does. So in heaven you better be ready to watch sports and never win or lose, and not to mind one way or the other. Again, no sense trying to be number one; up here that's last.

Not much in the way of movies and TV, either—gratuitous violence and pandering. Some folks discover that they have got a uncontrollable urge to catch the latest flick or maybe some *Baywatch* reruns. If you find that you are among that number, then maybe you should ought to ask yourself is heaven really the place for you. After all, there is another place in the afterlife just made to provide nothing but continuous entertainment, and for which a earthly life spent glued to the boob tube is the perfect training.

If—well, hopefully, when—you are admitted . . . . You can stay in your hotel room long as you want. Some folks, they like the room service. Sooner, later, 'most everybody starts looking around a place of their own. No housing shortages here. In your Father's house, there are mansions, and very many of them, and you can have any one you want. So, you ask, what's to stop you taking the biggest mansion of all? Two things. First, all the houses here exactly the same. Second, you won't feel no greed no more. Soon as you enter heaven, greed is washed away. Consequently, your craving for the biggest and best of everything is replaced by meek satisfaction with the smallest and humblest, comparatively speaking. Ain't it ironic—on earth most of us strive for a bigger house. And sometimes we get it. Here in heaven, there's no striving, and we're just given it, no questions asked. Funny life, right? The name of the real estate agent who will give you your mansion is Grace. Folks from New York like to refer to it as their Gracie Mansion.

Afford it? Hey, no problem. In heaven the earthly laws of finance and economics simply do not apply. Our money here ain't dollars or pounds or euros or yen. Our money here is goodwill. In Heaven, goodwill will get you anything you want. One goodwill is equal to one hundred kindly thoughts.

Tell you the truth, heaven ain't never been a exciting place to shop. While back, some developers tried to put in a shopping mall, but we got no blacktop up here; we do all our paving with gold. Besides, pleasures of the flesh, physical comforts, things like that are simply unheard of here, superfluous, as they say. You like to poke around some back streets and some yard sales, maybe you find some great deals. But be careful; don't buy nothing from some guy tries to sell you something for thirty pieces of silver.

Generally speaking, bargaining is disapproved of. Old Father Abraham, he just cannot seem to get it out of his system, you know? And in Abraham's case, the Heavenly Father, he don't seem to object to a little harmless negotiation from time to time. But most prices here are "no haggle." After all, since our money up here is goodwill, and since in heaven there is a unlimited supply of goodwill, why should you quibble? Take all you want, spend as much as you want. Freely receive, freely give.

Some folks are surprised to find out almost everything up here is taxed at a flat rate of ten percent. What can I say? We got a lot of tax collectors here—they was among the first in—and they like to keep busy. Besides, before this they ain't never collected no goodwill.

That brings us to the main item of business. Little while now, we going to be asking you a few questions. Take it easy! Take it easy! We got a broad-based immigration policy. I trust you have already read the Admissions Handbook, which is sold on earth as the Bible. I would like to call your special attention to the experience of my good pal Saul of Tarsus on the Road to Damascus. When the time comes, I would advise you to try to be found standing in with the sheep and not with the goats. We

THE STAR THROWER 189

handle each case on a individual basis, but it don't hurt none to be in with the right crowd, you know what I mean. And when your turn comes, I want you to just bare your soul and put your trust in God, OK? The Almighty, He don't want a empty heaven. All the same, it remains sadly true that many are called, but few are chosen.

You going to be asked to give a full accounting of your previous life and to explain why you want to enter heaven. Always tell the truth. No point trying to, shall we say, gild the lily of your past—already we know more about you than you know about yourself. We got a minute-by-minute computer printout of your entire life, birth through death, everything you ever done or ever thought about doing. In fact, only reason we bother to ask you the questions at all is so's you get a chance to tell your side of the story. We already know the facts. Make you feel any better, we ain't trying to trick you, so just stay calm and relaxed. (*Perhaps singling out a member of the audience*) Uh, you might want to try to get a little extra repenting in now, before it's too late.

Yeah, these here are the Pearl E. Gates. No, they ain't *made* of pearl, they're *named* for Pearl—Pearl E. Gates, the black lady architect who designed them. Incredible artist! I mean, what a sculptor! Just look at them gates. Puts Rodin and The Thinker to shame, don't it? You can see all the great scenes of the Bible carved on them gates. And when them gates open up, it's like the Red Sea parting, like the heavens opening before you, which they are, just the same as when our Lord ascended up into them. And inside!

(*Singing* to tune of Alford) O then what joyous greetings
On Canaan's happy shore!
What mending broken heartstrings up
Where partings are no more!

You ain't never seen no homecomings and no reunions like

what's waiting for you inside of them gates!

All the same, wonders like them gates don't exist without price. Them gates require constant maintenance which gets tougher every year. You can see over there the gradual sinking of the posts that support them gates. Them pillars is made out of adamantine rock quarried special in the Garden of Eden. They have stood the test of time very well, thank you, but time ain't stood them so good, or, at least, not the clouds of time in which them pillars is sunk. Furthermore, a couple millennia ago we found them gates was so loaded down with laws and legalism they couldn't be opened no more. I mean, that made a lot of people hold their breath.

These here keys? No, these keys, they wasn't no practical use from the very beginning. Yeah, sure I wear them, for identification—they are kind of like my badge of office. And for sentimental reasons. Our Lord, he give them to me himself, you know. But you look at them gates real close. See? Ain't got no locks. So: you want to enter heaven, all you got to do is go in by that little door over there on the left. Maybe you got to stoop down a little. Shaped like a man? Oh, no; that door ain't *shaped* like a man—that *is* a man. Yeah, that's him!—with the pierced hands and feet and side. He is the door. No, he ain't crucified no more. He holds his arms open like that to welcome you to heaven!

And that, my friends, is really all you need to know.

Tell you what. Me and some of the boys, we're going down to the pier, do a little fishing. I will stop inside and see what is holding things up. You just hang on, OK? Your number's going to be up real soon.

(EXIT singing) "Heaven, heaven! Gonna shine all over God's heaven!"

PAUL, A PRISONER

"Would I might free St. Paul, singing in chains
In your deep hearts."
—Vachel Lindsay

(*A prison cell in Rome. 65 A.D. PAUL, a middle-aged man in chains, kneels and chants:*)

Gam ki elech
B'gei tsalmavet
Lo ira ra.
Ki Atah imadi.

(*Paul becomes aware of the presence of the audience. He rises and approaches them.*)

You've come to visit me in prison. Good!

Be comfortable. Ha! You may find that hard, unless you have been, as I have been for these two years past here in Rome, Caesar's prisoner. We have no comforts here; but the God of all comfort is here. And I have learned to be content in whatever state I am, abased or abounding.

Everyone here—(*pointing to a gate*) even the soldiers of Caesar's Praetorian Guard who outside that gate daily wait their orders to take me and take my head—everyone knows I am in prison because I am a Christian.

This is all going to turn out for good. I live in eager expectation and hope that with full courage I will be able, now as always, to honor Christ in my body, whether by my life or by my death.

To live or die—I really don't know which is best. Sometimes I want to live, and other times I long to go and be with Christ— how much happier for me than being here! But the fact is I can be of some help to you by being here—to help you grow and become happy in your faith. And I have been in prison before— many times.

The first time was in Philippi. Silas and I . . . . On the Sabbath, Silas and I went outside the city gate to the riverside where we had heard there was a place of prayer. As we were going, a slave girl met us. She was possessed by a spirit of divination, and by her soothsaying she brought her owners much gain. She followed us, crying, "These men are servants of the true God, who proclaim to you the way of salvation!" She did this for many days. I became annoyed. I turned and said to the spirit, "I command thee in the name of Jesus Christ to come out of her." And he came out that very hour.

But when her owners saw that their hope of gain was gone, they seized Silas and me and dragged us into the marketplace before the magistrates. They said, "These men are Jews, and they teach customs which it is not lawful for us Romans to accept or practice." The crowd joined in attacking us. And the magistrates tore the clothes off our backs and gave orders to beat us with rods. And when they had laid many stripes upon us, they cast us into prison, charging the jailer to keep us safely. He thrust us into the inner dungeon and clamped our feet in the stocks.

But about midnight Silas and I were praying and singing hymns to God—and the prisoners were listening to us—and suddenly there was a great earthquake, so that the foundations of the prison were shaken. And immediately all the doors flew open, and everyone's shackles fell off.

When the jailer woke and saw that the prison doors were open, he supposed that his prisoners had escaped, and that according to the law he himself would be put in our place. He drew his sword and was about to kill himself, but I cried with a loud voice, "Don't harm yourself; we're all here!"

He called for lights and rushed in, and trembling with fear he fell down before us. And then he brought us out and said, "Men, what must I do to be saved?" And we said, "Believe in the Lord Jesus and you will be saved, you and your whole household."

THE STAR THROWER   193

He washed our wounds. Then he brought us into his house, and set food before us. And we spoke the word of the Lord to him and to all that were in his house, and he—our jailer!—was baptized at once with all his family, and he rejoiced.

The next morning, the magistrates sent the police, saying, "Let those men go." But I said, "No. They have beaten us publicly, uncondemned, men who are Roman citizens! And they have thrown us into prison. And now they want us to creep away secretly? Never! Let them come themselves and release us!"

The police officers reported this to the magistrates who feared for their lives when they heard that we were Roman citizens. So they hurried to the jail and apologized and begged us to be free! And they escorted us out and desired us to depart.

There had been a time when I myself cast many into prison. I had been convinced that I ought to do many things in opposing the name of Jesus. Educated according to the strict manner of the law of our fathers, being zealous for God, I persecuted those of this way to the death, binding and delivering both men and women into prisons. And when they were put to death, I gave my voice against them. And in raging fury, breathing threats and slaughter, I persecuted them even to foreign cities.

Thus I journeyed to Damascus to take those who were there and bring them in chains to Jerusalem to be punished. As I made my journey and drew near to Damascus, about noon, suddenly there shone from heaven a great light round about me. I fell to the ground. I heard a voice saying to me, "Saul, Saul, why persecutest thou me?" And I answered, "Who art thou, Lord?" And he said unto me, "I am Jesus of Nazareth, whom thou persecutest." And I said, "What shall I do, Lord?" And the Lord said unto me, "Rise, and stand upon thy feet; for I have appeared unto thee for this purpose, to make thee a minister and a witness."

I was not disobedient to the heavenly vision. Immediately in the synagogues I proclaimed Jesus, saying, "He is the Son of God!" And all who heard me were amazed, and said, "Is not this the man who made havoc in Jerusalem of those who called on the name of the Lord? And he came here for this purpose, to bring them bound before the chief priests." The Jews plotted to kill me. They were watching the city gates day and night, to kill me. But my converts took me by night and lowered me down over the wall in a basket!

I departed into Arabia for the space of three years.

And it came to pass, when I was come again unto Jerusalem, while I prayed in the temple, again I saw the Lord saying unto me, "I will send thee unto the Gentiles, to open their eyes, to turn them from darkness to light, from the power of Satan unto God, that they may receive forgiveness of their sins."

So being sent out by the Holy Spirit, Barnabas and I went on our missionary journeys, always going first to the synagogue in whatever city we came to—as we did that time we came to Perga in Pamphilia.

On the Sabbath Barnabas and I went into the synagogue. After the usual readings from the books of Moses and the prophets, those in charge of the service said to us, "Brethren, if you have any word of exhortation for us, come and give it." So I stood up. "Brethren! Sons of the family of Abraham! And you Gentiles who fear God! We bring you good news! What God promised to our fathers he has fulfilled to us their children by raising Jesus. In this man Jesus there is forgiveness for your sins."

As we left the synagogue, the people begged us to return and speak again the next week. The next Sabbath came almost the whole city to hear the word of God. But when the Jews saw the multitudes, they were filled with jealousy, and they cursed and argued against anything I said. But we spoke out boldly, saying, "It was necessary that the word of God should be spoken first to you. Since you thrust it from you, and judge yourselves unworthy of eternal life, why, we will offer it to the Gentiles, for so the Lord commanded us." When the Gentiles heard this, they were glad and rejoiced in our message. And as many as were ordained to eternal life believed. And the word of the Lord spread throughout all the region.

But some men came down from Judea and began teaching the brethren, "Unless you are circumcised according to the law of Moses, you cannot be saved." Circumcised! Circumcised! I wish these troublemakers would *emasculate* themselves! Beware the dogs! Beware the evil workers! Beware those who mutilate the flesh! For *we* are the true circumcision, who worship God in spirit, who glory in Christ Jesus, and who put no confidence in the flesh. For in Christ Jesus neither circumcision nor uncircumcision availeth anything, but a new creature. We had no small debate with them. Henceforth let no man trouble me, for I bear in my body the marks of the Lord Jesus!

And when Simon Peter came, I had to oppose him publicly, to his face. When Peter first arrived, he shared table fellowship with the Gentile Christians. But afterwards, when some Jewish friends of James came, he would eat with the Gentiles no more, because he was afraid of what these Jewish legalists, these Judaizers, would say. Then all the other Jewish Christians—and even Barnabas—became hypocrites, too, following Peter's example, although they certainly knew better.

But when I saw that they were not straightforward about the truth of the gospel, I said to Peter in front of all the others, "You have long since discarded the Jewish ceremonial laws; so why, all of a sudden, are you trying to make these Gentiles obey them? We Jewish Christians know very well that we cannot become right with God by obeying laws, but only by faith in Christ Jesus to take away our sins; for by works of the law shall no one be justified. Is God God of Jews only? Is he not God of Gentiles also? Yes, of Gentiles also, since God is one; and he will justify the circumcised on the ground of their faith, and the uncircumcised through their faith.

I through the law died to the law that I might live to God. Circumcised? I have been crucified with Christ! It is no longer I who live, but Christ who lives in me. And the life I live now in the flesh I live by faith in the Son of God who loved me and gave himself for me. If we could be saved by keeping laws, then there was no need for Christ to die!

Finally we decided that Barnabas and I would go up to Jerusalem to talk about this question with the apostles and elders there. I laid before them the gospel that I preach among the Gentiles because I wanted them all to understand just what I had been teaching and, I hoped, agree that it was right. And they did agree. The great leaders of the church had nothing to add to what I was preaching. On the contrary, when they saw that I had been entrusted with the gospel to the Gentiles, just as Peter had been entrusted with the gospel to the Jews, James and Peter and John gave Barnabas and me the right hand of fellowship, that we should go to the Gentiles, and they to the Jews.

And, dear friends, when I came to you I did not come preaching profound words or high-sounding ideas. I determined to know nothing among you save Jesus Christ, and him crucified. Yet I know very well how foolish it sounds to those who are lost when they hear that Christ died to save them, for it is written, "Cursed is he who hangs upon a tree." But we who are being saved recognize this message of the cross as the true power of God, for it is also written (*reading from a scroll*):

> I will destroy the wisdom of the wise, (saith the
> Lord)
> And the cleverness of the clever, I will thwart.

So what about these wise men, these scholars, these brilliant debaters of this world's great affairs? Has not God made foolish the wisdom of the world? For God in his wisdom saw to it that the world would never find God through human brilliance. It pleased God through the folly of what we preach to save those who believe. Jews demand signs. Greeks seek after wisdom. But we preach Christ crucified—unto the Jews a stumbling block and unto the Greeks foolishness. But this so-called "foolish" plan of God's is far wiser than the wisest man, and God in his weakness—Christ dying on the cross—is far stronger than any man.

God chose what is foolish in the world to shame the wise. God chose what is weak in the world to shame the strong. God chose what is low and despised in the world—even things that are not!—to bring *to* nothing things that "are," so that no human being might boast in the presence of God. For it is from God alone that you have your life through Christ Jesus.

(*He moves to peer through the gate.*) I look through the gate every now and then to make certain that my guards have not escaped! Or fallen into too deep a slumber—their centurion would not take that kindly. It's weary work, waiting. These are men of action. They would much prefer to march a man out to the Appian Way, stretch out his neck over a block, and . . . .

Am I afraid? I am afraid—for you. I am afraid that you will somehow allow yourselves to be led away from your pure and simple devotion to our Lord. You seem so gullible! You believe whatever anyone tells you—even if he is preaching a different Jesus than the one we preached, or a different spirit than the Holy Spirit you received, or shows you a different way to be saved. You swallow it all.

Yet I don't feel that these marvelous new preachers— "messengers from God," as they call themselves—I don't feel they're any better than I am. No. I am in no way inferior to these "extra-super apostles," even though I am nothing! And if, as they say, I am a poor speaker, at least I know what I'm talking about!

Those who boast that they are doing God's work in just the same way as we are—such are false apostles, disguising themselves as apostles of Christ. And no wonder, for even Satan disguises himself as an angel of light—so it isn't strange if his servants disguise themselves as godly ministers. Their end will correspond to their deeds.

But whatever they can boast about, I can boast about it, too— I'm talking like a fool! Do they brag that they are Hebrews? So am I. Are they Israelites? So am I. Are they servants of Christ? I am a better one—I'm talking like a madman! I *am* a better one, with far greater labors, far more imprisonments, with countless beatings, often near death. Five times I have received at the hands of the Jews the forty lashes less one. Three times I have been beaten with rods. Once I received a stoning and was left for dead. Three times I have been shipwrecked. A night and a day I have been adrift at sea. In journeyings often, in danger from rivers, danger from robbers, danger from my own people, danger from Gentiles, danger in the city, danger in the wilderness, danger at sea, danger from men who claim to be brothers in Christ but are not. In toil and hardship through many a sleepless night. In hunger and thirst, often without food. In cold and exposure. Then, besides all this, there is the daily pressure upon me of my anxiety for all the churches.

This boasting is all so foolish! But I will go on to visions and revelations of the Lord.

(*Kneeling*) Fourteen years ago I was taken up into the third heaven. Don't ask me whether my body was there or just my spirit; I don't know, only God knows. But I know that there I was in Paradise! And I heard—things beyond a man's power to put into words.

That experience is something worth bragging about, but I'm not going to do it. I'm only going to boast about how weak I am and how great God is—to use such weakness for his glory.

(*Rising*) I will say this: because these experiences I had were so tremendous, God was afraid that I might be puffed up by them; so I was given a sickness which has been a thorn in my flesh—a messenger from Satan to rack and harass me, to prick my pride. My pride!

Three different times I begged God to make me well again. Each time God said, "No; but I am with you, and that's all you need. My power shows up best in weak people." Now I'm glad to boast about how weak I am. Instead of showing off my own power and abilities, I'm glad to be a living demonstration of the power of Jesus Christ. For this cause I, Paul, the prisoner of Jesus

Christ, was made a minister. Am I not an apostle? Am I not an ambassador for Christ? Am I not free?

(*Again he looks through the gate*) How their centurion lords it over them! But our Lord says it must not be so among you. Whoever would be great among you must be your servant.

(*He sits, takes quill and ink, and writes on a piece of parchment. Satisfied, he puts them down and speaks to the audience.*)

In the church God has appointed first apostles, second prophets, third teachers, then workers of miracles, then healers, helpers, administrators, speakers in various kinds of tongues. Is everyone an apostle? Of course not. Is everyone a prophet? Are all teachers? Does everyone have the power to do miracles? Can everyone heal the sick? Of course not. Does God give all of us the ability to speak in tongues? Can just anyone understand and interpret tongues? No. But for yourself, earnestly desire the greater gifts and graces. Let me tell you about something that is better than any of these.

Though I speak with the tongues of men and of angels, and have not love, I am become as sounding brass or a tinkling cymbal. And though I have the gift of prophecy, and understand all mysteries and all knowledge; and though I have all faith so that I could remove mountains, and have not love, I am nothing. And though I bestow all my goods to feed the poor, and though I give my body to be burned, and have not love, it profiteth me nothing.

Love is patient and kind; love envieth not; love vaunteth not itself, is not puffed up, doth not behave itself unseemly, seeketh not her own, is not easily provoked, thinketh no evil; rejoiceth not in iniquity, but rejoiceth in the truth; beareth all things, believeth all things, hopeth all things, endureth all things.

Love never faileth; but whether there be prophecies, they shall fail; whether there be tongues, they shall cease; whether there be knowledge, it shall vanish away—vanish away! For we know in part, and we prophesy in part. But when that which is perfect is come, that which is in part shall be done away. When I was a child, I spoke as a child, I understood as a child, I thought as a child: but when I became a man, I put away childish things.

For now we see in a glass, darkly; but then face to face. Now I know in part; but then I shall know even as I also am known. And now abideth faith, hope, love, these three; but the greatest of these is love. Make love your aim!

(*A spell of his sickness strikes him. He partially recovers.*)

We have this treasure in earthen vessels, to show that the transcendent power belongs to God and not to us. We are afflicted in every way, but not crushed; perplexed, but not driven to despair; persecuted, but not forsaken; struck down, but not destroyed; always facing death just as Jesus did, showing forth within our mortal bodies the power of Jesus Christ.

Because of my preaching, I face death. But it has resulted in eternal life for you!

That's why we never give up. Though our bodies are dying, our inner nature is being renewed every day. These troubles and sufferings of ours are after all quite small and won't last very long. This slight momentary affliction is preparing us for God's richest blessing for ever and ever. So we don't focus on what we can see right now—the troubles all around us—but we look forward to the joys which we have not yet seen. The troubles will soon be over, but the joys to come will last forever.

We know that in everything God works for good with those who love him, who are called according to his purpose. What then shall we say to this? If God be for us, who is against us? Who shall separate us from the love of Christ? Shall tribulation, or distress, or persecution, or famine, or nakedness, or peril, or sword? No! In all these things we are more than conquerors through him who loved us!

(*We hear the sounds of marching feet, a door being opened, then slamming, a key turning in a lock, a gate squealing on its hinges.*)

My friends from Caesar's Praetorian Guard have come for me, and you must excuse me.

THE STAR THROWER

(*Kneeling*) Now I am on the point of being sacrificed, and the time for my departure is at hand.

> (*Chanting as at opening*)
> Yea though I walk
> Through the valley of the shadow
> I will fear no evil,
> For thou art with me.

(*He rises, steps toward the exit, then speaks to the audience.*) Thank you for coming to me. I have fought the good fight. I have finished the race. I have kept the faith. Henceforth there is laid up for me a crown of righteousness which the Lord, the righteous judge, shall give me—and not to me only, but to all them also that love his appearing. (*He retrieves his scroll, looks about for someone to whom to entrust it, at length gives it to someone in the audience, perhaps a young person or child.*)
The Lord will deliver me from all evil and will bring me into his heavenly kingdom.
The grace of our Lord Jesus Christ be with you.

EXIT

DONNE TO DEATH

A Meditational Drama

(*Dr. John Donne's study in St. Paul's Cathedral, London, 1631. A funerary urn, a Bible, a cape and plumed hat, a winding sheet, and vestments. A bell sounds. Enter NARRATOR/ PERFORMER. As noted above, the play is designed to be and was originally performed by a solo actor.*)

NARRATOR: The bell has rung, it's time to begin. We have an audience, a playing space, an actor. All we need is a play. I shall compose a play—a play about the death of the Reverend Dr. John Donne, late Dean of St. Paul's Cathedral, London—England's greatest preacher, and the English tongue's foremost love poet—the priest and the poet, the minister and the minstrel. A play about the death of Donne—death and Donne, Donne to Death; a play composed about a death composed. No haphazard death, no unconsidered, accidental death, and no death such as *you* die—your mortality measured by meters, your death described by digits. No, thank you! But a composed death, a Christianly death with tolling bells and fervent prayers and last words. A death designed, a death artistically arranged so as to reveal, and perhaps renew, the life, the meaning, the essence, the soul of the man who dies, of this Dr. John Donne, this Jack Donne. And in this composing to compose myself. In revealing Donne, perhaps reveal myself. And you—can you not find your life in his, your death in his? And therefore no hidden death, neither, but a death displayed—with classical restraint, of course: no carcasses. But nevertheless a passing performed upon the stage for all to see and wonder at. Step right this way, Ladies and Gentlemen! For when our hero—

PERFORMER: [*Posing*] That will be me.

NARRATOR:—when our hero leaves this space, he goes to his place of execution—

PERFORMER: That will be to his pulpit. I pray God that I may die in my pulpit. And tonight I think God may grant my prayer. Am I prepared? Are you?

NARRATOR: What has John Donne's death got to do with you? Is it nothing to you, all ye who pass by? Are you not involved in this piece of mankind? I would like to inoculate you and myself with John Donne's death.

PERFORMER: You may think me vain, to cast myself in my own play. (*In a two-actor performance the previous line is the Narrator's and reads, "You may think Donne vain to cast himself in his own play."*) I have a desperate desire to be myself. How shall I be myself except I enact myself? The whole frame of the world is a great theatre, and here we all enact ourselves, here we all play ourselves before God. If I am to enact myself on this world's stage, I must as the final act perform that one obligatory scene, my own death. In this life, I never knew myself but in disguises. Death removes the masks.

NARRATOR: Therefore, I shall stage-manage my own life in a play showing John Donne stage-managing his own death in his last play—or, at least, his last sermon. But with Donne, who can tell the difference between a sermon and a play? Donne is the most dramatic of preachers. It will be the preacher's own funeral sermon, entitled, Death's Duell, in which the preacher wrestles, or, as Donne would say—

PERFORMER: "Wrastles"—

NARRATOR:—in mortal combat, in final fight against his enemy—his great, his obsessional, his last enemy, death. Who will win? Who always wins, Punch or Judy?

PERFORMER: (*Singing*) Punch and Judy
    Fought for a pie.
    Punch gave Judy
    A knock in the eye.

NARRATOR: Punch plants his boot in everybody's backside

and kicks us all out of the theatre. Who can outfly death's swift angel? The setting: I shall set my play's last scene here in John Donne's study in the Cathedral of St. Paul's, in the city of London, in the year of our Lord sixteen hundred and thirty-one—fifty-nine years after his birth in his father's house in Bread Street. All the properties we require is this funerary urn. For effects of course we shall have a tolling bell—"never send to know for whom the bell tolls"—that bell that told when a person died, and struck one stroke for each year of life. Scene the first! At rise: "Donne Composes His Last Sermon."

PERFORMER: My own funeral sermon. I have already died and speak to you a dead man. I died fourteen years ago. Yet it pleases me a little to have had a long funeral, and to have kept myself so long above ground without putrefaction. No, such a sermon will not repel my hearers; we are more familiar with death than you are—you who hide death the way a rake hides his pox sores from his bride, as if a person's passing spirit were like a person passing wind, an obscenity; as if the last page of the book should remain uncut, unread. I have not much time. I shall preach it at vespers tonight. You shall be my conjectural congregation, my anticipatory auditory, my audience invited for the dress rehearsal for my death.

NARRATOR: The Preacher Prepares:

PERFORMER: (*Picking up Bible*) This is the text for my funeral sermon: Psalm eighty-nine, verse forty-eight: What man is he that liveth, and shall not see death?

NARRATOR: The Introduction:

PERFORMER: (*Composing*) From the first minute that we began to live, we began to die. You were born under that law, upon that condition, to die. Death comes equally to us all, and makes us all equal when it comes—dust to dust. And if a dust devil blow the dust of a cemetery into the church, and the man sweeps out the dust of the church back into the church-yard, who will undertake to sift those dusts again,

THE STAR THROWER   205

and to pronounce, "This is the patrician, this the noble flower, and this the yeomanly, this the plebian bran." And if the wind blow it thither, the dust of a wretch will trouble thine eye as well as the dust of a prince. Death—that most deadly and peremptory nullification of man—death is in an old man's door, he appears and tells him so; and death is at a young man's back, and says nothing. Age is a sickness, and youth is an ambush.

NARRATOR: Five of Donne's twelve children have died.

PERFORMER: Shall I embrace them again, and shall I embrace again their mother, Anne? A sermon? Oh, no; my life story is no sermon, nor yet no play; my life story is a love song. I fell in love with Anne and Anne with me when first we met. I was then employed as secretary to her uncle, Sir Thomas Egerton, My Lord Keeper of the King's Seal.

NARRATOR: Donne was well prepared for that post.

PERFORMER: In my youth I had been infected by the worst voluptuousness, an immoderate desire of humane learning and languages—a desire more appropriate to a gentleman than to one of my own station; I ought to have studied a way to make a living. I had studied law—I had studied everything. But I took no degree, because my family was Catholic, and we could not subscribe to the Oath of Supremacy required for graduation. But I know enough law to write my own will—and to avoid lawyers! The Scripture is right: If any man will sue thee at the law, and take away thy coat, let him have thy cloak also—for if thine adversary have it not, thine advocate will! I studied divinity, too, but that was chiefly to settle my own mind whether to remain in the Old Faith of my family, or to become a member of the Church of England. At length—too late for graduation—I concluded, I hope on conscience alone, that I should join the Anglican Church. But I hold that all churches are beams of one sun.

NARRATOR: Flashback! Donne's Career As A Privateer! Donne's *Brief* Career As A Privateer!

PERFORMER: (*Donning cape and Cavalier hat*) I'm home and I'm through with soldiering. Two expeditions with Lord Essex, that ill-fated favorite of the Queen, and nothing to show for it but blisters and bare bones. Soldiering hath not brought me the knighthood I hoped for, although it hath brought many a knight to everlasting night—but not so many as before. For mankind have found out artillery, by which wars come to quicker ends than heretofore, and the great expense of blood is avoided, for the numbers of men slain now, since the invention of ordnance, are much less than before, when the sword was the executioner. (*Removes cape and hat.*)

NARRATOR: Good job Donne never got near enough to Essex to share his fate, although, in his capacity as secretary to the lord Keeper, Donne was present at York House when the Earl was arraigned there.

PERFORMER: As Sir Thomas' secretary, I was getting along well. But, like Essex, I was too confident. I was sure of advancement at court (that play within a play!). But then Anne came into the household. She was as I say Sir Thomas' niece, her father being Sir Thomas' brother-in-law, Sir George More. She was not yet sixteen.

NARRATOR: Donne was twenty-nine. "The Good Morrow:"

PERFORMER: I wonder by my troth, what thou, and I
Did, till we lov'd? were we not wean'd till then?
But sucked on countrey pleasures, childishly?
Or snorted we in the seven sleepers den?
T'was so; But this, all pleasures fancies be.
If ever any beauty I did see,
Which I desir'd, and got, t'was but a dream of thee.

NARRATOR: Yes! Yes! There he is—Jack Donne the poet!

PERFORMER: Poems—they spurted from me like blood from an open artery. I like to have bled to death of 'em. I published only one or two complimentary verses. The rest circulate among my friends in manuscript. But wherever they surface, wherever they are comprehended—rough, passionate, wayward verses—they spatter like so many gory stains to the icy eyes of those who would prefer their clergymen to be cold and immaculate men of snow. I cannot plead innocency of life, especially not my youth. My youth, like St. Augustine's, was a foil to my later life, but in a way, of a piece with it, too. Because my whole life has been a love song in four parts: (*Singing*) My love for God, my love for learning, my love for ladies, and my love for Anne. (*Speaking*) I knew that her father, a miniscule man with a mountainous temper; I knew he had other plans for his minor daughter than to marry her to Sir Thomas' secretary. But Anne and I, we could not bear to lose each other. Three weeks before Christmas, we eloped. A clandestine marriage. Her father erupted. For this breach of canon law, this technical violation of civil law, for this sin against the social code—for this Sir George had me thrown into Fleet prison, and he kept Anne locked up no less securely in his own home. I regained my freedom after four days, but it cost me sixteen months of legal proceedings to obtain my bride. The lawyer in me argued: "Sir George, since you have thrown me into jail for it, you yourself and the law have thereby recognized that Anne's and my marriage is a reality indeed. And my wife, therefore, by law, Sir, belongs with me! And now you have persuaded Sir Thomas to dismiss me! My Lord, by depriving me of my position you are depriving your daughter of the means to live. I beg you to forgive me." And at last he did relent, at least so far as to ask Sir Thomas to reinstate me— which Sir Thomas, although he valued my services and myself, declined to do. "It is inconsistent with my place and credit to discharge and readmit servants at the request of passionate petitioners." "Oh, Sir Thomas, if you let me go, it will cast a shadow on my character and my industry; no one else will employ me."

NARRATOR: Donne was right about that!

PERFORMER: So, Anne, we have given all for love, you and I. You have exchanged a life of privilege for a life of privation. I have forfeited all my worldly ambitions. My employment with Sir Thomas had been the first rung on my ladder of success, and it has snapped under the weight of our precipitous marriage. John Donne; Anne Donne; undone. We have less than nothing, but we have all the world, for we are each other's world. Twenty-four March, 1603, our first child is born. We have named her after our own love, Constance.

NARRATOR: In the same night in which Constance was born, Queen Elizabeth died. King James swept to the throne on a wave of hope. On that sanguine swell Donne's own skiff rose.

PERFORMER: I've found a patron, Anne! Sir Robert Drury! He has given us the use of a home in Drury Lane. We have a new lease on life . . . Travel abroad with you, Sir Robert? To be gone how long? But Anne is pregnant again! . . . Anne, you must not beg me not to go. I cannot refuse the man whose bread we all eat!

NARRATOR: "A Valediction: Forbidding Mourning:"

PERFORMER: Our two soules therefore, which are one,
  Though I must goe, endure not yet
A breach, but an expansion,
  Like gold to aeyry thinesse beate.

If they be two, they are two so
  As stiffe twin compasses are two,
Thy soule the fixt foot, makes no show
  To move, but doth, if th'other doe.

And though it in the center sit,
  Yet when the other far doth rome,
It leanes, and hearkens after it,
  And growes erect, as that comes home.

THE STAR THROWER 209

Such wilt thou be to mee, who must
    Like th'other foot obliquely run;
Thy firmness draws my circle just,
    And makes me end, where I begunne.

Anne, the fixt foot of my soul, stayed with her sister on the Isle of Wight, there to await the birth of our next child.

NARRATOR: But Donne saw her. Across those miles, on the Continent, he saw her.

PERFORMER: (*Excited*) Look! Look! See where she comes! She passes twice by me in this room! Do you not see her? Her hair hanging about her shoulders, and a dead child in her arms! And they were gone. It was tormented months before messengers between us confirmed my vision. At that very hour, the child had been stillborn, and I had been away. (*Quietly*) I think that there is no Phoenix, nothing single, nothing alone. God, who saw that all that he made was good, came not so near seeing a defect in any of his works, as when he saw that it was not good for man to be alone. Therefore, he made him a helper. And one that should help him so as to increase the number and give him her own and more society. Angels, who do not propagate nor multiply, were made at the first in an abundant number, and so were stars. But for the things of this world, their blessing was, Increase.

NARRATOR: Donne's family increased by the birth of a child with each year of his increasing age. But his income did not increase.

PERFORMER: I was past forty. We lived in poverty, sustained by the patronage of Drury and the gifts of friends—and the few pence I earned writing pamphlets for the Rev. Dr. Thomas Morton. It was Morton who first advised me to enter the church. "No, sir; I thank you, but no. I have no calling. I am not fit—my past life, like my love poems, could only be an embarrassment to the church and to me. The preacher is his own sermon. The infirmity of him which speaks diminishes the Word. And people will think I come into the church only to have a living. No; thank you, but no!" But Morton did persuade me to write, at King James' behest, a tract showing that subscribing to the Oath of Supremacy was a political, and not a religious, decision, and one therefore which every English Catholic might conform with in good conscience. The King approved my work—too much! The King got it into his Scotch skull that I would be an ornament to his kirk, and the King himself saw to it that all other doors of employment were barred to me except the door of the church. To take Holy Orders, to become a divine, one of God's conduits—I wrastled with that decision as Jacob wrastled with the angel.

NARRATOR: "Holy Sonnett Fourteen:"

PERFORMER: Batter my heart, three person'd God; for, you
As yet but knocke, breathe, shine, and seeke to mend;
That I may rise and stand, O'erthrow mee, and bend
Your force, to breake, blowe, burn and make me new.
I, like an usurpt towne, to'another due,
Labour to'admit you, but, Oh, to no end,
Reason your viceroy in mee, mee should defend,
But is captiv'd, and proves weake or untrue.
Yet dearely I love you, and would be loved faine,
But am betroth'd unto your enemies:
Divorce mee, untie, or breake that knot againe,
Take me to you, imprison mee, for I
Except you'enthrall mee, never shall be free,
Nor ever chast, except you ravish mee.

(*Bowing*) Your Majesty, being convinced, after such soul searching as I have been able to undertake, that no man, no imperfect man, is good enough to be an ambassador for God, and being convinced that no man, no matter how perfect, is too good for that office, if Your Majesty still desires it, I am now ready to put my hand to the holy plow. I am willing to become a

THE STAR THROWER

priest in the Church of England. Whosoever be the conduit, the water is the Holy Ghost's. I have sins incarnadine which, if He will, God will wash white. I shall have to work much harder than others to prove to God and to Your Majesty and to myself that I can be a profitable servant. (*Donning cassock and collar*) God stripped me of myself, and clothed me with himself. (*Kneeling*) Most Merciful Father, I beseech thee so to send thy blessing upon this thy servant that he may be clad about with all justice, and that thy word, spoken by his mouth, may have such success that it may never be spoken in vain.

NARRATOR: Donne first preached at Paddington and Sevenoaks, country churches. They didn't understand a word he said.

PERFORMER: But true to the King's promise, my preferment was rapid. At length I became Dean of St. Paul's Cathedral. Here I preach to comprehending, comprehensive crowds, to commoners and to kings.

NARRATOR: Vespers comes on apace! Compose! The Conclusion:

PERFORMER: I shall put the end of my sermon at the beginning, because we do not know else that we shall live until we reach the end—which, for anything we know, may come this minute, before we be at an end of this point, or at a period of this sentence. From the first minute that we began to live, we began to die. And then all our life is but a going out to the place of execution, to death. If you go to execution in a chariot, and I in a cart or by foot, where is the glorious advantage? But was there ever any man seen to sleep in the cart between Newgate and Tyburn, between the prison and the place of execution, does any man sleep? And we sleep all the way! From the womb to the grave we are never thoroughly awake, but pass on with such dreams and imaginations as these: I may live, as well as another; and, Why should I die, rather than another? But awake, says this text, awake and tell me *Quis homo*? Who is that other that thou talkest of? What man is he that liveth, and shall not see death?

NARRATOR: Interlude! Donne Designs His Tomb:

PERFORMER: The prebendaries have decreed that upon my death I am to have my own niche here in the Cathedral. Therefore, I have also been under the necessity of designing a monument to decorate the space. My remains will remain, buried beneath. Above, this urn—empty, but full of symbolism—this urn shall grace my grave. They have further granted that I shall have a bit of statuary of myself—a graven image of a grave man. It is to be carved by a sculptor with the marvelously apropos name of Mr. Stone. To that end, Mr. Nicholas Stone has been sketching me from life—for death. For this portrait, I don my costume. (*Struggling into the shroud*) My winding sheet!

NARRATOR: A Spurious Poem:

PERFORMER: And in these grave clothes
Every evening I pose
For Mr. Stone,
So that when I shall be decomposing
You may see
His granite ghost of me
Poised for posterity.
Shroud-haltered,
I'll strain eastward toward
The great altar
Till from my funeral urn
I'll rise (*standing on the urn so as to appear to rise from it*)
To greet my Savior in the skies. (*He lets shroud fall.*)

NARRATOR: "The Paradox:"

PERFORMER: Once I lov'd and dy'd; and am now become
Mine own epitaph and Tombe.

NARRATOR: In Donne's mortuary statue I glimpse the image of my own meaning. I, too, pose as a dead man that I may live. Donne is a poser. Come down!

(PERFORMER *steps down from the urn.*)
Remove that death mask! Unmask!

THE STAR THROWER   213

(PERFORMER *covers his face with a death's head mask.*)
NARRATOR: And behold the hollow-socketed skull. Why don't
you laugh at that! Donne laughs. His graven grin will outlive
St. Paul's Cathedral.
PERFORMER: (*Removing mask*) But my flesh-formed face,
superimposed on his, will momentarily melt in your
memory.
NARRATOR: But Donne himself, he will outlive cathedral,
statue, and all, in his words. And with his words, his love.
PERFORMER: I died when Anne died in childbirth. But this
manacle (*displaying bracelet of hair on his wrist*) mates us still.
NARRATOR: "The Relique:"
PERFORMER: When my grave is broke up againe
Some second ghest to entertaine,
. . .
   And he that digs it, spies
A bracelet of bright haire about the bone,
   Will he not let'us alone,
And thinke that there a loving couple lies,
Who thought that this device might be some way
To make their soules, at the last busie day,
Meet at this grave, and make a little stay?
(*A bell begins to toll.*)
NARRATOR: Finale!
PERFORMER: No; that is not the vesper bell; that is the passing
bell. I know it well. That tolling bell clangs incessantly
whenever the plague is afoot here in the city of London.
NARRATOR: (*Calling singsong*) Bring out your dead!
PERFORMER: In the compass of a mile, I believe there died of
the plague a thousand a day. In Constantinople, twice that
number died. But by reason that these plagues are not so
frequent with us, the horror, I presume, was greater here.
There were so many dead as that they could no longer be
buried according to form. The funerals became so many that
people could not toll the bell, mourn or weep, or wear black

for one another, as they did before; no, nor so much as make coffins for those that died.[27] The citizens fled away, as out of a house on fire, and stuffed their pockets with their best ware, and threw themselves into the highways, and were not received so much as into barns, and perished so, some of them with more money about them than would have bought the village where they died. A Justice of Peace, into whose examination it fell, told me of one that died so with 1400 pounds about him.

NARRATOR: Bring out your dead!

PERFORMER: When the Turks took Constantinople, they melted the bells into ordnance. I have heard both bells and ordnance, but never been so much moved with those as with these bells. I have lain near a steeple in which there are said to be more than thirty bells, and near another where there is one so big as that the clapper is said to weigh more than six hundred pounds, yet never so much moved as here. Here the bells can scarce solemnize the funeral of any person but that I knew him, or knew that he was my neighbor. We dwelt in houses near to one another before, but now he is gone into that house into which I must follow him.

NARRATOR: Bring out your dead!

PERFORMER: No man is an island entire of itself. Every man is a piece of the continent, a part of the main. If a clod be washed away by the sea, Europe is the less, as well as if a promontory were, as well as if a manor of thy friend's or of thine own were. Any man's death diminishes me, because I am involved in mankind. And therefore never send to know for whom the bell tolls; it tolls for thee.

NARRATOR: And now Donne is done.

PERFORMER: My sermon is composed.

NARRATOR: My play is composed.

PERFORMER: My death is composed.

NARRATOR: And I am composed. When Donne is done, I am Donne, and you are Donne. And all are Donne—enfleshed, entombed, enskyed with Donne! The exit finishes the character—or completes it.

PERFORMER: It remains only to ascend my pulpit. (*Beginning to vest himself*) Now death hooks me from this bright stage to his dark wings. O bear me up upon those wings!

NARRATOR: Rise, Donne! Soar, Donne!

PERFORMER: Soar, Spirit, on the ebony wings of words!

NARRATOR: Flash forward! Donne duels with death! Who will win—Punch or Judy? You decide!

PERFORMER: Death is the last, and in that respect, the worst enemy. When I lie under the hands of that enemy on my last bed, when the last enemy shall watch my remediless body and my disconsolate soul there; there where not the physician in his way, perchance not the priest in his, shall be able to give any assistance; when my delirious tongue shall cry out for my beloved Anne—Anne!—whom he hath savaged and ravaged from my side; and when Death hath sported himself with my misery upon that stage, my deathbed, shall shift the scene, and throw me from that bed into the grave, there to triumph o'er me God knows how many generations, till my Redeemer come—in that consideration, in that apprehension, Death is the powerfullest, the fearfullest enemy; and even this enemy *Abolebitur*, he shall be destroyed.

NARRATOR: "Holy Sonnet Ten:"

PERFORMER: Death be not proud, though some have called thee
Mighty and dreadfull, for, thou art not soe,
For, those, whom thou think'st, thou dost overthrow
Die not, poore death, nor yet canst thou kill mee.
From rest and sleepe, which but thy pictures bee,
Much pleasure, then from thee, much more must flow,
And soonest our best men with thee doe goe,
Rest of their bones and soules delivery.
Thou art slave to Fate, Chance, kings, and desperate men,
And dost with poyson, warre, and sicknesse dwell,
And poppie, or charmes can make us sleepe as well

Or better than thy stroake; why swell'st thou, then?
One short sleepe past, wee wake eternally,
And death shall be no more; death, thou shalt die.
[NARRATOR *dies. Exit* PERFORMER.]

FATHERS AND SONS

You can link a series of monologues together to make a play.

This gives you the advantages of direct address, concentrated focus, and potential stream of consciousness or interior dialogue that are typical of monologues. At the same time, a play composed of monologues allows you to create a Rashomon effect—multiple viewpoints from many characters.

This connected monologue form also offers acutely realized relationships between characters who, although they may never be face to face with one another, are according to the convention of soliloquy free to speak their true feelings. Further, this form continues the practical benefit of convenient rehearsal—no small consideration in today's busy congregations.

Using masks, one actor suffices.

The Prodigals may be presented on three separate Sundays, perhaps followed by sermons or discussions, or it may be presented, as I have twice seen it, all at one worship service. It was originally written to be simply a dramatized version of the Master's masterpiece story. Had Jesus never been known as the Savior of the World, the Son of God, had he never done any other remarkable thing in his life, the world would be bound to recognize the author of The Prodigal Son and The Good Samaritan as a master of literature.

If the three monologues are done as one play, the climax is the Father's "My boy!" After that we need to settle down to the point: love the Father, love the family.

Walter Williamson revived my interest in the father-son theme. Walter—"Chip"—is a former student of mine who is now in Hollywood, but was then acting in New York. He told me that he had written and was performing in his church a full evening of monologues entitled *Four Fathers* (music by Mozart!). I asked him to send me a copy of the script. As usual, Walter's work was fine, but it wasn't right for me to perform in my situation. Therefore, like any good teacher, I shamelessly stole Walter's idea—even used the same characters he had—and composed my own versions.

My method of composition was this: After researching my subject, I took a hand-held tape recorder into the sanctuary and began developing the script orally, as I customarily did sermons. But then on transcribing the tapes of the monologues, I was interested to discover that in two instances—Adam and David—the monologues had developed spontaneously in the form of blank verse. That seemed appropriate to me, and I left them that way, in defiance of the joke about the writer who put his whole mind into his blank verse.

The style of *Adam Remembers* is deliberately simple and plain. As a youngster browsing through my father's *Encyclopedia Britannica*, I had been fascinated by a picture of a sculpture group entitled, "The First Funeral." It showed Eve walking beside Adam carrying Abel's limp granite body. The story of mankind's death is ancient and basic.

Abraham I see, like Adam, as a man of the earth. In developing Abraham, I must have been mightily influenced by Cabot in O'Neill's *Desire Under the Elms*, because I was certain that for an American audience the nearest equivalent figure to Abraham would be a New England rock farmer. When I have performed this monologue, I have given Abraham a preponderance of what I hoped was Down East dialect—one or two audience members have even recognized it as such. Unfortunately my lack of facility with dialects is notorious, and I'm afraid there has probably been an admixture of every other regional rural dialect in the country! Once I performed Abraham for a ministerial association. I cherish the line its brutally honest secretary recorded in the minutes: "He talked like a hillbilly, but it was good."

Controversial King David! In *David Declines* we find him in age (I Kings 1:1-31). Bathsheba and Nathan have asked David to name Solomon his heir. This is one of those rare instances when the monologist ought to have another character on stage with him, even though Abishag plays more the role of a prop than a person. To my mind, the essential struggle in David's life has been between his warrior self and his psalmist self, between as it were his beast and his beauty.

For *Joseph Disappears* I chose a form of dramatic monologue, *prosopopoeia*, practiced from antiquity by school children assigned to write a letter that a historical personage might have penned.

Here is a Biblical mystery. Jesus knows no higher word than "Father." It is Jesus' name for God. We can only wonder at the image of "father" Jesus must have derived from Joseph. Yet Joseph slips softly out of the New Testament like an errant father or a knight errant slipping out the back door. If Joseph left willingly— a huge assumption!—surely he could only have been impelled by an irresistible force.

Although epistolary monologues have been common throughout history, I find the form difficult to perform. It helps if Joseph uses vigorously a huge quill pen and ink well. And of course he has his angel—the audience?—to talk to. Joseph keeps fluttering about like a moth between two candles. He is in a hurry to leave; he is in a hurry to finish his note. There is an air of pell-mell urgency.

THE PRODIGALS

SON

I was so bored! I thought I was going to die! We had 187 acres of boredom. Boring!

Maybe that's never been a problem for you. Maybe you're the stay-at-home kind. That's OK for some people, but "some people ain't me!"

"Some people" can never see beyond the fence rail. Hey, Baby, there's a world out there—a whole, big, beautiful, wonderful, exciting world out there! Maybe you know how I felt. Maybe you know what it's like to be young, to know there's a world out there. And to know it's all passing you by!

Stuck in the mud! That's my brother. He likes it! Can you feature that? I mean, he *likes* it! Mister Responsibility, that's my brother. Big brother, Mr. Know-It-All. Goody two shoes. He can walk through a field of manure and never get his goody two shoes dirty. No gumption. No guts. I mean, no imagination at all. Dull, dull, dull, dull, dull. Stick in mud, stay at home, eight o'clock sleepy time boy.

Get up in the morning; milk the cows. Now there's excitement for you, staring at the right rear panel of a cow! Whoopee. And watching olive trees grow! You think God put young men on earth to watch trees grow? I wasn't sure my heart could stand the excitement.

Yeah, sure. God gave me this body, and these muscles, and this hot, red blood in my veins, and these juices leaping inside me—God gave me all this so's I could sit and watch the trees grow! Oh, yeah.

So finally I said, "I have had it!" You know what I mean? I have had it! So I go to my Dad and I say, "Dad, I have had it! I simply cannot live like this, not one more day. Dad, I gotta get out there in the world and find my fortune. This life is not for me. Dad, I know I can make it! I can make it big! All I need is a break. Stake me to it, Dad. You won't be sorry. I know I'll make good!"

Old Man's always been a soft touch, and I think, you know, me being the younger son and all, I think maybe he remembers what it's like to be young and alive. After all, he made it big himself, didn't he? When he came here to this farm, it wasn't nothing, just a wilderness. And he made it. He created this whole spread all by himself. Why couldn't I do the same as him?

Anyway, make a long story short, Dad gave me my share of what I would have had coming to me, and I took off.

I mean, I took off! I put some serious distance between me and home. I wanted to show everybody I could make it all on my own, in a country where nobody ever even heard of my old man.

Before you make it big, I figure you gotta make some contacts, get to be known, known and liked. You know that's the way this world does business. Good clothes, that's important. And transportation, that's something people will notice. Nice apartment. Make the scene. Parties. Get to know the people who count. Then throw a good times bash yourself.

And chicks. At first I figured chicks were kind of window dressing, you know? I mean, you got a client, an associate coming in from out of town, you want to take him out someplace nice. And you gotta provide a little, you know, company, make him feel good, like a man. They like that. I mean, after all, it's routine.

Hey, I liked it, too, don't get me wrong. That's part of the good life, you know? Man and woman. Man and *women*. Nothing cheap, you know. Good, clean, high-class girls, chicks who know what it's all about. Expensive, sure, but it's worth it, right? Nothing to comfort you when things go wrong like a woman.

And things did go wrong. Not my fault. I had it made. I really did. Things were gonna break my way any minute. Then that famine hit. A famine! Who ever even heard of a famine in that part of the country! I mean, there's never been a famine there! They claim it was this El Nino thing. Moved the whole cotton-pickin' weather system 200 miles south. An act of God, already! How you supposed to predict a thing like that? How can you control a thing like that? Well, anyway, that's what happened. Wiped me out. Nothing I could do. Not my fault. Everything gone—totalled.

Friends? Forget it. I mean, in this world there's winners and there's losers, and that's the breaks. You catch a bad wave, you wipe out, and it's like all of a sudden you got leprosy. Nobody even knows your name.

So what can I do? I don't want to go home—some homecoming that would be! Puppy dog with his tail between his legs, big shot all shot, come crawling home to Daddy. And I could just see my big bro, Mr. Excitement. Oh, yeah.

With this famine, there's just no jobs. Nothing. So finally this guy does me some big favor. I can take care of his pigs. You got it? Pigs! You know I'm Jewish. Pigs! Talk about your insult! Man! So there I am. I got it all, all right. I got a famine. I got a job. I got pigs. And I still got debts. Like I owe plenty. And these guys I owe, you don't mess with. Every lousy penny I make, they take.

Chicks? Forget it. I don't even see 'em, except in my dreams. If I see 'em, what am I gonna do? I gotta eat. I need food. I am starving here, literally starving. I am looking at the slop the pigs got their snouts in, and I'm thinking, That slop don't look all that bad. I mean, at least it's food, right? And a man has gotta have food to survive, and there I am . . . .

And then it happened! For the first time, like in a flash of lightning, I see myself. I mean, I really see myself, the way I really was. It was not pretty. Here I was who had been one good hunk of a man, and now I'm down in the mud and manure pushing pigs away to slurp up their slop. Me! That's me!

And I'm like, This is crazy. This is impossible. I am going to die here. This is out of control. I have lost it. I am going down the tubes.

And I go, My Dad has got farmhands who are better off than me. My Dad's men, they got food, and clothes, and lives, and their own dignity. I mean, at least they are human. And I'm like, I'm going home. I'm gonna face the music. I'm gonna say, Dad, I know. I blew it. I blew it big. I disgraced you. Dad, take me back. Take me on as a hand. I'll be a good hand. Dad, I need help. Help me. Help me. Please.

BROTHER

The way I see things, you reap what you sow. Sow wild oats, reap the whirlwind.

On the other hand, you work hard, you keep your nose clean, you walk in the ways of righteousness, then things are going to work out right for you. That's what I've always believed. In this universe there's a kind of scales of divine justice.

I have always done my duty. Always. I have always honored my father and my mother. After all, they gave me life. They cared for me. And my father built this farm with his own two hands. Many's the time my father has said to me, Son, this is all going to be yours. And he says he's happy it's that way. He says it warms his heart to think he's going to leave all this to me. And for my part, I have always known that I will never let him down. When he is in his advanced years, I am going to take care of him just like he took care of me. He won't be sorry. I am going to be a good son.

After all, I'd even like to make it up to him a little for my brother. What my brother did to my father was devastating. Took off. Just took off. Probably figured being the younger son he'd never get this farm, so he got our father to give him his cash share of the estate, and he took off for parts unknown. Broke our father's heart. I don't know why he let him go. Always was maybe just a little bit too permissive with the kid. So he used to stand by the gate and stare down the road where he went. Just stare. Like he was trying to wish him back.

What we heard from travelers was that he was doing all right. Well dressed, nice apartment, well liked. Trading in futures or something like that. Never wrote home. Broke our father's heart, broke his heart.

One day, there Dad was, standing at the gate again looking down the road. Tears in his eyes. Maybe from the dust. Just staring, kind of like he was hypnotized; just staring, maybe remembering, maybe wishing. Brokenhearted. Tell you, almost broke my heart to see him. I went out into the South field.

About the time it's getting dark, I come back. What am I hearing? I'm hearing music. Music! Funny thing: we used to have music when we were growing up, you know, happy music, upbeat. But ever since the kid brother took off, the music's been—I mean, what music there's been—it's, well, subdued, you know? And now I'm hearing trumpets blazing away! And tambourines! And people are singing and yelling and clapping and dancing.

I grab a farm hand. "What's going on?" He says—get this!— he says, "Your brother's come home. He's dead broke, but he's alive, and your Dad's throwing a welcome-home party. Come on in! It's great!"

Whoa! Little brother's come home and he's broke and we're having a party? What's wrong with this picture? Peachy keen! And how come I'm not invited? If I was invited, I wouldn't come.

So I'm standing there, trying to take it all in, just trying to make sense out of what I'm hearing. My mind is blown away! And Father comes out. Father comes out and he says to me, "Son! Come in! Your brother's come home!" It is pathetic, he is so happy. He is happy that this kid has gone and blown all his money and now he's come crawling home. Oh, nice. Big deal. Thanks a heap. Looks to me like he got just what he deserved, going broke. How does he rate a hero's welcome for being a total failure? Where's the logic in that? Where's the justice in that?

So I look at my father. He's still got tears running down his cheeks, and his face is like a sunrise. I can't hold it in any more. So I scream, "Father! Look at me! This is me. I'm your son! I've been here with you every day of my life. I have done everything you ever asked me to do! Right down the line! This is me! I am the boy who is going to take care of you in your old age! Now you tell me—when did you ever just all of a sudden throw a party for me? Oh sure, birthday parties, that kind of thing everybody does. But did you ever give me a real blowout for no reason at all, but just because I'm here? Well did you?"

And I said, "Look, I'm not jealous. I've got nothing to be jealous of. You think I want to be like him? A no-good? A punk? A flop? A loser? No, thank you, I am not jealous of that zero! But I would like to have a little bit of justice around here, if you don't mind. I mean, just a little bit of basic fairness. Is that asking too much? I appeal to you in the name of everything that's right, is this fair—that you welcome him and you never even think to send somebody out into the field to call me in? What am I— sausage? You call this fair? Do you?"

FATHER

I love both my sons. I love all my children. Everything you see here, this whole place, I made for them, to be their home. That was the whole point. There wasn't any need for it, no reason to create all this just for myself. I didn't need it. Without my family, it would have been pointless. I love them.

Some folks look at me and think there's nothing I need, I own everything. In a sense that's true. But in another sense, I do have a need, if you can understand it. I need to be true to myself. And it's my nature to love. That's who I am. I am a loving person. Ask me the one word that describes me, that's it: love. To me the greatest thing of all is to be a father, a loving father.

Out of my love I created my family. And for my family I made all this.

And yet some people think I don't have feelings, think I can't be hurt. You know better than that. You know every time you love, you lay yourself open to getting hurt. Vulnerable—it's a risk. You've got a choice: you can take a chance on getting hurt, or you can play it safe and never love.

So I admit it: my younger son broke my heart. He did. He went over fool's hill. Children do that. Part of the risk. He made some poor decisions. He paid for them. But my love is stronger than his bad decisions. My love won. When the worst happened to him, my son remembered me, he remembered my love, and he knew he could come back home.

I was standing right here at the gate, staring down the road. I guess the dust blew in my eyes, because they were watering. You could see the wind whipping the dust up down the road. Then I thought, That dust devil out there looks like a man. I blinked. You know, my son used to have this walk, this kind of a lope where he rises up on the ball of his foot. And that dust devil looked to be moving just like that. I watched it come closer. And then—my heart knew it before my eyes could see it. My heart just, well, kind of leaped, yeah, leaped up. It was him! I knew it was him.

And I ran down that old dusty road; no, I ran—I can still run. And now I could see him. I could see him! My boy! And he saw me coming. And he stopped. And I ran to him. And he started—he started to kneel down. But I caught him in my arms and I hugged him and I wept! Tears of joy! Tears of joy!

He started to talk: "Father, I have sinned and am no longer worthy to be your son; make me as one of your hired servants."

But I just hugged him. And then I kissed him. And then I put my arm around his shoulder and started back to the house. By now the hands were coming out to see what was happening. I shouted out, "Bring a robe! Rings for his fingers! Kill the fatted calf! Prepare a feast! Music! Dancing! Rejoice! My son which was dead is alive and has come home!" And we began to make merry! Joy! Joy! Joy!

And then I asked, "Where is my other son?" And they told me he was outside and refuses to come in. Refuses? I went out and found him. I went to take him in my arms like his brother.

I said, "Rejoice!" He had this stone face. I said, "What's the matter?"

And he said, "You never did this for me, and I have been a faithful son."

I understood how he felt. I just kept holding him. And I said, "My son, my son! You are always next to my heart. Everything I have is yours. And your brother is yours, and mine. Surely you see how fitting it is we rejoice: he has been restored— to life and to us!"

Yesterday—he came home yesterday. Now I'm waiting to see how we will all behave. I love my family. I don't want anything else, except that my family should also love me and all the rest of the family, too.

FOUR FATHERS

ADAM REMEMBERS

Both your brothers died before you saw
The light of day, before we knew what that
Word meant or what it was—to die, be dead.
All I'd ever known was life—
Molded from mud, sculpted of cold clay,
Shaped by God's own hand to be like him,
Breathed by God's own mouth, my lungs inspired
With life.
Life from life! Life bursting forth with
Grass and trees, with hills and streams and great
Garden groves that grew eastward in Eden.
Life was good.
God gave the garden to me, to care for it.
Wonderful work!
Break a branch and snap it at the fork,
You have a tool to till the ground like dolphin
Plunging through the sea.
God made each fruit to carry its own seed.
Plant it, bury the seed in black earth,
Rain falls, sun shines, the dead seed springs to life.
The Lord gave all to me except the tree
Of knowing good and evil. Forbade to eat
Of that, for the Lord said to me the day I eat
Of that tree I shall surely die.
Die! I did not know what that word meant.
All I'd ever known was life.

The garden was home to beasts of every kind.
To me God trusted the naming of them all.

THE STAR THROWER   229

The Lord lent me his own great gift of words,
Then made the beasts pass by for me to name.
And God would laugh to hear the names I chose—
Ostrich! Zebra! Hippopotamus!
They all had mates, the beasts. They had, not I.
To speak their names and call them in was good.
But none of them could speak to me.
No voice shared the game of naming them.
No voice remarked the fragrance of the flowers.
No voice echoed the praise of our great God.
Until one night while I slept the Lord created
Eve, your mother,
Most marvelous of all the creatures made,
My mate. And she spoke—her lighter voice
And brighter mind made harmony with mine.
We two shared all the beauties of that place,
God's garden, and all delights of life.
I felt fulfilled, perfected, whole.
How shall I speak of her, your mother?
Of her feel, think, nor speak ill.
Beautiful and tender, warm was she.

The subtle serpent, envious snake, seduced,
Tempted her to eat forbidden fruit
Of knowing good and bad, but she said, "No,
The day we eat thereof we surely die."
The serpent soothed, "And what is that—to die?
You shall not surely die." And she believed.
Her innocent trust and frankness played her false.
She saw the fruit a thing to be desired,
A thing that we should have to make us wise.
And she gave me to eat the fruit and I
Did eat. We shared the fruit and then we shared
The shame. Never before had we known shame.
In the cool of the evening, God walked in the garden.

We hid ourselves from him for fear that he
Would know what we had done. But he found us.
The snake he cursed to crawl. For Eve, birth pangs.
The ground for me with thorn and thistle plagued.
Then lest we grasp and eat the fruit of life
And live forever—
What did that mean, to live forever?
Of course we'd live forever!—
He turned us out the grace-filled grove and placed
One with flaming sword to guard the gate.
We went forth free in the wilderness.

Then your mother bore your brother Cain.
I'd rejoiced when God created Eve,
Rejoiced again when our first son was born.
Not molded from the earth as I had been,
But formed and framed within his mother's womb.
And he was perfect, a miniature man.
We cared for him and loved him—Cain.
We showed him all our world: the gentle beasts,
The flowers. He brightened us, he lightened all
Our ways, made happy us who had been sad.
Of every shining day he was the sun.
And we rejoiced again to find new
Marvel, each day new meaning, to live
For him.
I taught him how to hoe the grudging ground.
We shared the work together, he and I.

And then your brother Abel next was born,
Every bit as beautiful as Cain.
Cain helped to teach his brother as he grew,
Although he may have envied him. Who knows?
Abel was younger and so was minded more,
Got all the coddling Cain had got before.

Time passed. Abel was the one I tasked
To care for those few animals we kept
To help us in our living, the sheep and goats.
Cain and Abel both I taught God—
Who he is, and how to worship him.
I loved them both.

But then between your brothers came dispute
Whose sacrifice pleased God the more.
And Cain killed Abel.
I found his body.
I had never seen a person dead.
I didn't know what death was.
I spoke to him, but he spoke not to me.
I touched him. I lifted him.
There was no life at all in him.
He lay limp in my arms.
And Eve his mother wept. And I wept.
We called his name.
Our son was dead, dumbly dead.
And Cain who killed him, Cain too was dead
In different sense, exiled away from us
To wander through the world, doubly dead.
Could God endure our pain—parents of sons who died?
Then the Lord sent you to us, Seth,
My son.
Learn from your brothers' deaths. Live in peace.

In night's dark day I sometimes question God.
I ask him, "Will there ever come a day
When Cain can be forgiven and come home
To me and live with us again, we four?"
And I have asked him if there'll be a time
When Abel my dead seed may live again.
God's answer I do not understand.

God tells me he is not God of the dead,
But God of those who live. With him all souls
Live. With him! And hear this, Seth, my son:
The Lord God says, "By first man death has come;
When time grows full, a second Adam comes
To bring his children life that never dies."
What do you think that means, "That never dies?"

Well, come now, Seth, my son. Remorseful night
Tempts us to turn in sleepless rest until
We rise with the sun to walk together in the light.

END

ABRAHAM FOLLOWS

Ayah! That's the place! Right over there! At the end of the field! Heh! That's it! That's it! Not much of a place, but ya see there, there! It's got that there cave in it! That's what I'm consid'rin', I'm consid'rin' that there cave. . . . Ah! Machpelah, huh? Ya call it Machpelah. Ayah.

Not much call fer caves, I reckon, but I've tuk a notion t' that there cave. Come 'cross it jes' this mornin' when we was herdin' the sheep. . . . No, not fer livin' in, fer buryin' in. That's right, buryin'.

M' wife, principally, m' wife. Sarah. Sarah were her name. Good woman. Now she's gone an' died, an' lookin' fer a place fer her final restin' ground. An' bein' as how we be strangers an' sojourners here in your country, had no place t' bury her, no place o' my own, an' I'd admire to buy me jes' a little spot. An' I visioned as how this here cave, bein' dry an' all, would be a good . . . good buryin' place fer her. Machpelah, ya call it. Ayah! All right. . . . . Oh, that's right neighborly-like o' ya t'offer, but, no, no, I couldn't take it as a gift. Really do want t' pay ya fer

THE STAR THROWER 233

it—a fair exchange o' value, so t' speak, t' make it all bindin' an' legal like—so's I kin prove it's mine, an' me an' m' people got a *right* t' be here.

Yestiddy. She died yestiddy . . . yestiddy. Good woman, Sarah, good woman. Better woman 'n I deserved, they's a-many'll tell ya that, better woman 'n I deserved. Ayah! Hard world out there, I'll tell ya that. Brimstone an' fire! It's a hard world. 'Tain't no playground out there.

Come a long way t'gether, me an' Sarah. Started out with next t' nothin'. Had prac'ly nothin'. . . . Ur. City of Ur in the Chaldees. I were pretty well along, too—seventy-five year old. The Lord God come an' speak t' me an' . . . an' . . . . The Lord God. Don't know 'im, huh? Peculiar kind o' individual, the Lord God. Chock full o' s'prises! Come t' me an' he said, "Abram"—Abram, he called me in them days—"Abram," says he, "want ya t' sell the lands ya got, pack up an' leave, 'count o' I got a new land I be aimin' t' lead ya to." So I left. "Abram!" Heered him callin' an' jes' ca'lated I had t' do what he said t' do, so I left. Lotsa folk figured I was crazy as a loon, but I done it. Jes' started walkin', started walkin'. "Abram! Abram!" Wherever he led me. Walked blisters on both m' feet. Set down upon a rock, rubbed them blisters, an' I said, "Is this what ya want I should be doin', Lord?" An' the Lord God said, "Yes, Abram, them blisters is part o' my plan. You jes' keep on awalkin'." An' I said, "M' feet's getting' mighty tired, Lord." An' he said, "Abram, you jes' pick 'em up, an' I'll put 'em down." So, been pretty well walkin' ever since. Walked m'self, m' whole household become nomads. Wherever the Lord God led us, we follered. "Abram! Abram!" Pick 'em up, put 'em down.

Tuk a journey down t' the land o' Egypt. That's how come I say they's lotsa folk'll tell ya Sarah's a better wife 'n I deserve. Got down t' the land o' Egypt, an' I ca'lated as how, bein' as I was a stranger an' a sojourner there, an' bein' as how Sarah was a beautiful woman, even at her age, an' I ca'lated some o' them Egyptian fellers might jes' take a interest in Sarah an' want t' get rid o' me.

So I told her, "Sarah," says I, "you jes' tell 'em yer m' sister. M' sister. An' sure 'nough they went an' tuk 'er into Pharer's own household. 'Course, when they come to find out she was really m' wife, Pharer was almighty put out an' he fetched her back t' me. But ya see, it turned out good, fer ya see Pharer give me lotsa goods t' make up fer it, sent me on m' way with lotsa animals an' silver fer a peace offerin', an' that were the beginnin' o' m' wealth—not that I got a great deal, y' understand. But ever since, ever'where I gone, follerin' where the Lord God told me t' go, I had good luck, t' the point where a certain amount o' this world's goods has accumulated t' me—not that I'm what a body'd call rich, y'understand.

So! While they's some'd say I done Sarah wrong, nothin' happened t' her. Fact is, only good things come t' her as a result of it all. So how kin ya say what I done was wrong? Hmm?

Sarah were a woman as could not have children, y'know. That were a burden on her most o' her life. An' a fair tolerable disappointment fer me, too. Didn't have no proper son. Sired a child on a slave woman, but 'twan't the same thing. Me an' Sarah together didn't have nary young'un. She growed old. Give up on the whole idea o' havin' children. An' then, then the Lord God come to me ag'in, an' the Lord God said, "Abram, Sarah be goin' t' conceive an' bear a child." Tell ya straight, I laughed at that. An' Sarah, she laughed, too. She were past the way of havin' children. Too old—anybody'd tell ya that, too old. But ya ain't never too old fer nothin' when it comes t' the Lord God, fer sure 'nough, right in keepin' with the Lord God's promise, Sarah conceived an' bore a baby boy. Isaac. Named 'im Isaac, the Laughin' One. So ya see good things happened fer her after all. Ayah! The Lord God keeps his promises. Isaac!

'Course, they's some'd tell ya I ain't been the father I ought t've been, neither. The boy growed. Our whole household continued t' grow, an' ever'thing was goin' fine until, until that day the Lord God come t' me an' said, "Abraham"—fer that was the new name he had fer me, Abraham—"Abraham," says he,

THE STAR THROWER   235

"how d' ya like that son Isaac I give ya?" an' says I, "Oh, fine Lord, jes' fine, he's a fine young lad!" An' the Lord God, he said, "Now, Abraham, now you take that young'un up t' the mountains where I show ya, an' there on the mountain I want ya t' . . . t' offer 'im t' me as a burnt offerin'." Well, what could I do? That's all I done all my life, were done what the Lord God told me t' do. An' so I, I tuk the lad up int' the mountains, an' cast me up an altar, an' bound the boy, an' heaved the boy up on the . . . on the altar, an' tuk m' knife, an' were fixin' to do what the Lord God said an' slay . . . slay 'im an' burn 'im as a burnt offerin'. An' then the Lord God stopped me. An' the Lord God said, "Abraham, do not harm that boy of yourn." I have puzzled as to why that should be. First the Lord God told me t' do it; then the Lord God told me not t' do it. They's some'd say soon's I made it up in m'heart t' do what the Lord God said, I become the same as a . . . a . . . whatever ya call a man as kills his own son. But 'twa'n't 'zactly killin'. 'Twere offerin' t' the Lord God as a sacrifice, an' I thought that's what the Lord God wanted. That's what he said! Ca'late as how the Lord God changed his mind, decided he don't want no human sacrifice.

Oh, yes, the Lord God does change his mind, y' know. Sometimes does, sometimes don't. Some is spared, some ain't. Some is chose. Some ain't. No playground!

'Course, if'n ya want the Lord God t' change his mind, ya got t' come at it proper-like. Got t' know how t' deal with 'im. Mind the time the Lord God tuk a notion t' wipe out the city o' Sodom. Terrible nasty place, Sodom. So the Lord God said he were goin' t' destroy it. So happened m' nephew Lot an' his wife lived there in the city o' Sodom. So when the Lord God said t' me, "I be aimin' t' wipe it off 'n the face o' the earth," I said t' the Lord God, says I, "Now wait jes' a minute, Lord. Suppose they's some *righteous* folk live there in the city o' Sodom. Ya aimin' t' wipe out them righteous folk 'long with all them evil folk?" An' I said to the Lord God, "Suppose they's, say . . . fifty of 'em, fifty righteous folk in the city o' Sodom; ya goin' t' wipe 'em out? Ain't ya goin' t' spare them righteous? An' fer the sake o' them righteous folk, won't ya spare t'others?" An' the Lord God, says he, "Well, all right, if'n I find fifty righteous souls in the city of Sodom, I will repent me o' that evil I were about t' do." An' I said, "That's mighty merciful o' ya, Lord, but would ya destroy a whole city 'count o' lackin', say, five people? Supposen we find jes' forty-five righteous people in Sodom?" An' the Lord God said, "All right, if'n ya find forty-five, I will not destroy the city." An' I said, "Thirty, thirty. Would ya preserve the city fer the sake o' them thirty?" An' at last I worked it down t' ten. "Only ten persons, would ya spare the city account o' ten persons?" An' the Lord God said, "Ya find ten upright, an' I'll spare the city." Got t' know how t' deal with him! That's how it be when you be a friend o' the Lord God! Ayah! . . . Could not find ten righteous people in that city. An' the Lord God wiped it out—fire and brimstone! No playground out there, I'll tell ya, no playground.

So ya see, that's pretty much the story o' m' life. Been doin' whatever the Lord God said, follerin' wherever the Lord God led. "Abraham!" An' now, now the Lord God be sayin' he's goin' t' make me the father o' all the faithful. Ayah! The Lord God said t' me, "Abraham, go out an' look at the night sky. Count them stars up there, Abraham, count 'em!" The Lord God said t' me, "Abraham, ever' one o' them stars is goin' t' stand fer a follerer o' the Lord God, account o' you been m' follerer." All them stars, sons an' daughters o' mine! Ayah! An' the Lord God'll keep his word. Oh, yes, he'll keep his word. Don't rightly know how, but I know he will! Why, he even . . . . He even . . . . (breaking off so as not to tip his hand).

I mean, who knows? One day maybe some o' them descendants o' mine might jes' happen t' come t' live right here in your land! Wouldn't that be a wonder! That's how come I be thinkin', y' know, if'n I could buy me a place here, even though I be jes' a stranger an' a sojourner, if'n I could buy me some buryin' place here that were, well, that'd be mine an' m' descendants. So if'n y'd jes' name yer price . . . . Eh? Four hundred shekels o' silver fer this cave? Heh! Now wait jes' a minute! Jes' now you was aimin' t' give it me! Say, 300. Ya drive a hard bargain. No. No. Done. Done! Three hundred an' fif . . . . Four hundred shekels o' silver fer this . . . cave . . . t' be a buryin' place—an' a kind o' monument, a memorial fer all time t' come—that I, Abraham, do believe the Lord God be faithful. I believe it 400 shekels o' silver worth! The Lord God will give me, he will do fer me, what he has promised! Ayah!

Maybe ya don't approve o' me. Maybe ya think I done some things I oughtn't t've done. Hard world out there—no playground. A man's got t' survive. Life makes ya do lotsa things ya don't maybe think is always "right." 'Tain't clean an' neat out there, I'll tell ya. So maybe ya think I ain't always done right, an' I got t' tell ya I can't rightly seem t' care what ya think. Think maybe I ain't been good enough, eh? Ya don't understand. That ain't the way the Lord God works. Brimstone and fire, the Lord God's got enough goodness fer us all! What the Lord God wants from us is faith! An' that means follerin'! So I ain't perfect! So I ain't done ever'thing right in m' life! The one thing I done right in my life, I follered the Lord God. Jes' as I were! This old man, this weak, tuckered-out old man, I follered wherever he said go. I believed 'im! I trusted 'im! I follered 'im! An' the Lord God, he counts that t' me fer righteousness! Ayah.

Done, then. It's mine. It's mine. I'll jes' be about m' buryin', an' then I'll be on m' way. That's where she'll rest.

Me? No. No, the Lord God be callin' me still. She's gone, but I got t' go on. The Lord God be sayin' t' me, "This here'll be a place t' come back t'. But don't you rest yet, Abraham, old friend." The Lord God be sayin', "Abraham! Abraham! I be goin' t' make you the father of nations o' follerers!" I kin still hear the Lord God callin' me: "Abraham! Abraham!" An' long as I kin walk, I'll foller. Lead on!"

I pick 'em up, an' he puts 'em down. Ayah!

EXIT

DAVID DECLINES

Cold calculation brings you begging here.
You reek of plot. How obvious you are!
His mother first, you next; same day, same hour.
Both come to claim my former voice that my
Son, Solomon, shall have my throne.
It's mine to give, then, is it—and not yours?
You prophets may anoint, as Samuel
Anointed me, but only kings can give.
Samuel anointed Saul, but God,
Heaven's king, made me Messiah-king.
Tell me now: would God have given me
The kingdom if I'd nothing in my hand?
Notice: God contrived to slip the scepter
Into this same right hand that held my sword.
What's Solomon got in his hand? An account book!
No; in this kingdom, the sword *is* the scepter.
God used my bloodstained, sacred scepter-sword
To carve his kingdom out of Canaan's land.
His scepter is the weapon in my hand.

God condescends that I be called king—
Great David!—but you and I, prophet and puppet,
We know who is the power behind this throne.
What kind of king am I who must keep
Over-the-shoulder watch to wonder whether
God's prophet Nathan approves of David's reign?
I'm sure you do approve. You nod your head.
The enemies of Lord and land lie dead.

But you, prophet, have been my enemy.
You've kept my crown empty as an idol.
That matter of Uriah . . .
Is there another king in any nation
In all the world who would abide your voice?

THE STAR THROWER 239

They would have nailed your tongue to the walls of Nineveh!
But into my palace you parade
And chide me that I took the Hittite's lamb!
And I confess that you, prophet of God,
Are right, and I, king of Israel, am wrong!
I must submit to you! And must repent!
Royal repentance! I meant it.
I was sorry. I'm sorry still.
And you forgave. You claimed that God forgave.
Hoaxer! In God's name you forgive a king?
Who gave you authority of sins?
Prove it! When did God anoint you?
But you were right about my sin, prophet;
And may be right about forgiveness, too.
But nothing—no one—could save the baby.
You let the baby die, you and God.
Does that satisfy your sense of justice?
The son must die for the father's sin? I prayed
For its life seven days and seven nights.
Good training! I was well exercised
In the art of grief. So when Absolom my other
Son who killed his brother Amnon died,
For David that was one more victory!
I go to them. They will not come to me.

Did God imagine that he'd punished me
When he—or was it you?—gave me the curse
Rebellious sword should never leave my house?
But the sword of the Lord has saved me—my scepter.
And you want me to hand it over to Solomon?
Can't you just see my son Solomon
Trying to lift this in his lily hand?
Let alone split a few skulls with it!
You may be right again. It may be time
The sword that carved a kingdom in Canaan slumbers.
The weapon for the days to come may prove

Solomon's account book after all.
Or cookbook! Kitchen king! He'll be a cook
To rule by recipe, his scepter a ladle,
When my right hand lays the sword to cradle.

And to my left hand God gave the harp.
The singing sword my key to the kingdom of Canaan;
The bloody harp my key to the kingdom of God.
Did God anoint his David prince or poet?
I'd rather be the singer than the swordsman.
Oftimes in the field after the battle of the day
I've strummed my harp and sung the songs of God.
When I wheeze now, the royal scribe
Scribbles every word. Too bad he can't
Capture too the tones, the shimmering sounds.
The words he has. He flatters me my words
Will be immortal. Hmm! We shall see—
Not we, but those who hear hereafter—they
Shall see which lives longer: kingdom
Carved by sword, or spirit sought by song.
I sometimes play for hours and never tire.
To sweep the strings and hear the harmony—
It soothed the soul of Saul—years ago!—
And nowadays so it soothes mine.
A little lad to sing! A killer king!
Solomon sings, too, that much
I'll say for him, love songs of a softer sort.
His mother sang when she was young.
Not now. Not now that she foresees herself
Queen mother of the king-to-be, Dame Ambition.
Nathan, good prophet, prophesy for me.
Why did God choose me to be the king—
For sword or song, or both? To conquer or to quest?
I believe God chose me, anointed me,
To suffer, Messiah of sorrows.
Years of flight and fight, hiding in the hills,

THE STAR THROWER

Incaved by night, then flashing forth to strike
Enemies like lightning cracking from the clouds,
Then vanish. After the battle's
Brutal screaming slaughter, stars brooding over
Blood—and God was in them all?
The baby, Amnon, and Absolom! Triumph?
David has slain his tens of thousands!
Great David! Dancing David! Praise David
With psaltery and with harp! Psalm and harp!
Embattled or embittered, not abandoned.
Improbable, impossible, and odd
As it may seem, in all of these was God.

It's done. The kingdom's won—for Solomon?
I'll prophesy for you, good prophet:
If my son Solomon take my flock,
He'll fleece it bare and leave it cold in winter.
The temple I had hoped to build for God
But you forestalled—let him build it, Nathan,
To shelter all those souls who'll shiver then.
My sword and song were dedicate to God,
But he'll parade before the world his wealth.
He has a lustful eye, his father's son.
A stabled stallion, he'd rather mount than kneel.
What can I do now more than I have done?
This weathered hand wanes weak to wield the sword.
These knotted knuckles disdain dexterity
To coax melodies from memory.
This voice which cried command by day and sang
God's praise by night with mighty music's art,
This voice begins to crack, alike my heart.

Give him my throne. Let Solomon be king.
Let his doting mother have her way,
And Nathan, prophet as you are, prevail.
Solomon shall reign, and David sing himself to sleep.

See to his coronation, prophet.
And that the folk may know the king's consent,
Send to my city Bethlehem in Judah;
Bring here my own royal beast, my mule.
Seat Solomon thereon and bid him enter
Jerusalem humbly, riding on an ass—
The king who comes, great David's greater son!
Yet know, if dying men do prophesy in truth,
In farther future David's shining star
Will sing yet one last, chosen, hidden king
To come—in the name of the Lord.
Where is Abishag? Here is gold.
Come, little one! Warm a king who is cold.

END

JOSEPH DISAPPEARS

(*To a Presence*) Yes! Yes! I'm coming! I'll be right with you! But I can't leave my family without a word. Shhh! I don't want to wake them. Give me just a moment and I'll be with you! Let me just write!

(*Writing*) Joseph, the Carpenter, to Yeshua, my son. My father's blessing be with you always!

I am about to undertake a journey full of danger. I do not wish to be away from home at this time of year, and I would not set out were it not for the most compelling inner conviction— and outward manifestation—that this is God's will for me. An angel, my son! An angel urges me forth!

Before I leave, I write this to you, my son. I will put it next to your mother's bed with a note that she is to give this to you only in the event that I fail to return before Rosh Hashanah.

If I should never return—of course I will, but if I should not—I would of course expect you, my eldest son, to care for your mother; to see that your brothers, James, Joseph, Simon,

THE STAR THROWER   243

and Judas, complete all their schooling in the scriptures; to see that your sisters, Miriam and Elizabeth, listen to and obey the instructions of their mother; and that the whole family as always remain faithful followers of our great Lord God.

You have learned our carpenter's trade well, we have our workshop and our home, and, if you apply yourself as you can, you should be able to manage. My affairs are in order. My accounts are where I always keep them, on the tablets in the box to the left of my workbench.

(*To the Presence*) Yes! Yes! A moment! A moment!

(*Writing*) Yeshua, there are a few . . . incidents . . . I have never before found occasion to inform you of. Naturally, a father hesitates to put notions into his children's heads. A father wants his children to grow up modest, unassuming, decent persons, never expecting special treatment. Of course each one of you has been special to me. I have loved you each as if there were only one of you.

Nevertheless, about your birth, Yeshua, about your birth God gave me special dreams. (*To the Presence*) O indeed! Thank you! (*Writing*) I have always paid attention to my dreams, because I know that in my dreams sometimes the Lord God speaks to me.

The first dream—as a man you will know how hard it is for me to write this to you—was the dream in which an angel told me to marry your mother. You are sure to say, "It needs no angel come in a dream to tell your father to marry your mother," and it is true that no man could have found a more wonderful woman than your mother. She was beautiful!—as she is now in a more mature way, but was then the most attractive of maidens. I think it was her laughter I loved most—you sound a bit like her when you laugh—and her singing. I loved to hear her sing.

So, in herself, Mary was a prize. But we did have a problem, and that problem was you. Your mother was pregnant with you before I knew her. I know you will be shocked to read this; believe me, I know how it sounds, as it sounded to me back then. But you would be wrong to think anything ill. Only ask yourself:

would that be consistent with everything else you know about your mother? Of course not! Yeshua, the unbelievable truth is this: your mother was as chaste when you were born as the day she was born! I know this. But it was first revealed to me in a dream by an angel of the Lord who said to me, "The child conceived in Mary is from the Holy Spirit." Yeshua, that angel told me that you were born not of flesh but of the will of God. And yet you really are flesh of flesh. I cannot explain this.

You have to admit it is puzzling to mortal minds. Of course I have been subject both to doubts and to ridicule, but the truth of this dream was confirmed to my complete satisfaction. When you were born while we were on our journey to Bethlehem for the census, shepherds from the fields came to the stable where we were and told us that angels had announced your birth also to them. These humble shepherds told us that one of the angels had used words so magnificent that I hesitate to write them here for fear that they may lead you astray. But your mother has kept these words and ponders them in her heart.

(*To the Presence*) Should I tell him how after his birth, you appeared in my dreams again, warning me to take him and his mother and escape into Egypt? I did it. I took him, tiny as he was, and his mother, and under cover of night fled to Egypt. I found work there and survived. Oh, thank you! Thank you! Imagine how I felt later when I learned that King Herod had ordered the massacre of every little male child in and around Bethlehem! Had you not warned me, Yeshua would have been one of them. Yes! Yes! I'm hurrying!

(*Writing*) I think you, my son, have little reason to ridicule me or doubt me. You know me for a practical man, although a dreamer, and, I hope, an honest man. I share these things with you now only so that, in the event I do not return, you may know I believe the Lord God has created you especially for his own purposes and has . . . significant . . . work for you to do.

If I am right about this, surely the Lord will guide you and direct you to that work, provided you are open to his leading, and I know you will be. He does speak to us! (*To the Presence*) You will guide and direct him, won't you?

I have prayed that the Lord God who now has sent his angel to tell me to venture forth on a mission of my own, a mission of great importance, will bring me safely back to you. In any event, know that about my own life I have no regrets. What I have built and what I have made I have done as best I could. I have cheated no one, lied to no one. I have tried to leave my little corner of the world better than I found it. For joy I have had your mother as my wife, you and the others as my children, and God as my Lord who has sent me my angel visitants. How could my life have been better?

(*To the Presence*) Yes! Yes! Just one moment more!

(*Writing*) Now I ask myself what are the last words I would wish my beloved eldest son to have from me. My last words to you, my son Yeshua, would be these: let the word of God dwell in you richly. Be what God wants you to be, do what God wants you to do. Whatever that is, be sure that wherever I am, I am well pleased with that and with you.

Born of the Holy Spirit, you are nevertheless my son. You know—but let me write it, it may be this one last time—you know how much I love you. Then think how much God, who is the Father of us all, loves us all. In my love, you know his love. And through you may others know it, too.

And so farewell, my son Yeshua!

(*To the Presence*) Yes! Yes! I am coming! I am with you!

WOMEN AND WONDERS

In matters spiritual I prefer the positive approach. But scripture obviously intends the story of Lot's wife to be a cautionary tale. It teaches, "Don't do this. Don't be like Lot's wife."

And although one might hypothesize dozens of reasons, some of them no doubt benign, why Lot's wife might have looked back, the plain meaning of scripture is "Don't." So our Lord understood it. So history has taken it. So I take it. Therefore I would hope that this purposely short monologue will often be followed by a positive message about followers who do *not* look back (Luke 9:62; 18:28).

Still, we may ask what were the values—or anti-values—that doomed Lot's wife. There was some attraction she felt powerless to resist, in spite of a warning straight from an angel of God. Her husband had wealth. They had vested interests in Sodom. Sodom—Sin City if ever there was one—must have offered all the considerable enticements that flesh can flaunt. Then there is the matter of her daughters' later incestuous behavior—perhaps (but here we conjecture) a reflection of the dishonorable morals her daughters learned from their mother.

As *Lot's Wife* is an admonition, *Mary of Magdala* is an inspiration. Unfortunately—outrageously—Mary continues to be maligned as a whore, which she never was. But nasty rumors die hard. Nevertheless, Mary Magdalene is one who does not look back. In spite of calumny, Mary lives on in the front rank of disciples. I ask the actress to present Mary with a light touch.

The Greatest Show on Earth is a Lenten or Good Friday play. It is made up of five monologues that may be presented in one performance, or may be presented, for example, one per week through Lent.

The stage world as circus is a venerable, not to say timeworn, theatrical metaphor stretching at least as far back as the clowns of Roman theatre and favored by such luminaries as Leonid Andreyev (*He Who Gets Slapped*), Berthold Brecht (Berlin production of *Arturo Ui*, and Franco Zeffirelli (*8½ et passim*) as well as Schwartz and Tebelac in *Godspell*. Here we'll view Eden as circus and the divine comedy as The Greatest Show on Earth.

The play features several problems or opportunities—what I call "probortunities."

One is juggling.

On one late-night whim, we piled into a car and drove the forty-five miles to Chapel Hill to go to a movie. This jaunt had nothing to do, so I thought, with the fact that both my sons were then studying, so I thought, at the University of North Carolina. It was merely that a group of us, after rehearsal, had movie fever. Besides, at the particular cinema that we were headed for, you could never tell what added attractions there might be. University students would sometimes spontaneously perform to entertain the gathering crowd until the midnight feature started.

And tonight's added attraction must be spectacular, because before we even got into the auditorium we could hear the cheering and applause inside. We found seats. Then we looked up front to see who was doing what to merit such clamorous approbation. Who, indeed, but my two sons and the spouse of one of them— juggling en masse if not ensemble. Juggling has been for them a delightful hobby they share with whomever. They are good at it. Regrettably, however, this talent apparently does not inherit retrogressively, and I myself know not the touch of it.

If the actor presenting the monologue of the Juggler does

have the touch—or happens to be my son or the juggler-spouse of my son—then let that actor go to it with a will. But if like me the actor is not a juggler, the actor may, as he did in our production, carry juggler items—apples, balls painted to represent Earth and other planets, or flaming swords would be good—and perhaps occasionally tease the audience as if about to juggle them, but never actually attempt it. I tried to build a device to simulate juggling, but I was unable to solve the weight-to-leverage equation. Alternatively, the Juggler may enter in the act of catching one of three balls, and on exit simply make a joke of it, toss them up, and miss them all.

I would prefer the actor of the Ring Master to portray that character as winsome, personable, plausible, reasonable, relaxed, and smiling—in a word, a director's verb, let the Ring Master *charm* the audience. In a Biblical word, *beguile* the audience. However, our experience showed that some perhaps naive audience members tended to trust the Ring Master. After all, how could the Master of Ceremonies at a circus be untrustworthy? Therefore we found it necessary to have the Ring Master give himself away as a bit of a con artist, or at least as a tad too arrogant.

An alternative presentation style, preferable when the monologues are being given in a single performance as one play, is to allow the Ring Master to frame the monologues by performing some introductions, sideshow-barker or ring-master style, indicated as optional in the text.

We found it interesting that the most controversial figure in the play was Emmett Kelly. There are some persons in our Hollywood-conditioned audiences who picture Jesus looking at least like a college football star, say, someone along the lines of The Gipper or a young Mel Gibson. But God has a preference for the weak and foolish. God casts against type. The scandal of the cross is with us still.

Of course, using a clown as a figure for Christ is nothing new. A happy (and therefore, presumably but perhaps superficially, hopeful) clown might be easier to accept. But Emmett Kelly—

THE STAR THROWER   249

Weary Willie? Yes, because in the kingdom of clowns, Kelly fits the role of the figure portrayed in Isaiah 53—one who had no comeliness that we should desire him, but rather a man of sorrows and acquainted with grief. This is Gruenwald's crucified Christ, or Joyce Kilmers's—"the scene shall never fit the deed."

This tramp, tattered and torn, takes it upon himself to clean up the mess so that the show may go on. Against earthly appearances and against fleshly judgments, precisely this rejected, tragic-comic, and crucified one is the true hope of the world.

Nevertheless, the play frustrates some popular expectations. Perhaps this can become an opportunity for discussion. Here theology denies theatricality. Theatre and the world prefer a "big finish;" go out on a high note, at least a bang, not a whimper. Weary Willie makes a humble exit and ends the play as so many other plays traditionally began, with a servant. But Christ, through his earthly ending, begins a new drama. There is no dynamite, socko final curtain. The play—one drama teacher complained—has no "punched up" ending. George Docherty had a great sermon titled "Slogging Through." Sometimes life is a matter of slogging through, of toiling. Christ slogs with us.

A director once described to me how he supplied a happy ending for *Romeo and Juliet*. To the end of Shakespeare's play this director added a film clip that showed Romeo and Juliet running up to a hilltop and embracing. Swelling music! Climax! The lovers are reunited in heaven!

His audiences did not need to dwell on those two inconvenient corpses.

Instead, it was the tragedy that died.

Still, Charles Dickens' Jenny Wren had a point when she said, "The public don't like to be made melancholy, I know very well."

We had the opportunity to present The Greatest Show on Earth only twice before our group broke up (for reasons not connected with presenting the play!). Therefore our experimentation was curtailed. As a director, I would have liked to experiment with letting the Juggler drop whatever it is he or she juggles and leave them on stage for Emmett to pick up as he/she talks about cleaning up. In fact, the cleanup probably ought to be imperfect. For even though Christ made the perfect sacrifice, nevertheless sin and death, principalities and powers, continue in our world—like dictators who defy a plebiscite and maintain their power even though another has been elected (God elects Christ) to be the ruler. Therefore, the untidiness of the stage, like the untidiness of the real world, reflects the situation in which we find ourselves.

Our Emmett actress used a push broom that was taller than she was. When the setting permits, of course Emmett Kelly's justly famous sweeping up of the spotlight's pool of light is in order. Or try reversing it—as *our* Emmett Kelly is himself the light of the world. On exit, Emmett carries the broom across his/her shoulders, even as Christ is depicted carrying his crossbeam.

LOT'S WIFE

The world's coming to an end? Yeah, right!

Who told you so—Chicken Little? Let me guess: some angel sent from God, right? How many times have we heard that one? The world's coming to an end, my eyebrow!

Oh, you mean just *my* world is coming to an end, huh? How lucky for you! Look, Honey, this world's been here a long time, and I guess it's going to be around at least a few more days. I know you're all excited, but this old world has outlived generations of doomsayers. But there's a sucker born every minute. "I can see the signs," they say. "The handwriting is on the wall," they say. Well, excuse me, but I just don't believe anybody knows when it will end. Oh, sure, it could happen. Anything's possible. That's why I say eat, drink, and be merry, for tomorrow—who knows? That's scripture, you know. There's your message from God! Life is too short to drink cheap wine. Meanwhile, nobody's going to stampede me. I'm not one to bolt at shadows.

I've got roots here. My husband and I moved here years ago. My husband—maybe you've heard of him—Lot? I thought you just might have. One of this city's leading citizens. That stone mansion inside the Kidron Gate, that's our home. But we weren't always rich. Believe me, I knew some hard times. When we first moved here, we were homesteaders. That's right, homesteaders—squatters! We lived in a tent. We couldn't afford a house, much less a house in town. We pitched that tent on the plain outside the city walls. But we knew what we were doing. We knew the city was going to grow. We saw the future and we grabbed it. We staked our claim on land nobody else would waste a backward glance on. And we made that scrub blossom like the rose. We made it produce. It's called irrigation, Honey, irrigation. We dug wells.

You can't irrigate crops with salt water. Here we are living on the banks of the Dead Sea. That's what we call it nowadays. I've got news for you. The old people, they used to call it "The Salt Sea." They say that once upon a time it was a volcano. Can you believe that? Well, if it ever was, now the volcano is as dead as the sea. It's still The Salt Sea, saltier than the ocean. Nothing much lives in it. But for us, it's a gold mine!

You know what you can get out of salt water? Salt! For centuries that sea has been laying down salt. And there it is, right smack on our property. And in our world, salt is worth almost as much as gold. Not as pretty, maybe, but pretty valuable. And that little property of ours just happens to sit right on top of layers of salt, Honey, salt—pure rock salt—salt the Salt Sea has been laying down there for centuries. Ours! The city grew. Our development developed. So it didn't take long—living outside the city, yearning for the city, envying all those grand folks who parade around in the city. The fine ladies in their luxury, their designer clothes, their stone houses, their cedarwood floors, their shopping sprees. Well, Honey, now those gals envy me!

And I love it! I've been poor and I've been rich. Rich is better. I never ask, How much does that cost? I want it, I buy it. I'm entitled to whatever I can get. Want it? Go for it. And never look back—that's my motto.

Clothes, jewels, horses, houses. You heard me: that's a plural, houses. Work? I paid my dues. That's what servants are for. Not that they can't be good for more specialized duties than just plain old ordinary work, if you know what I mean. Some of these boys have got bodies to die for, smooth and hard, but I mean hard. And believe me, Honey, they never ever complain about being overworked. Interested? There's plenty to go around. Come on over to my next party. You haven't lived! Do you good.

I include my little girls, too. Sure I let them in on it. I'm not going to raise my daughters to be slaves to some prehistoric moral superstitions. My little girls know what it's all about from the start. They're not out running around with God knows what kind of trash. Why should they? They can get everything they want right here at home—at Mama's knee. Here at home I can keep an eye on them, give them the guidance I wish I'd had. I know who they're with and I can show them how to take care of themselves. Don't think I don't know what my husband's doing, either. And the girls know, too. I don't shock you if I speak frankly, do I? Don't be a fuddy-duddy. This is the modern world.

So you see I really don't have any use for this "world is coming to an end" stuff. Perpetual hysteria! Sure, I can see how it appeals to the down-and-outers. After all, what've they got? Their lives are miserable. They haven't got anything in this world. No wonder they'd like it to end. Wishful thinking—spiteful, really. If they can't have a good time, nobody can have a good time. Fantasy! They believe some God is going to destroy this world and give them a better world. Let them believe it. Keeps them in their place, comforts them, contents them. It helps them bear their lot. Well, I can bear my own Lot. That's a little joke, see? Bear my Lot. (*Laughs.*)

But my eyes are open. I see how things are. And I like what I see. And I don't look back! We eat, we drink, we buy, we sell, we plant, we build. I've got the good life. So you can go peddle your prophecies of doom someplace else.

Look, Honey. Your house catches fire. And I'm not talking a hovel, Honey, I'm talking a mansion with cedarwood floors. And it catches fire. You going to run away and leave it, just run away? Tell me you're not going to stop just long enough to grab your treasures, your jewels, your money. You can't take it with you? Then I'm not going! (*Laughs.*)

I'd have to be crazy to leave all this, go out and start all over again from scratch—and all because of some superstitious blather? And if I leave, who's just waiting to move in? Trash from the plains! Thank you very much!

(*Looking at the sky*) Red sky tonight; sailor's delight. It'll be fair tomorrow. Warmer, too, maybe.

So, Honey, you can just toddle along without me. And do have a lovely time. Drop me a line. And if you're ever back in the neighborhood, do come by, you hear?

(*We hear a distant but ominous rumbling as of a mountain bestirring itself.*)

END

MARY OF MAGDALA

Once upon a time I was possessed by demons.

I know—you don't believe that. You don't believe in demons. You've never seen a demon outside of cartoons and fantasy movies. You've never seen scientific evidence for the existence of demons. As if you had ever seen scientific evidence of anything! Oh, you were subjected to a few oversimplified experiments in science classes, and after that you just took someone else's word that such-and-such was so.

But you won't take my word. You think those ancient descriptions of demons must be only the superstitious mythology of primitive peoples. And of course, if it was someone who lived centuries ago, it was bound to be somebody ignorant—some ignorant soul like Socrates, for example, or Plato, or Aristotle, or Goethe, or Joan of Arc with her voices, or Yeats—ignorant, superstitious people like that, right? Well, let it go.

Let me see if I understand the way you think. What I call "demon possession," you explain away as neurosis, right? Something wrong, something a little bit out of alignment with my ego and my id and my superego, as Freud put it; delusions bubbling up from my unconscious or my subconscious. And what I see as vision or insight you dismiss as hallucination. Have I got that right? And of course that settles that, doesn't it?

Tell me: these things you're so sure of, how many of these egos have you actually seen with your own eyes? How many ids? Tell me, what does a superego look like? Have you got a picture of it? Oh! You've seen what you assume are the *results* of these things in the way people behave! You've *felt* them working inside of you! But you mean to tell me you've never actually seen the things themselves? Well, of course that's very different from demons, isn't it? And your subconscious, you've never seen that either? How about a neurosis? Have you ever seen a neurosis on a dissecting slab? Or in an electronic microscope? How many micrograms does a psychosis weigh? When have you ever taken a photograph of this schizophrenia thing? What is the atomic charge of a paranoia? Isn't it true, in fact, that as far as you actually know, all these things are merely words, words you use to describe the way you see human beings behave? Yes, certainly that's all very different, very superior indeed to the superstitious notion of demons!

Have you ever been cured of a neurosis? Allow me my primitive way of talking, but hear me when I tell you this: I was set free from the grip of seven demons. They had me under their control, just as surely, just as miserably, as if they had been neuroses. A psychiatrist? No; he was a carpenter. Five years of analysis? No; he just touched me. And I was healed. And the demons were gone forever. He gave me back myself.

And I gave myself to him. No, not sexually. There you go again! Talk about neurotic! With you, if I say I gave myself, you automatically think I said I gave him my body, instead of my self. Is body the only part of self you understand?

Or is it that old rumor again? That vicious rumor? Sorry to disappoint you, but it's not true. I never was a harlot, no, not even when I had the demons. It so happens that scripture tells my story immediately after it tells the harlot's story. And because the one story follows the other on the page, hasty—or over-imaginative—interpreters linked our two completely different stories, mine and the harlot's. Men—of course they were men— men who couldn't see a transition in front of their nearsighted eyes! Actually, I knew her, too, the harlot—and she was one terrific woman. Before you look down your blue nose at her because she was a whore, I'd like to tell you that that woman has now entered the Kingdom of God before you. But, no, it wasn't me.

Did I say I gave myself to Jesus? I threw myself at him—my self, my heart, my soul, my personality, my being. I loved him, I loved him with an absolute love, a perfect love. Oh, yes, *that's* true, too—I did give him my money. (*Ironically*) You can't separate

THE STAR THROWER   257

body from self, but you *can* separate *money* from self, hmm? You leave *your* money in the bank—or in your investments. I put *my* treasure where my heart is. The Carpenter didn't have any money. I helped to pay for his ministry. It's that simple. Others did, too. It wasn't payment for my healing or anything else; it was a way of coming to life, it was coming alive. You think you're saving money, do you? Well, my money *got* saved, same as I did. And where my treasure was, my heart was.

And my body. I followed him. Everywhere—through the countryside, in the towns. I watched him heal others. I saw him cast out more demons. I heard him teach about another kind of world, a better world, a kingdom of the Spirit, a realm of the heart. He was Raboni, my teacher. He made the blind see and he gave me new eyes, too. I see so much more to life than I ever did before!

See this coin? Do you really see it? Lose it, you'll get down on your hands and knees and look for it. But if you see that this coin stands for eternal riches—eternal riches!—*then,* if you lose it, you'll sweep out your entire house, you'll move every stick of furniture, you'll roll up every rug until you find it. See this candle? Really see it? It stands for the flame of life. We're supposed to put it up high to give light to all. See this bread, this wine? Do you really see them? Something to eat? This bread is the presence of God, this wine is the life of God poured out for you. But only if you can see—only if you have eyes of faith, eyes of vision, eyes of insight. Or do you call it hallucination, self-deception?

Where do you get eyes of faith? Follow him as I did. Live every day at the Carpenter's side, and you'll begin to see with his eyes—not through his eyes, but with his eyes—think with his mind, feel with his heart, trust with his faith. No secret. It's simple—simple!—not easy, simple. Just go with Jesus. Go with Jesus, everywhere, all the way. The road winds uphill all the way to the end.

I said it's not easy. When you go with him, you go to the cross with him. I did. And it was horrible. Oh, I went good places with him, too—green pastures, still waters. But then there were the rocky roads, for the sake of the honor of God. Roads that ran through enemy territory, roads through the valleys of death. But even there—even in the shadow of death—even there I found a feast, a table prepared—and a blessing, because I was with him and he was with me.

I loved him. And when you love someone, you just want to be with him wherever he is, but most of all, be with him when he needs you.

The worst was the cross. If you have ever watched someone you love die . . . and he wasn't just dying. He was tortured to death, executed like the scum of the earth, like a rat. His pain, his suffering, I can't . . . . He died. And so did I.

Know what I found out? I found out they could kill him, they could kill me, but they could never kill what had happened between us. Death could never cut off our relationship. They could break his body and they could break my heart, but they could never, never break our love.

I wasn't through yet. They put his body in Joseph's garden tomb. They say the body of an executed man pollutes the tomb. Today millions of people crowd into that tomb for blessing every year! They sealed it. They guarded it. He was crucified. He was dead. He was buried.

As soon as the Sabbath was over, we took the embalming spices—Mary, Joanna, and I—and we went to the tomb. We were going to pay his broken body the respect due to a just man. Mary and Joanna stopped to rest—Joanna wasn't young anymore. I went ahead. The tomb was open—open!

Right away I knew—I thought I knew—what had happened. Someone had taken the body away. I ran back to where Peter and John were and I told them. They ran to the tomb. They went inside. (*Deliberately*) They said it was empty. They said the burial cloths were folded up. Peter and John didn't know what to think or what to do. They went home.

I cried. I looked into the tomb. I saw two figures in white.

THE STAR THROWER

They were sitting on the slab where the body had been, one at either end. They asked me why I was crying. I told them, "They have taken my Lord away, and I don't know where they've laid him." I turned away. And I saw—I thought I saw—the gardener. (*Accelerando poco a poco*) He said, "Why are you crying?" I said, "Sir, if you're the one who took him away, tell me where he is." And he said, "Mary." "Mary"! I knew! "Mary"! I threw myself at him. (*Crescendo*) "Raboni!"

(*Held back*) But he said, "Don't try to hold me." I knew what he meant. He wasn't rejecting me. He was going to God. God is always with us, always with us. Raboni taught me that. I couldn't anoint his body. I said, "Lord, if you ascend to the Father, if I no longer have you, how can I show my love? How can I keep our love alive?" And I seemed to hear him say, "Mary, you can do for others what you would have done for me. You can do those things you know I would want to do."

You know what moves me the most? That it was me. Who am I? That he cares that much! He spoke to *me*, he made his risen, living presence known to *me*! Who am I?

I'm that poor, ignorant, deluded woman. I'm that schizoid. I'm the one with the hallucinations. I'm the one who loved him 2,000 years ago. I'm the one who had the demons. I'm the one Jesus healed. I'm the one who followed him all the way to the cross, all the way to the tomb, all the way to the garden. I couldn't find him. He found me. "Mary"! I'm the one who lives today. I know. And I tell you, "*He* lives!" And because he lives, I live.

You want to call that hallucination? Wish fulfillment? You know! What do you know? I know this faith has proved itself in the lives of millions for 2,000 years. Jesus saves lives. He heals the sick. He makes the broken whole. He restores the lost. You know! I know! "He lives!"

END

THE GREATEST SHOW ON EARTH

A Play in Five Monologues

[*Optional*] RING MASTER

Ladies and Gentlemen, boys and girls, children of all ages! The Greatest Show on Earth takes great pride and pleasure in presenting for your amazement and amusement that world-famous tamer of wild animals, greater than Gunther, better then Beatty or Buck, that Miracle of Mammals, that Jupiter of the Jungle, that Crown of Creation, Adam of Eden! (*Drum roll*)

TAMER

Yeah, I know you were expecting something exciting, but I'm, well, to tell you the truth, I'm feeling a little bit flat today. I guess I'm a little homesick. I miss, I miss the jungle.

The jungle was great. No streets, no buildings, no cars, no trucks, no cities, no so-called civilization—just nature, nature the way the Owner created it. Rain forests, rivers, lakes, savannas, mountains—what a paradise!

And the wild life! Ha! You go to the zoo, I bet. And what do you see there? Artificial, quote, natural environments. Some natural! Moats, cages, tanks, tourists and restrooms and ice cream stands. Be sure to take some digital pictures of the kids. Stand over there by the monkey cage, kids! And be sure to buy some stuff at the souvenir shop.

The jungle has got everything a person really needs. Soon there won't be any more jungles. But that jungle, that jungle was home. Don't give me that Tarzan-and-Jane business, either. There weren't any movie cameras. I wasn't swinging on vines and yelling, "Ayoooah!" I wasn't rescuing Jane from the white traders. I was farming, I was raising crops. But the work was easy because I loved it. I was where I was meant to be. I was doing what I was meant to do. I was friends with the Owner. Oh, the Owner is so wonderful! Anyone who could create all that—wonderful!

And the animals! I really liked the animals! That was the other part of my job, taking care of the animals. I named them all. I am brother to the animals. I've got some of them inside of me. No, not that way—back then I was a vegetarian. I mean sometimes I feel like I'm a lion—a king. Other times, truth is, I'm a hyena—a coward. Then sometimes I'm subtle—a snake. Clever—fox. A builder—a beaver. Fierce—a tiger; gentle—a lamb; swift—a gazelle; slow—a sloth. I'm a whole menagerie all by myself. No wonder I'm at home in the jungle!

Jungle life was great. I belonged in the jungle. I was made for the jungle. And the jungle was made for me. The thing about the jungle was that there you felt close to the Owner. There in all that wonderful, wild beauty, there I knew the Owner. The Owner used to walk in the jungle in the cool of the day. And I would walk alongside. And we would talk. Or we were quiet. And we understood one another, the Owner and I.

Of course the Owner is *here*, too, but I don't know—things aren't the same here. Anymore, I just don't seem to be able to connect. It's not the same. Here it's all . . . strange. I don't feel like I belong here. I've got no roots. This isn't home. Oh, I've got a nice enough place to stay, all kinds of food, nice clothes, nice things. But it's not the same. I miss our walks, our talks, I miss knowing who I am, knowing what I'm supposed to be doing, I miss knowing that I'm doing what I was made to do.

Maybe someday I'll go see one of those career counselors. You know, things just don't fit together anymore. I don't fit.

Every day I put on my show. I do my act, I go through my routine. But the animals, the animals are different, too. I've got them all tamed now. They jump through their hoops. The crowd applauds. I get my paycheck. But it just doesn't feel right . . . at the end of the day when it cools off, and I go out in the dark and just walk—alone.

I have a wonderful woman, my wife. She makes it better. We're together, but together we're alone. She feels pretty much the same as I do. Maybe it's worse for her. Because the boys are gone. Both our first born and our second born, both of them are gone now. I stay with her. I cry. I cry for them. I cry for her. I cry for myself.

Maybe someday soon I'll move on. Do something different, something different with my life. I don't know what. I . . . I don't know.

[*Optional*] RING MASTER

And now, Ladies and Gentlemen, boys and girls of all ages, here she is, that Reptilian Rhetorician, that Python Provocateur, that Hedonistic Herpetologist! She walks with serpents, she talks with serpents, she dines with serpents—Madame Eve, the Snake Lady!

CHARMER

Some people don't like to look at snakes. I think snakes are beautiful. Some people are afraid. Some people don't like to face the facts. There are snakes in the world. They're part of creation. Some of them are dangerous. And some of them are beautiful— gorgeous, shimmering, iridescent. Still, some people just don't like snakes, don't even want to think about them. Me, I always was a bit of a daredevil.

Maybe you don't want to hear my story. I don't blame you. It's painful. In fact, it's the story of pain—my story, my pain. It's painful for me even to tell it. It's painful for you to hear it. So if you'd like, you can just switch your mind off, tune me out. Think about some attractive person or something you like to do. Watch TV, go to a movie. Plan dinner. Laugh . . . laugh and the world will laugh with you.

You don't laugh a lot when your son dies. You don't laugh

when your son is murdered, murdered by his own brother. See? You don't want to think about that, do you? You don't want it to happen to you. Neither did I. But I can't help it. It's what happened. It's what I live with. He died. I died then, too. You've already read my story, or someone read it to you, or you heard it when someone told it to you. "Cain killed Abel." That's the story. You know it. You think you know it. But you don't really know. They weren't your sons. You didn't love them. Well, they were my sons and I did love them. I love them still. And Cain killed Abel—and me.

He didn't know any better, Cain. He was hurt, he was angry. Because Lord God accepted Abel's sacrifice, but Lord God rejected Cain's sacrifice. And Cain didn't know why. Do you? And Cain, jealous, frustrated, angry the way boys will be—Cain rose up and killed his brother Abel. No one told him it was wrong. Back then there was no commandment. Back then there was no "Thou shalt not kill." There was no commandment against killing. The only commandment back then—the only commandment!—was "The fruit of the tree of the knowledge of good and evil, you shall not eat of it lest you die." But think about that. Since we did not yet know good and evil, how could any of us know if obeying the commandment or disobeying the commandment was good or evil? *Cain didn't know it was wrong!* You see? He literally did not know right from wrong. The only commandment was *against knowing* right from wrong! And now Abel is dead, and Cain is banished—gone! Both of them are gone.

"Lest *you* die," the commandment says, "lest *you* die." Cain didn't break that commandment. I did. But I didn't die. Abel died. Why should Abel die for my sin? Is it fair that Cain should be condemned because I transgressed?

Every one of you here has knowledge. You know right from wrong. You have learned. You were taught. Or you learned from experience. Would you give up your knowledge? Would you erase from your brain everything you've learned, everything you know?

You dread a disease that would wipe away the records of your mind.

Which of you would not teach your child the difference between right and wrong?

"Knowledge is power," you say. That is part of *your* knowledge. "Wisdom is more to be desired than rubies or much fine gold," you say. Why? Because you believe that wisdom is good. You crave wisdom for yourself, you crave education for your children. Then is it fair that I should be condemned because I saw that the fruit of knowledge is good and a thing to be desired? That is my sin. Which of you would withhold knowledge from your children? You believe knowledge of good and evil to be one of the most precious gifts you can give your children. Then why should the Father withhold it from me? Why should the Father prohibit knowledge to me, his daughter? And for knowing why should he take away my children?

It's true. I tasted knowledge. I shared it with my husband. And for that transgression—transgression, yes, civil disobedience of an arbitrary, an unreasonable prohibition—for that transgression I am condemned, expelled. Because my sons did not know right from wrong, my son Abel is dead and my son Cain wanders the world. And me, I charm snakes.

RING MASTER

They were two babes in the wood. They wanted to improve the place. Imagine that—improve on paradise! It is a beautiful dream, to improve on paradise. Man and woman have got a bit of the creator in them.

Creator put the man in charge of the place, made him the caretaker. Then he gave him the woman to be his teammate to help him win the game of life. I like the concept—teamwork, cooperation! I cooperated with the woman, helped her get the knowledge she needed. Knowledge is the power to turn your dreams into reality. Without the power of knowledge, all your good intentions are just that, merely good intentions.

When he was just starting out, the Creator had never had to deal with anyone else before. He was a bit lacking in tact, diplomacy, subtlety. He tried threats and brute force. He told the man and woman, "Don't eat that, for in the day you do, you die." It was a bluff. I called the bluff and I called it right. See for yourself. The woman ate the fruit, the man ate the fruit, and in that day did they die? They did not.

They ate the wonderful fruit and their eyes were opened and then . . . and then . . . Oh, come now, children, what a disappointment. Did they build laboratories? Did they build schools? Did they philosophize? Did they write books? Did they write symphonies? They took fig leaves and covered themselves.

Don't blame me if you human beings don't know how to use power when you get it, whether it's power of sex or money or knowledge. I didn't come here to exonerate myself. No need. Everyone of you here, in spite of all the lies you have been taught about me, everyone of you here knows deep down in your heart that the man and woman tried to make me the scapegoat, the patsy, the fall guy. Because the man and woman don't want to grow up and accept responsibility for their own desires and deeds.

Come, let us reason together. If the Creator had created Eden a level playing field, if instead of resorting to threats and brute force the Creator had stayed in the paths of sweet reasonableness and gentle persuasion, then I would have prevailed, man and woman would still be living in the garden, and they would know that the garden was good, and day and night they would bless my name.

I think I hear you know who coming. Excuse me, I can't abide his presence. I've seen his act and it's boring. You can hang around if you want. But don't be fooled!

JUGGLER

That's right, don't be fooled. The Ring Master is not the owner. He wishes he were. He'd like to take over. There are serpents among us who walk on two legs.

Me, I'm just a juggler. I hope you're in the juggler vein today.

I imitate God. God juggles everything. God controls them all—the planets that parade and plunge through their orbits, the galaxies that gyre in space, the subatomic particles and the quintessential quarks that leap in their places. God juggles infinite space and infinite spaces. God juggles infinite universes, infinite infinities. God never misses. And yet you imagine that God might drop you? No way.

The Ring Master, he would like to persuade man and woman that they can be gods, that they can juggle everything all by themselves, that they don't need God. According to him, if they only have knowledge, man and woman can juggle the genomes, nuclear weapons, biological warfare. According to the Ring Master, man and woman can ignore God. I don't think so. Man and woman need to learn from the Master Juggler. If they don't, they drop the ball.

Man and woman must choose. They can trust and obey the Master Juggler and live in paradise, or they can disobey and bring death and destruction on the earth.

(*Pointing to audience*) Watch that woman walk the high wire! She balances! She juggles herself! Her family! Her career! Her friends! Her mate! Her life! She falters! She makes it!

(*Pointing*) Look at the human cannon ball! Boom! He arcs! He's safe!

(*Pointing*) See the trapeze artists! They somersault through the air! So graceful! So beautiful! They leap! They fly! They fall! Saved! At the last second!

Come and join the circus! It's the greatest show on earth!

EXEUNT marching to circus music.

EMMETT KELLY

(ENTER *sweeping. Pauses, looks up.*) The show's over, folks. You can go home now, if you'd like. Maybe you'd like to get some refreshments on the way out. You got your money's worth. More. This show costs the Owner an awful lot to put on. Costs me, too. Blood, sweat, toil, and tears. Me, I sweep up after hours. Pretty big mess—usually is—pretty big mess. Folks are careless, you know. Just don't care, don't care. I care. So that's my job, clean up after, get things ready for the next show. Yep, that's what I do. My Daddy did it before me. One day he dropped dead and I caught his broom. Been doing it ever since. I'm good at it. I mean, either you can clean up or you can't. I can. I just start wherever I am, and I keep on sweeping until it's clean. Same thing tomorrow. Just one of those things got to be done. The show's got to go on. 'Bye, now. (*Weeping*) Have a good time!

END

NOTES

1. Loren Eiseley, *The Unexpected Universe*, Harcourt Brace Jovanovich, Inc., New York, 1969.
2. Paul Brockelman, *Cosmology and Creation: The Spiritual Significance of Contemporary Cosmology*, Oxford University Press, New York, 1999, p. 52.
3. Keith Johnstone, *Impro: Improvisation and the Theatre*, Routledge, New York, 1989.
4. John A. Sanford, *King Saul, the Tragic Hero: A Study in Individuation,* Paulist Press, New York and Mahwah, 1985.
5. Julian Jaynes, *The Origin of Consciousness in the Breakdown of the Bicameral Mind*, Houghton Mifflin Company, Boston, 1976 and 1990, pp. 306ff.
6. Oscar G. Brockett, *The Theatre: An Introduction*, Holt, Rinehart and Winston, Inc., New York, 1969, p. 116.
7. Frank M. Whiting, *An Introduction to the Theatre*, Harper and Row, Publishers, New York and Evanston, 1961, p. 56.
8. See Viola Spolin, *Improvisation for the Theater: A Handbook of Teaching and Directing Techniques*, Northwestern University Press, Evanston, Illinois, 1963, and Dan Cheifetz, *Theater in My Head*, Little, Brown, and Company, Boston and Toronto, 1971.
9. Phyllis Hartnoll, *The Theatre: A Concise History*, Revised Edition, Thames and Hudson, London, 1997, p. 31.
10. One couple complained to their pastor's judicatory officer, "If we want drama, we'll go to the theatre!" But after a choir anthem they did not threaten that if they wanted music they would go to the concert hall, and after a church supper they

did not threaten to take their gustatory business exclusively to restaurants.

11. J. Michael Walton, *Greek Theatre Practice*, Methuen, London, 1991, p. 53.

12. Oscar G. Brockett, *The Theatre: An Introduction*, Holt, Rinehart, and Winston, New York, 1969, p. 59. I quote Dr. Brockett's paragraph at length not only because he makes his point clearly, but also in order to call attention to the putative "necessary" dramatic feature of conflict, supposedly "impossible" in solo performance. In theatre, absolutes are elusive. What one generation judges "necessary" another generation blithely omits, while particular theatres routinely perform the "impossible."

13. Jordan R. Young, *Acting Solo: The Art of One-Man Shows*, Apollo Press Limited, London, 1989.

14. Paul Ricoeur, *Oneself as Another*, trans. Kathleen Blamey, University of Chicago Press, Chicago and London, 1992, p. 248.

15. Keith Johnstone, *Impro: Improvisation and the Theatre*, Routledge, New York, 1981, p. 17.

16. A caveat about "character building." At times it has been tempting to fancy that portraying a noble personage could somehow ennoble the character of the actor. (See Thomas Keneally's *The Playmaker*, Simon and Schuster, New York, 1987, and Timberlake Wertenbaker's stage adaptation, *Our Country's Good*, The Dramatic Publishing Company, Woodstock, Illinois, 1988.) Perennial show biz celebrity scandal headlines ought to be enough to spike that pleasant but unwarranted supposition. Playing Saint Joan no more transforms an actress into a saint than playing Barabbas turns an actor into an insurrectionist. Acting makes one an actor; that is good—or bad—enough!

17. But beware Matthew 7:6: "Do not give what is holy to dogs, and do not throw your pearls before swine, or they will trample them under foot and turn and maul you."

THE STAR THROWER 271

18. William Erwin, ed., *Seinfeld and Philosophy*, Open Court, Chicago and LaSalle, Illinois, 2000, pp. 92-93.

19. See Jonas Barish, *The Antitheatrical Prejudice*, University of California Press, Berkeley, Los Angeles, London, 1981.

20. Marie MacLean, *Narrative as Performance: The Baudelairean Experiment*, Routledge, London and New York, 1988, pp. 17ff.

21. A "beat" is a small unit of action, a step of the dramatic journey. Or think of beats as "tacks" a sailor takes when sailing against the wind towards a destination.

22. See my "Rehearsing Creatively—Freeing the Natural Actor within Us," *Dramatics*, November/December, 1978.

23. John Miles Foley, *The Singer of Tales in Performance*, Indiana University Press, Bloomington and Indianapolis, 1995, pp. 42f. et passim.

24. Simon Callow, *Being an Actor*, St. Martin's Press, New York, 1984, p. 51.

25. Angela Devine and Rory Fellowes, *Heaven: A Guide*, Unwin Paperbacks, London, Boston, and Sydney, 1985.

26. Kimberly A. Christen, *Clowns and Tricksters: An Encyclopedia of Tradition and Culture*, ABC-CLIO, Denver, Colorado, Santa Barbara, California, Oxford, England, 1998, p. 181.

27. Daniel Defoe, *A Journal of the Plague Year*, New American Library, New York and Scarborough, Ontario, 1960, p. 169.